All About The

PARROTS

by Arthur Freud

First Edition—Second Printing

1981

HOWELL BOOK HOUSE Inc.
230 Park Avenue
New York, N.Y. 10169

To Ms. Mildred Bobrovitch of the American Museum of Natural History Library and Mr. Bill Meng of the New York Zoological Society Photo Lab for their invaluable help.

My special thanks to my wife, Hannah, who suggested the book and whose encouragement and moral support made it possible.

Library of Congress Cataloging in Publication Data

Freud, Arthur, 1927-
  All about the parrots.

  Bibliography: p. 299
  1. Parrots. I. Title.
SF473.P3F73   636.6'865   79-25568
ISBN 0-87605-815-2

ALL ABOUT THE PARROTS

Pigmy parrot. *Lydekker*

The parrot family has fascinated man for centuries. In cultures primitive and advanced parrots have been objects of worship, reverence, admiration status and pleasure. Today, as in the past, the parrot tribe holds a prominent place in the affections of bird lovers and serious aviculturists alike. *M. Morrone/S. Rosenblum*

Contents

Arthur Freud with his Moluccan Cockatoo, Rosie.

About the Author

THE MODERN CAGE-BIRD ENTHUSIAST is better informed about his hobby because of Arthur Freud's deep commitment to aviculture.

A recognized authority on parrots in the United States and Great Britain, Arthur Freud is a prolific contributor to the literature on all members of the parrot family. He writes a monthly column on parrots for *American Cage-Bird Magazine* and has been a contributing editor for *Pet News* since its inception in 1975.

An educator in the sciences, Arthur Freud brings the discipline of his profession to the enjoyment of his hobby in this, his most recent writing accomplishment. In ALL ABOUT THE PARROTS the reader can readily discern Mr. Freud's tremendous mastery of his subject, and also his lively enthusiasm for members of the parrot family.

From the bird room in the Freud family home on eastern Long Island comes the inspiration for many of the charming personal anecdotes that add so much warmth and appeal to this book. Here is Bill, the Yellow Naped Amazon, whose acquisition was exciting and whose acclimatization was very memorable. Here is Frodo, the huge Scarlet Macaw, who takes a dim view of rivals for the author's attention. Here are Duda and Jaco, the African Greys, a charming pair that cherish Mr. Freud and each other. And there are many other avian members of the Freud family circle that have helped their owner produce what is the most charming and at the same time definitive book on the ever growing hobby of parrot-keeping.

In his involvement with parrots one of Mr. Freud's deepest interests is the potential good parrots represent for the well-being of senior citizens. Here is a pet that can give and receive affection, that is relatively easy to care for and is not as demanding as a cat or dog. He says that a pet parrot can bridge the generation gap for an older person because of the natural attraction of people to these delightful birds. The parrot therefore serves as the focal point for the senior citizen; something to look after and something to share affection with. This in turn leads to a brighter outlook on life and the older parrot owner often finds him or herself better able to relate to family, friends and the world at large.

Arthur Freud is a co-author of a book on the earth sciences and has been teaching for over 25 years. He is currently an administrator in a public high school in Nassau County, New York.

Purple Capped Lory. *Lydekker*

Foreword

MODERN SOCIETY thrusts complexity into every aspect of our lives. This also carries over into pet keeping. With ever-accelerated life-styles and ever-shrinking living spaces an interest is created in indoor pets that can be housed easily within the confines of small homes or apartments. This factor and the ever-present human quest for beauty has resulted in an unprecedented interest in all members of the parrot family.

From the blithe Budgie to the lordly Macaws, members of the parrot family are becoming more in demand as pets than ever before. The relatively easy care of these birds combined with their innate beauty, their capacity for training and their celebrated ability to mimic human speech and other sounds has brought them a host of new, devoted admirers.

With the increased interest in parrot-keeping comes the need for a modern book on the subject to assist today's owner. With ALL ABOUT THE PARROTS, that need is admirably satisfied.

ALL ABOUT THE PARROTS, by Arthur Freud, provides accurate, intriguing descriptions of many psittacine species—some familiar, some obscure. The personalities, breeding habits and histories included shed additional light on the habits of these birds. There are frequent references to the observations of early and modern authorities and many of the author's charming anecdotes dealing with his own personal experiences with his own birds and those owned by others. These, in themselves, will be a delightful treat to those who already share their lives with hookbills. For those who do not, the personal accounts of a life shared with these exotic beauties will speed the transition from parrot admirer to parrot owner.

There is sound guidance also on every aspect of what the parrot-keeper should know to keep his pet happy and healthy. Advice on cages, food, toys, training and all the basics are clear and easy to follow. How to deal with illness and how to venture into breeding will also be found in these pages.

Here is all the essential guidance the reader seeks—what kind of bird to get, what sex, age, training it to do tricks, to talk and so much more. And all this comes from one of the best known modern writers in aviculture. The author is not only the expert the reader expects, but he is an enthusiastic fan who loves his birds and parrot keeping and demonstrates his surging enthusiasm on every page of ALL ABOUT THE PARROTS.

The expert text is made even more enjoyable and meaningful by a beautiful gallery of photographs—many in full color to bring you the parrot family at its most dazzling.

We hope ALL ABOUT THE PARROTS will prove the most complete, helpful book for everyone interested in these wonderful birds. We know it is the most fascinating.

ELSWORTH HOWELL
Publisher

Acknowledgement is made to the following publishers for their permission to use copyright material.

LIFE magazine for "The Old Bird Won't Sell" by Russell Sackett.

Harper and Row Publishers, Inc., for excerpts from *King Solomon's Ring* by Konrad Z. Lorenz.

Biographical Notes on Researchers Cited

THROUGHOUT the text of ALL ABOUT THE PARROTS there are numerous references to various researchers and their findings and observations on the species of parrots discussed herein. To assist the reader, we offer some brief biographical notes on many of these people together with some of their accomplishments in the world of aviculture.

Charles Barrett is an Australian ornithologist whose book on the Parrots of Australasia successfully established important relationships between the Cockatoos of this region of the world.

The Duke of Bedford (known under the title Marquess of Tavistock until he succeeded to the full title in 1940) was well known for his collection of Parakeets which were considered to be among the finest in the world. His birds were kept with other animals at Woburn Abbey where the Duke bred many rare varieties, including his famous Blue Ringnecked Parakeets. He was awarded many medals for first breedings by the Avicultural Society. His book is a standard in the field and he wrote scholarly articles for many journals. The Duke died in a tragic accident in October, 1953.

Edward J. Boosey founded the Keston Foreign Bird Farm in 1927. Along with his partner Alec Brooksbank, Mr. Boosey made Keston famous for its first breedings. He was a talented artist as well as a fine observer and writer.

Neville W. Cayley was a former President of the Royal Zoological Society of New South Wales, Australia and the Royal Australian Ornithologists' Union. His book on the habits of Australian parrots is vital to any serious study of these birds.

Jean Delacour has had a career in aviculture with origins dating back to before the first World War. Dr. Delacour is an expert on many bird families but is probably most highly famed for his work on pheasants. He is President of the British Avicultural Society and still maintains important posts with the American Museum of Natural History, the New York Zoological Society and many other organizations devoted to the natural sciences.

R. Meyer de Schauensee is Curator of Ornithology at the Academy of Natural Sciences of Philadelphia. He is an authority on the birds of South America and his books on these neotropical birds have helped to fill wide gaps in our knowledge of their behavior, life histories and habits.

Reverend F. G. Dutton was Vicar of the beautiful English village of Bibury in the Cotswold Mountains. The keeping of parrots was a hobby which engrossed him. Reverend Dutton was the second President of the Avicultural Society, serving in this office from 1896 until his death in 1920. He contributed material to Dr. Greene's famous books and wrote many articles for the *Avicultural Magazine*.

Joseph M. Forshaw is an Australian ornithologist with a special interest in parrots. Several of his books on parrots are already considered classics in the field.

W. T. Greene wrote prolifically on the topic of foreign birds. His three volume *Parrots In Captivity*, written between 1884 and 1887 has immortalized him among parrot lovers. The books have been reprinted at least twice. Although a smaller fourth volume is difficult to find, a copy can be seen in the Library of the British Museum.

Konrad Z. Lorenz is a behavioral scientist whose keen powers of observation have been frequently linked with his philosophical speculations on the behavior of animals. He provides fascinating, scientifically accurate and highly readable descriptions of the intimate activities of birds and other animals.

Rosemary Low is known not only for her books but also for her columns in the British weekly, *Cage and Aviary Birds*. Ms. Low is an expert on Lories as well as the South American parrots.

Malcolm MacDonald was High Commissioner for the United Kingdom in India from 1955 to 1960. He is the son of the late British Prime Minister, Ramsay MacDonald. His trained eye and graphic prose make us wish that he had chosen an avicultural career rather than one in government service.

K. A. Norris was a past President of the Foreign Bird League of Great Britain. He had made a life-long study of exotic birds and possessed an extensive range of aviaries.

A. A. Prestwich was for many years President and then Secretary and Treasurer of the Avicultural Society of Great Britain. Mr. Prestwich's books on the records of parrot-like birds bred in captivity as well as the origin of parrot names are important tools for any individual engaged in research on members of the parrot family.

Cyril H. Rogers has been keeping and breeding foreign birds for more than 40 years. He is a successful exhibitor as well as a celebrated judge at major British cage-bird exhibitions.

Dr. Karl Russ wrote several books and many papers dealing with exotic birds. He was also editor of the German ornithological journal, *The Feathered World* which is still published and which is the oldest journal of its kind in the world. Much of Russ' work has been translated into English. He was a comtemporary of Dr. Greene's and both men appreciated each other's talents.

A. Rutgers is a highly qualified Dutch aviculturalist, judge, author and exhibitor. His own successful maintenance of a large collection of birds is based on a thorough knowledge of their natural habitat as well as their feeding and breeding habits.

Prideaux John Selby wrote the volume on parrots for the famous Naturalist's Library Series produced early in the 19th century by Sir William Jardine. Selby was accurate in his descriptions and well ahead of many others of his day in noting the relationships between many of the parrots about which he wrote.

George M. Sutton is a Research Professor Emeritus of Zoology and Curator of Birds at the Stovall Museum in the University of Oklahoma. He is a gifted author, artist and teacher as well as an expert on the birds of Mexico.

This portrait of a Hyacinth Macaw was painted around 1884. *Greene*

Introduction

THE WHITE COCKATOO postured gracefully while fully extending her wings to show the wash of yellow on their under surface. She erected her yellow crest and then gave an ear piercing scream to make sure that she had the full attention of everyone in the room.

* * * *

Bill, the Yellow Naped Amazon, peered out at his guests with a wild and mischievous orange eye. The startled audience was delighted when he greeted them with a deep-voiced, "Hi Bill, what's your name?"

* * * *

Duda, an African Grey, stopped all activity and more or less froze in her most recent position. Since she was upside down and hanging by one claw with a little brass bell in her beak and a well chewed block of wood in her other claw, it was easy to see that she had been quite actively engaged in parrot games.

* * * *

Fiorello is a large Scarlet Macaw whose habit it is to dance up and down the length of his perch in typical, lumbering Macaw fashion. When his door is opened he exits willingly if he has finished dancing but if interfered with in his performance, he bites.

17

* * * *

These descriptions of whimsical Parrot behavior are real and taken from life. A tame parrot wishes to please and because of his intelligence knows that humans find his comical behavior charming and almost child-like. The cleanliness, relative ease of care and longevity of these birds make them ideal pets. Add the potential for speech with the illusion that the parrot understands some of what he says, and it is not hard to comprehend why parrots have been popular as household pets for centuries.

The birds described above have not been subjected to intensive training nor are they unusual. They have benefitted from good care, love and common sense training over a period of years. The purpose of this volume is to help you make a wise choice of your own parrot and to guide you in properly housing, feeding, training and caring for what may well be a life-time companion.

"Here's looking at you." This sleek African Grey personifies the puckish charm the parrot family is universally famous for. *Photo by author*

18

Beyond all, Psitaci repeat mens' words, and even talk connec-
tedly. India sends this bird, which they call Psitace, with the whole
body green, marked only by a scarlet ring upon the nape. It will
pronounce "Hail Emperor," and any words it hears; it is especially
sportive after wine. The hardness of the head is the same as of the
beak. And when the bird is being taught to speak, it is beaten with
an iron rod, else it feels not the strokes. When it flies down it re-
ceives its weight upon its beak, and supports itself thereon; and thus
lightens itself to remedy the weakness of its feet.

Caius Plinius the Elder in his
Historia Naturalis about 50 A. D.

A 16th Century illustration showing a variety of bird cages of the period including one "mechanized" model (bottom center). *The Pierpont Morgan Library*

1

A History of

Parrot Keeping

REFERENCES to the keeping of parrots can be found in many old records. These sources are sometimes unclear as to which specific parrot they refer as the nomenclature they use is often archaic, but there is no doubt that it is parrots they are alluding to. They are ancient birds and their parrot-like ancestors probably evolved as early as the Oligocene era, about thirty-five million years ago.

Parrots in Early Literature

Parrots have long been associated with seafaring men as it was the trade vessels of early days which made it possible for Europeans to visit South America, Asia, Africa and Australia and thus have an opportunity to see, describe and capture these unusual birds. In a very old volume titled, *Natural History of Africa* and dating back to the early nineteenth century, an anonymous author noted that ". . . The Greeks and Romans became acquainted with the parrot kind, in consequence of certain species of these birds having been imported from the east soon after Alexander's Indian expedition." The passage goes on to note that the Alexandrine Parrot arrived in Europe from ancient Taprobane, an island we know as Ceylon or Sri Lanka. He further describes how these highly valued birds were lodged in superb cages of silver, ivory and tortoise-shell with the price of a parrot frequently exceeding that of a slave. The Roman poet Ovid actually wrote a memorial elegy on the death of a parrot belonging to a lady friend.

Friends who are studying in Italy recently brought me two prints from the sixteenth century masterpiece, *Natural History*, written and illustrated by Ulisse Aldrovandi. Aldrovandi was a naturalist and professor of natural history at the University of Bologna as well as a founder and director of the Bologna Botanical Gardens. Both prints are of Macaws and one appears to be a Military while the other looks very much like a Green Wing. The prints are actually pages from chapters dealing with parrots and although I agree with those antiquarian book sellers who frown on such works being sold by the page, I must confess that I was pleased to get the prints.

Aldrovandi describes how one of the Macaws would tear apart apples and then seek out the hidden seeds. It devoured these with great pleasure and then discarded the rest of the fruit. This parrot would also cling lovingly to those individuals whom it knew and give them kisses with its beak and tongue. Strangers who attempted familiarity received a savage bite. Apparently parrot personalities have not changed at all in four centuries.

Descriptions and illustrations of those parrots known to the Greeks and Romans prior to the time of Nero are almost always of Ringnecks from India or the islands near the Indian sub-continent. In fact Aristotle refers to the parrot that he was familiar with as "The Indian Bird."

Exploration Brings the Parrot to Europe

Parrots have always been popular among residents of the New World. Edward A. Armstrong notes that Columbus found that the natives of the West Indies raised Macaws for food (much as we do with poultry) in addition to keeping them as pets. Armstrong also describes the fascinating experience of the nineteenth century explorer, Alexander von Humboldt, who came upon an old parrot which had once lived among a tribe known as the Atures. Humboldt's Indians were extinct but the parrot still spoke phrases in Ature and thus apparently was the last living being to speak the language.

Credit must be given to English explorers for much of the knowledge gained about the parrot race during the nineteenth century. Trade and exploration vessels frequently carried individuals with strong natural history backgrounds. Sometimes the whole pur-

An early 19th Century Italian bird cage made in the shape of a Greek temple. *Cooper-Hewitt Museum*

A delftware and wire cage from Holland, circa 1830. *Cooper-Hewitt Museum*

23

pose of their being aboard ship was to study the fauna of distant lands or, as in the case of the great Captain Cook, they possessed an avocation which ultimately assumed an importance equal to that of their main occupation.

Parrots began to appear with greater frequency in Europe after Vasco da Gama discovered a sea route to India. The same voyages which brought spices from Africa also began bringing parrots from Africa, India, Malacca, and Java. Birds were now reaching Europe directly instead of having to come through Egyptian or Arab third parties. This lowered prices and made the birds available to more people.

With the discovery of the New World, Amazon parrots of Central and South America were brought to Spain and from there to the rest of Europe.

Columbus was reported to have brought a pair of Cuban Amazons with him on his return to Spain and these beauties were given to his patron, Queen Isabella.

The nineteenth century was an era of great European interest in geographic and zoological phenomena with Great Britain leading the field in colonization and expeditions. It was a romantic period and exotic parrots became particularly favored creatures. Their behavior was engaging, they evoked foreign shores and their ability to speak was startling. Representations of parrots could be found decorating many household objects in a manner not unlike the Mickey Mouse or Little Orphan Annie mugs which many of us can fondly remember.

Parrot Pets of the Famous

Parrots were often associated with famous personages of the day which could not help but add to their popularity. Robert Lacey's description of Charlotte, the grayish-pink (probably a Rose-Breasted Cockatoo) pet of George V (grandfather of Queen Elizabeth II) makes one anxious to own a parrot such as she. She traveled wherever he went and even joined him at breakfast where she would hop from his finger and then range over the breakfast table sampling jam, butter or eggs as the fancy took her. Charlotte also had a special stand so that she could take up her station next to the King's desk in the office where he did his paper work.

Many returning veterans of the Boer War of 1899 brought African Greys home with them. Around the same time Coco, an African Grey resident of the royal household, was being taught to greet Queen Victoria with the expression "God save the Queen."

Parrots were also associated with earlier British nobility and royalty. One parrot, an African Grey which had been the pride of the Duchess of Lennox, had the distinction of being interred with an effigy of his mistress next to her tomb in Westminster Abbey. The Grey succumbed to grief and survived his mistress by only a few days when she died in 1702. The Duchess and the parrot had been together for over forty years and apparently had great affection for one another.

Henry VIII, the sixteenth century king, who thanks to Hollywood is best remembered for his bad table manners, kept an African Grey which is reputed to have had a temper which matched its owner's. There is considerable documentation of the bird's existence at court. We therefore have proof that African Greys had been imported into England and kept as pets over four centuries ago.

Parrots in Art

Parrots have always captured the imagination of artists. Ancient Indian paintings show Kama, the God of Love, riding a parrot. One of the panels on the famous and beautiful Bronze Doors of the Baptistry in Florence is engraved with what appears to be a Conure getting ready to attack the fruits of the plant he is perched on. Mark Catesby and Antoine DuPratz immortalized many of America's Southern birds at a time when the United States did not yet exist and the region along the Mississippi was still virgin territory. If one wishes precise descriptions and views of the now extinct Carolina Conure which DuPratz called *Papagai à tête aurore* (the parrot with the sun on his head), he can refer to these early 18th century artists and be sure of accurate information.

John J. Audubon also included the Carolina Parakeet in his huge folio on the birds of America which appeared between 1827 and 1838. Working at almost the same time as Audubon, Edward Lear used the new art of lithography to create his masterpiece *Illustrations of the Family of Psittacidae or Parrots*. A facsimile version of Lear's work has recently been published. Lear occasionally worked with John Gould, another well know Victorian artist, who frequently used parrots as subjects.

Parrot Keeping into the Twentieth Century

As crossing the ocean became less expensive and more common, keeping full-sized parrots was no longer restricted to the wealthy. Parrots became the rage and a parlor with a green or gray beauty

A parrot in the public eye at the turn of the Century was Eli, the Hyacinth Macaw pet of Theodore Roosevelt, Jr. This photograph, taken in 1902, shows Eli and his young owner in the White House Conservatory. *Library of Congress*

glaring from his hoop was not an uncommon sight. This vogue continued well past the turn of the century but apparently sophistication and the increase in activities outside the home affected parrot keeping along with many other hobbies. While the birds were still popular and desirable pets, interest no longer grew at its earlier, rapid rate.

During the 1920s a relatively large number of cases of psittacosis (parrot fever) frightened off many prospective owners of hookbills. In the United States laws were enacted to restrict the importation of parrots in 1930 and to completely ban their introduction in 1946. Thus, they began to become quite rare as pets.

The keeping of parrots (and other pets) in Europe during World War II was a problem of serious dimensions. This was not only due to the destruction (which caused the ruin of many famous collections such as those of the Berlin Zoo and the Gardens of Jean Delacour at Clères in France) but also because individuals who were just getting by on a heavily rationed diet found it very difficult to provide seed and other types of food for their birds. Various techniques were tried including rationing food for the bird or offering substitutes just as was done with the human population. Unfortunately, this did not always work out and many parrots could not survive the reduced or altered diet. Some birds were released to fend for themselves while others (no doubt the rarest specimens) were sent to countries which were still fortunate to be at peace during the early years of the war. Of course, some individuals were able to muddle through by growing a small amount of seed such as sunflower and sacrificing their own meager supply of fruits and vegetables to their birds.

Public Health and the Quarantine Question

Following World War II, two things happened which helped parrots to regain their popularity. These were the discovery of new drugs which could quickly cure psittacosis and the realization that the disease was not solely a parrot affliction but one which could be carried and spread by all fowl. In fact, today, psittacosis is considered a misnomer and bird fever or ornithosis are used as more appropriate terms.

On the negative side the relatively inexpensive method of transporting livestock by air which became common after the war posed new problems. Birds now arrived in the United States so rapidly that there was little time for disease to incubate and illness to be recognized.

In 1967 when the effectiveness of using seed medicated with chlortetracycline in treating ornithosis became evident the government lifted the total embargo. Parrots which had been through a 45-day quarantine and chlortetracycline regimen were permitted to enter the country. Unfortunately, these quarantine stations were in the exporting country and thus U.S. control over them was limited.

Interest in parrots and their importation from South America, Africa, India and Asia again grew at a rapid rate. In 1971 a highly contagious disease of birds called Newcastle virus, caused the loss of many chickens and other birds in Southern California. This threat to the poultry industry resulted in an emergency ban on parrot importation which was not lifted until a new set of quarantine regulations took effect in 1973. The United States Department of Agriculture came up with rigorous guidelines which provided that imported parrots must be quarantined and medicated at closely controlled quarantine stations within the United States. The birds are kept in the quarantine stations for 30 days, after which they are released to the importers who own them. Should any of the quarantined birds die of Newcastle virus, the entire group must be sacrificed or returned to their country of origin. The stations operate on an "all in, all out" rule which means that new birds may not enter once the 30-day period begins. If an exception is made the 30-day quarantine period begins all over again for all birds. Even this arrangement is far from perfect. Too high a percentage of birds die in transit and disease outbreaks still occur.

This entire problem has been under review by appropriate agencies of the United States government for a number of years. In May, 1975 a bill (H.R. 6631) was offered in the House of Representatives by Representative Dingell of Michigan to establish a Federal Zoological Control Board.

H.R. 6631 had a number of purposes. It was designed to provide for more humane conditions for animals imported into the United States. It would also have regulated the importation, interstate shipment, public exhibition, and maintenance of all wild animals to assure humane treatment for them as well as to prevent the spread of any exotic diseases associated with these animals. One section of the proposed bill described a licensing procedure for individuals keeping wild animals. It specifically mentioned hobbyists as individuals who would have to be licensed. H.R. 6631 generated considerable opposition. It apparently never got out of committee and died when the 94th Congress adjourned.

Some startling points were predicated in a paper prepared for the Secretary of Health, Education and Welfare. The paper, written in March, 1978, notes that 80,000 to 85,000 psittacines are legally imported into the United States each year and between 25 to 40% die in quarantine after arrival. The report goes on to indicate that parrot-like birds are commonly infected with psittacosis. Human psittacosis generally results from exposure to pet birds, poultry, pigeons and various wild bird species. Almost 600 cases of psittacosis were reported in the period 1967-1976. Of these psittacosis cases 42% were attributed to imported and domestically-bred parrots. More than half the cases (58%) were, however, associated with poultry and other bird species. It seems logical to assume that cases of psittacosis associated with pet parrots would be reported more often and with greater regularity than psittacosis caused by poultry or wild species. Thus, the above figures may be somewhat biased against psittacines.

The issue paper further notes that the use of the chlortetracycline (CTC) treatment has an adverse effect on the health of the birds which were treated making them more susceptible to fungus infections. This and other adverse effects of CTC treatment may be contributing to the high mortality rate in imported birds. The recommendation by the author of the paper, Julius B. Richmond, Assistant Secretary for Health, is a rather drastic one. It speaks of prohibiting importation of all psittacines with limited exceptions which would generally be for individuals engaged in scientific research, conservation purposes or zoological exhibitions.

Should the recommendations become law it would be another major turning point in the history of America's romance with parrots. Importation would virtually cease and the effects on the pet bird industry and allied suppliers could be far-reaching.

Of course, if the hobby moves in the direction of breeding parrots to replace those which are no longer imported then the effect would not necessarily be completely negative. More and more individuals are successfully breeding parrots and reporting success with species which were once thought almost impossible to breed in captivity.

Turquoise Grass Parakeets. *Lydekker*

He spoke single words and sentences in the Dutch language and also introduced Dutch words . . . when he did not know, or had forgotten the German equivalent. He asked questions and returned answers, made requests and returned thanks; and used words correctly in relation to time, place, and persons.

"Polly wants to kluk kluk" (drink): "Polly wants something to eat". If he did not receive what he wished for at once . . . he flung everything about to show his anger!

He sang several songs and would frequently place a phrase from one into the other. This mischief amused him so that he would laugh quite loudly.

Dr. W. T. Greene, *Parrots in Captivity*, 1887

Throughout Latin America, parrots and other birds can be easily purchased at public outdoor markets. The Blue Fronted Amazon shown here is often found at such markets in Brazil. *Reed*

A prospective buyer looking over the Blue Fronts at a Brazilian market. *Reed*

32

2

Purchasing a Parrot

WHEN HE IS READY to purchase a parrot the buyer should not over-pay but should remember that a bird is not a bargain if it is in poor condition or is untrainable. To enjoy a new pet, it is very important to select a hookbill that is healthy and of sound temperament.

How to Find a Parrot

Parrots may be purchased from breeders or dealers or from a private seller. Buying privately requires extra caution. Individual owners do not usually wish to part with tame and talking birds. After all, if you had a loving parrot who spoke would you offer him for sale? Unfortunately, many "broncos"(parrots which are almost impossible to tame) move from family to family with their dispositions getting worse with each change.

Although advertising of parrots is limited, ads do appear on a regular basis in many newspapers. The pet page of the Sports Sections of the Sunday *New York Times* has the largest volume of parrot ads in the country. Another regular source of parrot offerings is the *American Cage-Bird Magazine* (3349 North Western Avenue, Chicago, Illinois 60618) which appears monthly. Of course the shopper can also run his own "parrot wanted" ad. Because of the danger of theft many breeders keep a rather low profile and one may be pleasantly surprised to find sources surprisingly close to home.

I would recommend that anyone of limited experience with birds try to have an experienced friend accompany them when they shop. Buying from a reputable dealer may cost a bit more but in return one will get the benefit of the dealer's experience and advice as well as the security of doing business with someone who has a reputation to protect and who will stand behind his livestock if there is a reasonable complaint.

The ideal way to select a parrot dealer or breeder is by recommendation from a satisfied customer. Ask a friend or associate who has purchased a parrot about the dealer he or she used. Was the bird healthy? Did it live up to the claims of the seller? Did your friend enjoy doing business with the seller? Is he or she happy with the purchase or are there misgivings? Don't be afraid to pile on the questions. Parrot owners generally like to talk about their pets and usually are glad to help a novice learn the ropes.

Once a dealer is located, selection of the bird is the next step. The following check list is meant as a quick way to help evaluate a parrot for possible purchase.

Choosing a Healthy Parrot

Health should be the first consideration in choosing a pet parrot. Feathers should be clean and smooth. The only time a healthy parrot will have a ragged look is during the molting period, which occurs during the summer months. It is not normal for a bird to be missing so many feathers that bare spots exist and such a bird should be avoided. In the case of Macaws and other large or very active birds some damage to the tail feathers in the form of fraying or breaking may be due to the bird being confined in a cage which is too small.

The bird's stools should not be watery. A healthy parrot normally has a semi-solid stool which is a mixture of white and dark matter. A large area of soiled vent and tail feathers may also indicate very loose droppings.

Examine the seed dish. Note whether or not the bird has been cracking seed. Empty hulls are a good sign as sick parrots generally eat less or stop eating entirely.

Temperament and Trainability

Temperament is second only to health as a factor in the choice of a bird. Select a bird which is calm and gentle. Approach him slowly and watch his reaction. Parrots are intelligent creatures and naturally will be wary of strangers; so don't be put off if he doesn't treat you like an old friend. However, beware of the parrot who goes into a rage on being approached. Extend a hand cautiously; if the parrot attempts to deliver a vicious bite, he will probably do the same in a new home and thus is not a good pet prospect. On the other hand, excessive calmness may be lethargy and a bird who fails to have any reaction to a stranger may be ill.

Naturally, most shop owners will charge somewhat more for a calm parrot or one which is semi-tame. If price is a factor it might be necessary to take a chance on a lower-priced but less friendly bird and do all of the work of taming yourself.

Speaking ability is the most difficult aspect to check. If the dealer says that the parrot can say several words and phrases but will not perform for a stranger, he is probably being accurate. In fact, it may take several weeks for the parrot to become accustomed to his new owner and new home. He probably will not regain his old vocabulary (if he had one) or start learning new words until the acclimation period is over. Although most people link parrots with the ability to speak, not every parrot has this potential. They do, however, possess other endearing and whimsical traits plus the important ability of being able to return your affection. Thus, a parrot should not be rejected as a possible pet merely because he does not talk.

Cost and Availability

A number of factors will determine which parrot one actually buys once the decision to own such a bird is made. Cost and availability are two of the most important criteria.

The elements which determine the cost of a parrot are rarity of the species, potential talking ability and whether or not it is an imported bird as opposed to one which was bred in this country and possibly hand-fed from infancy by the breeder.

Large numbers of Double Yellow Heads, Green Cheeked Amazons, Blue Fronted Amazons, Yellow Naped Amazons and related species are currently being imported from Mexico as well as Central and South America. These are, at the moment, the least expensive full-sized parrots with good potential for mimicry which can be purchased as they are relatively abundant and, with the exception of certain rare species, few restrictions are placed on their export. The gaudy, ferocious looking Macaws, which also come from South America, are three or four times as expensive as the smaller parrots, since they are harder to capture and transport and because, unfortunately, their numbers are diminishing. A number of countries have also begun to place restrictions on the export of some species of Macaws.

The most common birds being imported from Africa are the Senegal Parrot and the African Grey. Both make fine pets although the Senegal is only nine or ten inches long and generally does not learn to speak very well. The Grey, on the other hand, is considered the parrot with the greatest potential for speech. It is also extremely clever and a healthy one will remind you of a monkey as you watch it climb and swing from perch to perch in its cage.

There is a total embargo on the export of parrots from Australia and this is truly unfortunate as the Cockatoos which make up the bulk of the Australian species are as highly desired in the United States as they are detested by Australian farmers. Until they were designated as protected birds (in most, but not all, of Australia) farmers thought nothing of killing them by shooting or using poisoned bait in an effort to protect their crops. Parrots are particularly irritating to the farmer as they have the infuriating habit of taking one or two bites of a piece of fruit or corn and then discarding it and selecting another choice morsel.

Double Yellow Heads, Yellow Napes, Senegals, African Greys, and many Cockatoos are all being bred successfully in small numbers in the United States. Many breeders are located in the Southwestern and Western portion of the country although a few talented individuals have accomplished some amazing breeding results in Illinois, Tennessee and even the colder areas of upper New York State.

Those breeders selling hand-fed birds generally have a waiting list if they have achieved the reputation for producing tame and healthy young stock. Such hand-fed babies are fed on demand in very much the same way a modern mother feeds her own offspring. Psychologists believe that this type of relationship produces the phenomenon of "imprinting." A parrot reared this way considers the breeder its mother. These hand-fed babies must be seen to be appreciated. They are fearless of humans, learn to talk more readily and soon perform the captivating little tricks we all admire in performing parrots seen on television or in the movies.

It is best to discuss the cost of parrots in terms of price ranges within each species with individuals at the high end representing the less-readily-available and smaller number of locally bred and hand-fed babies. In addition to their desirability, the time that the breeder spends demand-feeding these creatures will cause their price to be higher than the more commonly available imports which pass through the quarantine stations in large numbers. This is not to say that only a hand-fed baby can be outstandingly lovable or talented. Attention and affectionate care should work with any parrot which has not been previously mistreated.

Sometimes fads will affect prices. The appearance of Fred, the Triton Cockatoo on the television series, *Baretta,* caused the price of Tritons and closely related Cockatoos to double several times. Early in 1978 restrictions on the export of Hyacinth Macaws made their prices comparable to that of a new car. When only a few people were willing to purchase at that unrealistic price, the bubble broke and by the spring of 1979 Hyacinths were selling for less than $2,000.

The chart which follows gives an idea of the price ranges for the more costly parrots. Bear in mind that the prices may fluctuate as well as vary in different localities. They can be helpful, however, in letting the buyer know whether a quoted price is realistic or outlandish. The comments are also meant to be a helpful guide but, of course, as with all living things, some individuals can vary from the norm. Only parrots which are readily available to all have been listed.

Species	Price Range	Comments
Yellow Fronted Amazon	$200–$400	Relatively abundant as an import. A fair talker.
Green Cheeked Amazon	$175–$300	Abundant as import. Tame, cute and pleasant but not much of a talker.
Double Yellow Head	$250–$450	Abundant as import with a good number also being domestically bred. They tame nicely and have high potential for talking.
Blue Fronted Amazon	$200–$400	Not particularly common. Some talk, some bite, some bite and talk. Make sure it really is a Blue Front if you pay these prices and not an Orange Wing.
Orange Winged Amazon	$150–$250	Imported in very large numbers. Pleasant little pets with not too much talking ability. Frequently mis-labeled as Blue Fronts.
Yellow Naped Amazon	$350–$550	A good number are imported and some are also domestically bred. They are excellent talkers, tame readily, and seem to enjoy physical contact and learning tricks.

Hyacinth Macaw	$1,500–$5,000	Export restrictions in countries of origin do not seem to be rigorously enforced. Many are offered for sale and the prices bear a definite relationship to supply and demand as these large birds are not particularly easy to keep while awaiting buyers. They are truly beautiful and make excellent pets.
Scarlet Macaw	$500–$1,000	Look for gentleness! These beauties talk and are playful but a mean one cannot be intimidated. Imports are slowing down, local breeding is up.
Blue and Gold Macaw	$500–$1,000	A bit more striking than the Scarlet. Some people consider them brighter. I find them much the same in intelligence and temperament. Imports are diminishing but there is some local breeding.
Greater Sulfur Crested Cockatoo	$800–$2,000	The lower priced birds are generally Tritons which are a subspecies with a blue eye ring. Take advantage of the low price if you can as basically the Triton is the same as the true Greater. These are bright and affectionate creatures who for some reason prefer acrobatics to talking but who can learn to speak.

If noise is a problem, forget this bird. No true Greaters can be imported as they come only from Australia and the export ban is strictly enforced. Fortunately, a reasonable number of both types are bred in the United States.

Lesser Sulfur Crested Cockatoo	$500–$1,000	Apartment sized Cockatoos. Very similar to their larger brethren and a wise choice if space and funds are factors in making a selection. Imported as well as locally bred birds are readily available.
Moluccan Cockatoo	$800–$1,500	Big, lovable, gentle and loud. Many imports as well as an occasional locally bred bird are available.
Umbrella Cockatoo	$800–$1,500	About the same as the Moluccan but I don't find them as attractive since they lack the pink tint. These birds are readily available as imports.
African Grey	$400–$900	They are the finest talkers and possess the added virtue of not screaming. Although somewhat high strung, they are not vicious biters. Many are available either through import or local breeding.
Miniature Macaws	$250–$750	The more common miniatures are, naturally at the low end of this price range. Many species are available and although they generally lack the Amazon's talent for speech they do have interesting personalities and are a good choice if the buyer does not have the space for the full-sized variety.

Some birds may not be purchased because of their special status as endangered or threatened wildlife. A list of endangered and threatened wildlife and plants is up-dated and reprinted annually by the United States Fish and Wildlife Service. The following is the 1979 listing for parrots. Kakapo, Glaucous Macaw, Spix Macaw, Forbes'

Parakeet, Queen of Bavaria Conure, Golden-Shouldered Parakeet, Mauritius Ringneck Parakeet, Ochre-marked Parakeet, Splendid Parakeet, Turquoise Parakeet, Orange-Breasted Parakeet, Cuban Amazon, Paradise Parakeet, Ground Parrot, Imperial Amazon, Australian Night Parrot, Puerto Rican Amazon, Red-Browed Amazon, Red-Capped Parrot, Red-Spectacled Amazon, St. Lucia Amazon, St. Vincent Amazon, Thick-Bill Parrot and the Vinaceous Amazon. Unless you have a certificate exempting you from the restrictions (sometimes issued to breeders and zoos) you should not attempt to purchase any of the above species.

Ringneck Parakeet. *Animate Creations*

This bird, a household goddess, lived in our dining-room at Eton. Her cage . . . had a green baize hood for the night. She made a window in this cover with her strong beak whence to see what was happening on and around the mahogany table, especially when the decanters in their trays were circulating after the removal of the cloth. Her bright eye set in a pale wrinkled cheek witnessed these proceedings. Then, dinner ended, and the guests filing out, she would sum up by a mysteriously whispered comment (or was it a blessing?) and instantly vanished for self communion upon her dark perch.

E. L. Warre's Foreword to Brian Reade's *Edward Lear's Parrots*, 1949

Cockatoos in an outdoor flight cage. An enclosure of this kind allows birds the freedom to exercise properly with no risk of their escape. *Photo by author*

3

Cages, Toys and Construction Projects

WHEN SELECTING a cage for your pet it is well to keep in mind that a cage is also a home. Most of the larger parrots can engage in a considerable amount of exercise in a cage designed to permit them activities such as climbing, hanging and the extension and flapping of their wings which can be compared to stretching in human beings. The majority of parrot owners (other than breeders) have neither the space for building flight cages for their pets or the intention to do so. For these parrots, cages of adequate size plus frequent opportunities to exercise outside the cage are vital.

The Right Cage

Parrot cages can be purchased at any large pet shop or department store with a well-stocked pet department. Properly designed cages are made with both owner and bird in mind. Cages for parrots range in size and availability from the common and inexpensive 17 inch square by 24 inch high version to the equally popular and more suitable 19 inch square by 29 inch high variety. The latter is not only bigger but is also constructed more cleverly and features a deeper tray. This means that the tray and its contents (usually dirty and crumpled newspapers plus assorted seed hulls and bits of fruit) can be removed and emptied by anyone without opening the cage door to do

The cage shown here measures 5' × 5' × 4' and is appropriate for the three-foot-long Scarlet Macaw it houses. *Photo by author*

A cardboard box makes a very temporary playpen. *Photo by author*

so. This can be very important if the owner is away for a day or two and a timid relative is giving basic care to the parrots. Much larger cages are available using size formats which include: 36 inches wide by 28 inches deep by 48 inches high, or 48 inches wide by 28 inches deep by 40 inches high. These are known in the trade as "Sweetheart" cages and their heavy duty construction and size make them quite expensive but also provide an eminently suitable lifetime home for a parrot. The taller of the two is ideal for Cockatoos which love to hang and swing as well as climb while the wider variety is excellent for Macaws who can turn and move freely in such a cage without damaging their long, beautiful tails. A less expensive chrome wire version is made by the General Cage Company and it is 36 inches square by 48 inches high. I would not recommend it for particularly destructive Macaws (as so many are) as they can bend the chrome wire if they discover the right leverage. It would make a fine cage, however, for a Cockatoo or a smaller Macaw.

Most cages are equipped with a metal grid designed to slip in just above the bottom of the tray. Remove this grid and store it for possible use in the construction of a toy or exercise device at a later date. It is definitely not needed in a parrot's cage and, if anything, it will prevent your bird from walking, investigating or playing on the bottom of the cage.

In place of this grid (which is provided to make it easier to clean the cage) four sheets of newspaper can be used. For the average-size cage the tabloids are perfect; however the paper should be allowed to "age" for about a month so that the ink is dry and does not soil a bird's feet or harm him if he chews paper. For larger cages it is preferable to use larger newspapers rather than overlapping small sheets. If your own newspaper supply cannot keep up with the demand have friends save copies for you. Make sure your paper suppliers know what the paper is intended for so that they do not inadvertently give you paper which may have been exposed to poisons or lawn chemicals.

Yet another alternative is available. Some news publishers will sell surplus *unprinted* paper in sheets or rolls at reasonable prices. With this plan the parrot owner need have no fear of damage to his pet from news print or pesticides.

Most cages will come complete with a perch and a swing. For a large parrot (16 to 18 inches long) it would be wise to replace the standard swing with a larger one which can be homemade. A smaller swing frequently forces the bird to sit with his head touching the top of the cage, and until a larger swing can be provided it would be kinder to remove the swing completely. Side bars for a good sized

**The height and width of this cage (4' × 3') makes it
quite suitable for housing a large Macaw.**

General Cage Corp.

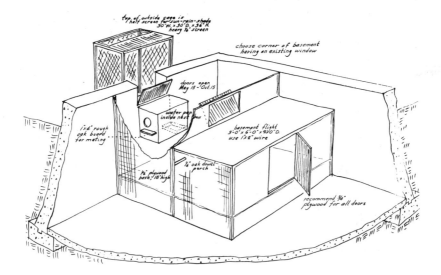

top of outside cage is
1/2 half screen for sun-rain-shade
30"W, x 30"D, x 36"H
heavy 1/2" screen

choose corner of basement
having an existing window

doors open
May 15 - Oct. 15

water pan
inside nest box

basement flight
3'-0" x 6'-0" x 3½'0"D
use 1x2" wire

1x4" rough
oak board
for mating

1/2" plywood
base, 18"high

½" oak dowel
perch

recommend ¾"
plywood for all doors

**For those interested in breeding their birds, a basement
set-up such as this is a highly practical arrangement.**

A large, hand-made cage makes a roomy home for this Cockatoo. *Photo by author*

Noisy, satisfying toys can be found almost anywhere. *Parrot Jungle, Miami*

Nuts must always be on the opposite side of beaks! *Kelley*

48

swing can be made from brass welding rod of about ⅛ inch diameter. The length of the bars should be sufficient so that there is enough stock to crimp for attachment hooks to the cage and still provide a comfortable amount of room for the parrot from the swing to the top of the cage. The swing should be wide enough so that the bird can turn around on it.

Drill holes in the wooden portion of the swing which are slightly smaller than the bars. If you then place the bars in a vise you can gently tap the base of the swing on with a hammer. The forced fit which is achieved in this manner will last indefinitely.

In addition to the perch that comes with the cage, friend parrot can be made happier by being provided with a second perch made from a tree branch. Apple or willow branches are recommended, but caution is advised. Some authorities believe that substances found in the branches of certain trees and shrubs can be harmful to birds.

It's simple to cut a perch from a tree branch and to notch it using a hand or power saw. Always cut the branch longer than you need to allow for errors in measuring and sawing. For the 18 inch cage mentioned before, a branch of about twenty inches would be a good starting point. The diameter of the branch should be anywhere from ½ to ¾ inch. Saw the notches at the ends of the branch just large enough to provide a tight fit when you slip them over the bars of the cage. (Parrots resent perches which wobble and will not use them.) This extra perch can be positioned below the regular perch and somewhat in front of it. This prevents the parrot from soiling the perch if he is seated above it.

Most birds will peel the bark from this new perch and probably destroy it over a period of time. This should not be a problem as this natural branch is easily replaced and chewing is a fun activity that is also useful in keeping a parrot's beak worn down.

Incidentally, don't worry if the branch does not have a regular diameter. The varying thickness of the perch makes it more valuable. Parrots who spend their lives perching on a uniform wooden rod rarely get the opportunity to change the position of their claws. This can be tiring and should be prevented by providing perches with different diameters.

The majority of parrots, unlike most birds, do not build nests out of grass or twigs. In a natural setting parrots will nest in hollow trees, cave-like openings in rocks or the ground or even in termite mounds. Individuals who breed parrots provide nest-boxes for them which are generally designed to simulate the hollow tree arrangement. The nests will vary with the size of the bird and range from

A well-designed, self-constructed aviary that makes wise use of translucent panels. These admit light and help retain heat, but are not easily broken. *Kelley*

This home aviary, located in the Pacific Northwest, was designed, situated and built to provide the birds living in it maximum protection from all extremes of weather. *Kelley*

boxes which are only seven inches square by about ten inches high (for Budgies and Love Birds) to huge affairs referred to as the "grandfather clock" type because their shape and dimensions resemble such a clock cabinet. For the larger species many breeders prefer to use large barrels or even suitably cut twenty-gallon garbage pails. The use of these large nest boxes would, of course, occur in a flight as obviously they would take most of the room if one attempted to use them in a regulation-size cage.

Toys from Many Sources

Toys for parrots generally fall in the categories of objects which can be chewed, manipulated or banged against the sides of the cage to produce a loud noise. Although many toys are made for Budgies, you will find virtually nothing on the market for parrots since their destructive nature and powerful beaks quickly reduce most toys to wreckage. By using your ingenuity and a few simple hand tools, you can create toys which will be popular with your birds and which will last a reasonably long time. Twigs from willow or apple trees are as excellent for toys as for perches. If cut to finger lengths, they can be easily managed by a pet bird. Green twigs are ideal and both owner and parrot will take pleasure from the way the bird delicately removes the bark in one piece from a willow twig and then reduces the juicy twig to splinters. I have mentioned apple and willow specifically because I know they are safe. If these are not available to you, I strongly recommend that you check with your local poison control center before offering branches of other plants. Only use twigs from trees which you know have not been sprayed with insecticides for several years. If in doubt, forget that particular toy.

Small pieces of pine about two inches square by one half inch thick will make a fine chewing toy. The parrot keeper can cut his own or have a large number cut at the local lumber yard very inexpensively. The quality of the pine does not matter although wood with knots is much harder to cut and impossible for a parrot to chew through. Naturally, the wood should be paint and chemical free. By drilling a small hole in the center of the wood and hanging it from the top of the cage the parrot is provided with a chewing challenge which will not fall to the bottom of the cage to be soiled or lost. If a leather thong is used to hang the wood, be sure it is thick enough so the bird cannot create a noose and injure himself. A chain (which I much prefer) should have links large enough so that beak and claws cannot be trapped. Don't discard the broken pieces which the parrot will

51

create from these blocks as they can be reused as claw-held chewables. If after a while it is found that the parrot is neglecting his block, extra holes can be drilled through it. Strange shapes and textures seem to attract parrots and a new hole or two which is just the right size in which to nestle a beak will rekindle his interest.

Split pieces of wood are also particularly encouraging to lazy birds. These chewing games are valuable not only for recreation but also help to keep the beak in shape.

Wooden spools are rapidly becoming extinct as more and more manufacturers move to plastic versions. Ask your friends and relatives to save all the wooden ones they can for you as parrots love to play with and then split these soft wooden objects.

A small cowbell or any other sturdy bell will prove an object of delight to a bird. When it is hung from a chain in his cage, he not only rings it by smashing it against the sides of the cage but he will also hang from it and ride it in an effort to create a maximum amount of noise. A spoon with a hole drilled through the handle so it can be hung in the cage makes a fine toy as parrots find this shape is pleasant to manipulate. A baby spoon or demitasse spoon is even more fun.

Clean stones about the size of a large marble will be rolled, banged, and eventually thrown from the cage but they cost nothing and provide activity.

Just about every parrot loves a mirror but, finding one that will withstand his attentions is difficult. Auto supply stores usually carry vanity mirrors with frames. Gluing one of these to a hard oak block and using the spring clips which come with the mirror to attach the block to the bars of the cage usually work out quite well. For really destructive parrots a larger mirror can be hung outside the cage.

Rawhide or other leather toys made for dogs are also very useful. A ball-shaped rawhide toy drilled through and hung in the cage will last for a very long time. The same is true of the large leather or rawhide bones. If you have friends who work in leather, or if you have access to a craft shop, ask for the scraps which would normally be discarded. Providing the material has not been dyed, it can be quite valuable as toys for a pet parrot.

Toys which provide exercise as well as diversion are especially valuable. A large trapeze falls into this catagory and can be easily and inexpensively constructed out of safe materials. To make it usable by all sizes of parrots I recommend dimensions of approximately 36 inches for the side bars and approximately the same for the perch portion upon which the parrot will sit. Brass welding rod of ¼ inch diameter may be used for the sides while the perch portion can be

At this Long Island aviary, birds benefit from the spacious design of the structure and other features which protect them from the elements. *Photo by author*

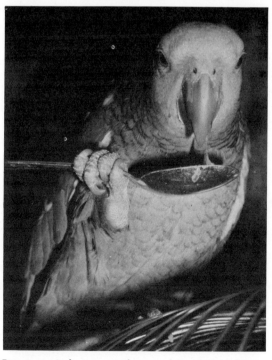

Parrots can make toys out of an amazing variety of objects, as demonstrated by this inventive Double Yellow Head.

Kelley

made either of electrician's conduit, a hard wooden dowel or a sandpapered portion of broom or mop handle. The construction technique is much like that for the making of the swing described earlier. Bending brass rod of this diameter may not be possible for the average individual, but the loops or hooks can be bent at the same time the rod is being purchased. If it is impossible to find someone with the proper bending tool then the loop can be hammered into shape. Use the same forced fit technique as mentioned earlier, but if you are using electrician's conduit as the base of the trapeze, attempt to peen the welding rod so it cannot slip out and then file off any rough bits of metal which remain. An alternative to peening would be to drill the rods and insert cotter pins. I have used both techniques and find that the cotter pins seem to attract inquisitive beaks.

For maximum pleasure the trapeze should be hung from the ceiling and you can use the standard decorative hooks with which people generally hang plants. Your trapeze loops can fit over these hooks and you may then squeeze the hooks with large pliers (using care to avoid breaking them) so that the trapeze is permanently mounted but can still swing back and forth. My smaller parrots climb the sides of the trapezes and tap the ceiling with their beaks when they reach the top much in the manner of a rope climber showing he has reached his goal. The Cockatoos and Macaws actually fly around the bars by holding their claws in a loose position. My Greater Sulfur Crested Cockatoo flaps her wings with such abandon when she is on the trapeze that she frequently brings it to an almost horizontal position.

Other Parrot Playthings

An old pole lamp with the lamp fixtures removed can make the basis for a fine climbing toy. The poles will expand or compress to fit any ceiling and cross bars can be added at intervals which should be determined by the size and agility of the parrots that will use it. Once again, keep safety in mind. Smooth off any rough edges and fill in any tiny holes where a claw might catch. The holes can be filled in with a tightly threaded sheet metal screw driven flush with the surface. A planter pole can be used if you don't happen to have an old pole lamp. The toy can be made even more interesting by wiring a section of tree to it. This is the next best thing to having a small tree growing in your birdroom.

The spring and fall tend to be fence building time in many parts of the country. When fence sections are installed on irregular terrain a large number of useless pieces of four inch posts may be discarded.

Natural perches are most preferable for parrots. The irregular surfaces and varying diameters of branches are more comfortable for them than man-made perches.

Photo by author

Chewing comes naturally to a parrot, so toys and furnishings should be chosen accordingly. The soft wood upon which this mirror was mounted shows the effects of a hookbill's play. *Photo by author*

If you can get permission to collect a number of these they can be nailed or glued together in an intricate shape that the typical, inquisitive parrot will find intriguing. Make the base extremely wide so that there is absolutely no chance of the little tower collapsing or anchor it so that it cannot fall over. A similar toy (which will also help in keeping nails worn down) can be made of cement blocks.

Always be on the lookout for objects which can serve as parrot playthings. The alert parrot keeper may come across them in the most unexpected places. For example, my doctor recently mentioned that he was discarding a large box of wooden tongue depressors because the lid had opened and they were no longer sterile. I asked if I could have them and for months my parrots were splitting tongue depressors until their cages looked like toothpick factories.

Before offering a parrot any toys or devices with which to hang the toy, give some thought to whether or not the objects pose any danger to the bird's safety and well-being. If there are any doubts, discard the device.

In purchasing a cage for a parrot, one must be sure to select one strong enough to house its tenant properly. Here is a graphic example of what can happen when the wrong cage is used. This Hyacinth Macaw was able to bend the ¼ inch steel bars all around the cage.

Photo by author

They are exceedingly docile and talkative. The specimen which I have seen imitated everything that was said, called all of the family by name, and was exceedingly obedient, faithful and good-tempered.

J. M. Bechstein on Macaws, *Cage and Chamber Birds,* 1794

A fresh, well-designed mix of seeds will lengthen your parrot's life.

8 in 1 Pet Products

Water soluble, liquid vitamins can be added to the parrot's drinking water and will be readily accepted. *Lambert Kay*

4

Feeding for Health, Vigor and Longevity

IF YOU OWN A PARROT it is up to you to provide the same degree of thought and care regarding his diet as you would for any other member of the family. Contrary to popular myth, parrots cannot subsist solely on hard biscuits and sunflower seeds. They are independent creatures and each has its own individual tastes. To insure good health, however, a parrot should receive a balanced, well chosen mixture of foods.

Seed

The person who owns only one parrot and lives in a fairly large city, can probably buy parrot food in ready mixed packages at the local supermarket or pet shop. Adequate mixtures are put out by a number of companies that pack foods for cage birds. Avoid buying parrot seed from stores which do not seem to turn over their inventory very quickly. These seed mixes have a short shelf life and if kept around too long the seeds will become "webby," a condition caused by a small moth which completes its life cycle in the seeds. While the moths are not harmful to the health of a parrot they are an unnecessary nuisance. Old seeds won't hurt a parrot but they won't do him as much good as fresh ones because aging tends to diminish the nutritional value of seeds.

The owner willing to go to a litte trouble, can provide a much better parrot mix by buying seeds in bulk and doing his own mixing. Most of the seeds needed can be located at a feed store or pet shop. Mixing the following seeds together will yield a blend that hookbills find pleasing and nutritious:

Sunflower seed—Sunflower seed has been fed to cage birds for centuries. There are a number of varieties such as dark, gray and striped but basically sunflower is an oil-rich seed which is high in fat and protein content. Virtually all parrots will eat sunflower in large amounts. This is fortunate as the fats are important in the role they play as a storehouse of reserve energy and in furnishing protection against cold weather. On the other hand, excessive fats can interfere with digestion. Proteins are crucial for growth and repair of cells and tissues and animals must have proteins to survive. Sunflower is physically, highly suitable for parrots as its size is convenient for them to hold and it opens easily and cleanly to yield its contents. Sunflower is frequently referred to as "polly" seed.

Canary seed—If you examine the physical appearance of canary you will note its resemblance to grass seed. This is not strange as canary seed planted will actually grow into a species of grass. Virtually all seed-eating birds will eat and benefit from this good source of carbohydrates and proteins. Carbohydrates include the substances we refer to as sugar and starch. Carbohydrates can be stored in the form of starch and then converted by a parrot to sugar for use as energy.

Millet—Millet is frequently fed in either the white or red form. Although the seeds are quite small, parrots can handle them due to their great dexterity. A parrot who turns up his nose at the carbohydrate-rich millet seed may show interest in it when it is in the form of a millet spray. It is typical of the parrot personality that they will make an edible toy of the interesting millet spray.

Rape—This small dark seed is related to the cabbage family. It is not always popular among the parrots but is worth trying as it is a rich source of fats and oils.

Hemp—In recent years the *Cannabis* family has come into disrepute. The hemp seeds which can be purchased in the feed store have been sterilized to prevent them from being purposely or accidentally used to grow new plants as *Cannabis* is the source of marijuana. The seeds lacks the hallucinogen but was frequently considered by older authors as a dangerous seed which might induce plucking or feather mutilation. This concept is generally disregarded today. Hemp is a nourishing and valuable source of proteins, fats and carbohydrates. Its size, physical structure and pungent odor make it a popular seed with most parrots. Although quite expensive it is worth including in the mix in small quantities.

Safflower—This valuable seed has become quite popular in recent years. It is a good source of oil and protein and can prove especially valuable for the occasional parrot who is hard to get started on sunflower seed. Safflower seed is large enough to make it easily handled by parrots.

Oats and groats—Groats are simply hulled oats. In general, oats are not particularly popular with parrots but you will find them in many mixes. They are quite fattening and if your parrot happens to enjoy them they should only be given in limited amounts.

A suitable seed mixture would be about ¼ cup of sunflower seeds with the remaining ¾ cup to be made up of a blend of as many of the other seeds mentioned which can be obtained. Sunflower, canary and safflower seeds are musts in a well-balanced diet.

A full-sized parrot should eat about a cup of seeds a day, however, a smart owner should not wait for his cup to empty before feeding him again. Parrots have a habit of depositing empty seed husks in their food cup giving the false impression that the cup is filled with seed.

Treats

One or two peanuts (in the shell) a day are a treat for the bird and also a treat for you. You can watch him carefully open the nut while holding it in one claw without dropping a bit or falling off his perch.

Small dog biscuits may also be included in the mix two or three times a week. I recommend the type which come in assorted colors and shapes as parrots find this attractive. If feeding peanuts or dog biscuits interferes with the normal seed diet, cut back on the amount and the number of times a week you provide these treats.

Fruits and Vegetables

Fruits and vegetables are also important as they form the basic natural diet of many parrot species. Apples, grapes, pears, peaches, corn on the cob and cherries are all suitable for parrots. A single grape and a small slice of apple a day is sufficient fruit for smaller parrots. Larger parrots such as Macaws can safely consume two to three times this amount of fruit. Carrot and beet tops, including the leaves and stems, are relished by parrots and are highly nutritious. A word of caution: It is vital that any fruits or vegetables be thoroughly washed to remove residues of chemicals with which they may have been sprayed before being offered to a bird.

Parrots have highly individual tastes so one can feel free to experiment with any kind of fruits and vegetables. Just make sure all produce is fresh and unwilted. If in doubt do not use it.

In warm weather the newly washed, dripping greens can be put on top of the bird's cage. Not only will he get nutritious food, he will also get the added treat of a gentle shower as he pulls them into the cage.

Seeds should be fed at night and fruits and vegetables the following morning. In this way fruit and vegetables can be removed the following evening after friend parrot has eaten as much as he wants. This routine also assures that the fruits and vegetables do not lie around the cage long enough to spoil.

The Importance of Water

Fresh water in a clean cup is very important to any bird. For many years people were not aware of the parrot's need for drinking water. They assumed that these birds got all of their moisture from their food. Actually many parrots do not drink large amounts of water but they do require it and in the wild can usually be spotted near water sources. Dr. Greene, a well-known 19th century writer, campaigned for many years to improve conditions for parrots in the London Zoo. He was extremely unhappy because the keepers of that time seemed unaware of the parrots' need for a regular supply of fresh water.

Vitamins and Minerals

Vitamins and minerals are only necessary in very small quantities. A good, fresh mix of seeds plus fruits and vegetables should take care of this requirement. Since a captive parrot does not have access to all the foods he could select from in the wild many people choose to give vitamin supplements in an effort to enhance the parrot's diet. A water soluble, liquid vitamin added to the parrot's drinking water rather than to his seed is most preferable. In this way he will not be deprived of seeds if he is not in the mood for vitamins.

Other Essentials

Although parrots are seed eaters they lack teeth to grind their food. It is up to the owner to provide gravel which the parrot's digestive system uses in lieu of teeth. Number two gravel is an appropriate size and can be purchased quite inexpensively at any pet shop. Sprinkle some on the bottom of the cage and also put a pinch or two into the seed cup.

62

Cooked rice is an excellent transition food for young birds that have passed the baby food stage and are just learning how to handle hard seeds. *Photo by author*

Handling large amounts of seed is made more convenient with the storage system illustrated here and discussed in the text. A dehumidifier in the storage area helps seed to remain fresh and palatable. *Photo by author*

Cuttle bone and ground oyster shell are important sources of calcium which should be provided for a pet parrot. Unfortunately, many parrots will ignore the rather expensive cuttlebone offered them. I find that breaking the cuttlebone into five or six pieces and placing a piece in the cage each night to be more effective (and cheaper) than mounting the whole cuttlebone on the side of the cage. Many parrots remove the cuttlebone from its clip in a few moments anyway. Ground oyster shell is cheap and a pinch or two can be added to the seed cup each evening.

The "B" vitamins are as vital to parrots as they are to people. A sprinkle of brewer's yeast or a 7½ grain tablet in the food dish each night will help your winged companion to retain his health and live a long and active life.

The Problem Eater

Some parrots are very much like children in that they are problem eaters. Birds who restrict themselves to one seed will survive but will not necessarily fulfill their potential for a long, healthy life. Do not attempt to starve such a bird into eating properly as this does not work any better with parrots than it does with children. One technique that can be used, however, is to color rejected seeds with a variety of natural food colors. Parrots have a limited sense of smell and taste but excellent color vision. They are attracted to colorful objects and may try a red sunflower or a blue safflower which was rejected in its normal state of coloration. Another technique to use with recalcitrant eaters is to change cups and locations. A bird may be rejecting seeds because he is unhappy or uncomfortable with a particular dish or the location of the dish. Exhibit patience and ingenuity and you will probably be delighted when you eventually find the empty hulls of previously rejected seeds.

Seed Storage and Vermin Control

When purchasing seeds in bulk to make your own mix do not hesitate to stress to the merchant that you want fresh seeds. If moths or insects appear within a relatively short time ask about returning the remainder of the seeds for a credit.

Several elements of good housekeeping will help diminish the number of insects and rodents which commonly exist where seed is stored in large quantities. As an initial step always store large amounts of seeds in new, clean, galvanized garbage pails. A 20-gallon pail can easily hold 50 pounds of seed. The pail should first be lined with a

This gaudy gaggle of Macaws consists of (above, from left) a Catalina hybrid, a Scarlet and a Blue and Gold. Arrayed on the lower branch (from left) are a Military, and, flanked by two Scarlets, another Blue and Gold. *Parrot Jungle, Miami*

Tres Marias subspecies of the Double Yellow Head. *Andrews*

Double Yellow Head. *Freud*

Green Cheeked Amazon, or Mexican Red Head. *Goyanes*

St. Vincent Amazon. *New York Zoological Society*

Mealy Amazon. *Kelley*

Blue Fronted Amazon. *Reed*

Yellow Naped Amazon. *Freud*

Yellow Fronted Amazon. *Kelley*

Green Winged Macaw. *Kelley*

Military Macaw. *Egbert*

Left: Viewing a group of adult Hyacinth Macaws in full, glorious plumage is a never-to-be-forgotten experience. *Parrot Jungle, Miami*

African Greys, popular favorites for generations. *Kelley*

Red Fronted Macaws, intriguing rarities. *Crimmson Star*

Noble Macaw, smallest of all Macaw species. *Kelley*

"Long distance, please." *Parrot Jungle, Miami*

A patriotic way to start the day. *Parrot Jungle, Miami*

71

The Scarlet Macaw and the Blue and Gold Macaw rank high among the most colorful of all birds and are the best known of all Macaws. *Parrot Jungle, Miami*

heavy duty plastic bag large enough to overlap the rim and with enough excess to fold down the plastic and close the bag once all the seeds have been poured into it. Never store the pails of seed directly on the floor of the bird room as the resulting moisture formation can ruin the contents. A few cinder blocks or two by fours make excellent racks to keep the pails off the floor. As a general rule it is also best to avoid buying very large quantities of seeds just before summer as in many parts of the country hot, humid weather accelerates the development of any larval forms whose eggs may already be present. It is practically impossible to avoid a certain number of these creatures. However, these candy moths (as they are called in the seed trade) do no harm and because they are attracted by water tend to kamikaze on a regular basis into your parrot's water cups or any other open containers of water which may be kept in the bird room. If their presence becomes really annoying or if they start to migrate to other parts of the house, keep several shallow pans of water around the bird room.

Mice present a second major problem in the storage of seed. Obvious techniques in the battle against mice are preventive. Be sure that no openings exist from the birdroom to the outside. A good way to check for such openings is to stand in the room with lights out while there is still a small amount of sunlight available. Close examination of areas where floors and walls meet will show cracks of light if an opening exists. These openings should be stuffed with steel wool and then plastered or cemented shut. Floors should be swept and vac-uumed nightly as mice will generally not appear from their hiding places while a person is in the room. Avoid the temptation of storing material which could be used as a snug nest for a mouse family. If in spite of all of your precautions extremely cold weather or a garage door which has been carelessly left open brings you unwelcome visitors, you must remove them or they will multiply rapidly. Simple, old-fashioned mouse traps placed in parts of the room which are not accessible to the parrots do a creditable job. Be absolutely sure, however, that they are situated where no inquisitive beak or claw can reach them or your bird may be severely injured. Caution other members of the household about their location as well. Poisoned bait should not be used under any circumstances. Such material is generally in the form of seed and if accidentally tracked by a mouse into the bird room, tragedy could result. If you feel you must use methods other than simple traps check for points of entry you may have missed or investigate the new sonic devices which many farmers are using to keep barns and other areas completely free of rodents.

"Long distance, please." *Parrot Jungle, Miami*

Speke, Parrot
WITH my becke bent, my lyttyl wanton eye,
My fedders freshe as is the emrawde green,
About my neck a cyrculet lyke the ryche rubye,
My lyttlyl leggys, my feet both fete and clene,
I am a mynyon to wayt uppon a quene;
My proper Parrot, my lyttyl pretty foole,
With ladyes I lerne, and go with them
     to scole.

John Skelton, English laureate poet, 1512

5

"Polly Wanna Talk?"

M ANY PEOPLE WONDER why parrots and a few
other bird families have the ability to speak or mimic. There seems to
be something to the theory that this particular talent helps paired or
mated birds to remain linked when separated by distance. This can
even be noted in the home aviary or birdroom when a member of a
pair is taken to another part of the house. The particular screeches
and calls of one parrot will be returned in an almost identical fashion
by the other.

Perhaps the words a parrot speaks are attempts on his part to
link himself to his owner or to remind his owner that he is there.
Groups of parrots practically explode in speech when a beloved
owner arrives in the bird room and virtual bedlam ensues when the
owner starts to leave as the birds chatter away in an effort to entice
him to stay.

The Parrot's Vocal Mechanism

Parrots have large, thick tongues and like all the other birds
possess a well developed syrinx. The syrinx is the vocal structure in
birds and is a modified portion of the lower windpipe. In man, sound
is produced in the larynx which is a structure similar to the syrinx.
The lips and tongue then modulate the sound in such a way that it
becomes speech and is capable of imparting information. Parrots, of
course, lack lips and observers note that there is not much tongue

movement when they speak, thus the speech may partially originate in the syrinx. Some parrots actually whistle but a great many more imitate the sound of a whistle by screaming in a high-pitched voice.

Do They Understand?

Many people wonder whether or not parrots truly understand the significance of the words they use. Obviously, they sometimes do form patterns of association between words and the time of the day or certain activities. On the other hand, they will repeat things at inappropriate moments and are also guilty of inverting words and phrases without showing any awareness of having done so. It is safe to say that a parrot who says "Good morning" in the morning and "Good night" at night has learned to associate these sounds with a particular time of day but does not realize that they are actually greetings. Before you can teach your parrot to talk you must win his confidence by convincing him that neither you nor anything else in his new surroundings pose a threat to him. When he is calm he can concentrate on learning.

Acclimating the New Parrot

When you and your new, large-beaked friend return home from the bird shop, bring the parrot, in his cage, directly to the room where he will live. Try to avoid having him receive a clamorous greeting from other members of the family, including pets. Once acclimated, screaming children and barking dogs will not bother him at all. As a matter of fact, he will probably imitate them. But in the beginning avoid unnecessary stress and pressure.

It is only natural that you will want to pet your new parrot or even take him out his cage to play with him. This could be a mistake as at this point, your home is a totally new environment and he will probably feel insecure because he has been taken away from a place that was more familiar to him. Go slow and keep in mind that the first step is simply to make friend parrot feel comfortable and secure in his new home.

Start with his Name

No doubt you will have chosen a name for the bird by this time (names of one or two syllables are easiest for the parrot to learn) and repetition of phrases such as: "Good Boy Jaco," or "Pretty Boy Jaco," can be the start of his vocabulary. (Jaco is the time-honored parrot

76

name given by Portuguese sailors to the African Greys they captured. They chose the name because the echo of the bird's natural cry sounded very much like "Jaco" to them.)

The Logical Approach

Many parrot owners make the mistake of using a hit-or-miss approach to try to get their pets to talk. While it isn't necessary to drill one word and not advance until the parrot has learned it perfectly, a planned and logical approach will reap greater and quicker rewards.

Make a list of the words and phrases that you say to your bird frequently. The list will probably include the phrases mentioned before and others such as "Supper time," "Hello," "Good Night," and the like. Since the bird will hear you say these words or phrases frequently without your making a conscious effort to say them, you can further reinforce the learning experience by attempting to use these phrases as much as possible. The only drawback to this technique is that the parrot may learn to say the phrases at inappropriate times.

One of the most delightful characteristics of talking birds is their ability to speak words and phrases in such a way thay they appear to actually know what they are saying. This is, of course, conditioning or sometimes just chance. The bird will say, "Good Morning," in the morning because that's when you say it to him. If you use the technique mentioned here your parrot may develop a large vocabulary but one which doesn't make much sense in a given situation.

Do not expect your parrot to always pick up a complete word or phrase. Many times you will have to settle for only part of a word. I purchased a Scarlet Macaw who arrived with the ability to say "Butter." When I had the oppoutunity to talk to his former owner, I discovered that the parrot was not expressing an interest in the high-priced spread but was calling his former master's dog whose name was Buttercup. Parrots are also guilty of inverting or transposing parts of words or phrases. Birl, my Mealy Amazon, earned his name because when he gets excited he combines "Hello Boy" and "Hello Girl" to produce "Hello Birl." He also says "Helli" whose origin is easy to figure out. The fact that my family and I laughed and made a big fuss over these cute errors reinforced the phrases and made them a constant part of his vocabulary.

In general, it is a waste of training time to teach a parrot to whistle. It is much like teaching a fish to swim. Common whistles such as the "wolf whistle" (a natural jungle cry of the African Grey which confused many GIs during World War II) are indeed a waste of time.

77

Teaching a simple tune, however, is possible and can be quite amusing. The best tunes to teach are those that are easily recognized. *Pop Goes the Weasel* or the *Woody Woodpecker Song* are good starts. Don't try for all the verses and choruses and remember that the bird will not add his own skills to those of his trainer. If the trainer whistles poorly or cannot carry a tune, somebody else should handle the musical end of the bird's education.

Patience is a Virtue

Teaching a parrot to talk requires great patience. If you are serious about training, be ready to spend about 30 minutes a day repeating words and phrases to your parrot. The time of day you choose is not important. Just pick a time that is convenient for you. You can also break the total time into several sessions.

Patience is very important because it sometimes takes weeks and perhaps even months before the fruits of the trainer's labor are seen.

It is difficult to say how long it should take for a parrot to learn. On the average I estimate that it takes about a month to teach a new word to a parrot. However, I have had parrots that learned a new phrase in a day or so. I would say that if after eight to twelve months of trying you haven't succeeded, resign yourself to the fact that your parrot is not going to talk.

Factors for Success

The bird's age, degree of tameness and previous vocabulary will all be important factors in the parrot's progress. Although there are exceptions, as a general rule parrots must be taught to speak before they are 18 months old. It also appears that tame parrots learn to speak with greater ease than wild birds. Thus, if a bird is mean and untameable, he is not as good a candidate for speech class as a friendlier bird.

Even though it is doubtful that a parrot who is more than two years old can learn to speak, a parrot who has uttered a few words during his first two years of life can always increase his vocabulary throughout his life. This is the reason why talking parrots are so desirable and so expensive. They have already proven their ability.

Teaching a parrot to talk is basically a matter of repeating a word or phrase until it is picked up by the bird. Begin with a single phrase and stick with it until the parrot learns all or part of the phrase. However, if he doesn't respond, introduce other words and phrases. Parrots seem to repeat some words more quickly than others.

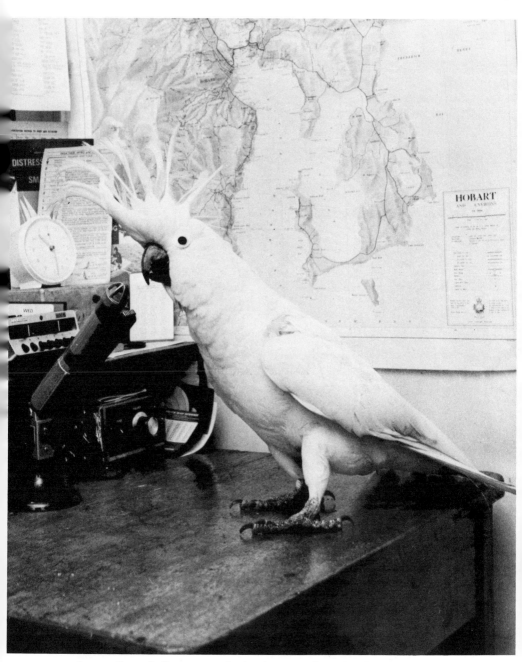

Can a really good talker operate a ham station? *Australian Information Service*

Parrots tend to repeat those things which please them. The pleasure may lie in the sound of a particular word or phrase or he may attempt a word and then repeat it often when he notes your excited reaction to his mimicry.

I sometimes wonder who is being trained. Bill, my Yellow-Naped Amazon discovered that when he calls my name loudly I come running with a treat for him. The urge to respond to an animal who is calling your name is irresistible! Of course, I realize that Bill doesn't know that he's saying my name but he does know that this particular sound is associated with me and also that he is rewarded when he says it.

Mechanical Aids

With the advent of inexpensive tape recorders, it is now possible to teach a parrot to talk even when no one is home. Do not make one long tape. Instead, buy an endless tape loop. This is a cassette which repeats the same message over and over again. A good quality tape loop is manufactured by TDK in one minute, three minute, six minute and longer formats. It can be purchased at any well-stocked electronic supply store.

Before making the recording, the owner should actually prepare a small script. Otherwise the loop will be filled with pauses and grunts. The recording should be made in as clear a voice as possible. The loop should not be filled; if it is, the bird will never get a moment's peace during the day as the loop will chatter away at him constantly. A parrot should be spoken to in a normal voice. One should resist the urge to sound like a parrot, or worse, how he imagines a parrot should sound.

Additional Points

A number of old wives' tales have persisted through the years regarding the techniques of teaching parrots to talk.

It is not necessary to isolate a parrot from other birds to teach him to speak. In fact, keeping him with other talking birds may actually enlarge his vocabulary because he can learn from his parrot neighbors.

With few exceptions female birds are as adept as males in learning to talk. Contrary to what many of the older books state in most species sex bears no relationship to speaking ability. I have actually owned female parrots who spoke better than males of the same species.

Do parrots really talk? *Kelley*

An endless tape loop is a useful teaching aide. *TDK Electronics*

Parrots do seem to prefer to emulate high pitched sounds but it is not vital that their instruction be given by women or by young children.

It is of no value to cover the parrot's cage while teaching him to speak. This is recommended by some to avoid distraction. Actually, the act of learning does not occur only when one is actively teaching the parrot, and covering the cage can itself be distracting, especially if it is not normally done. It can actually impede progress instead of helping to reach a goal.

Profanity and other rude expressions are not funny if a bird repeats them in front of children or strangers. Since such expressions are generally short and easy to say, parrots do pick them up easily. Avoiding them at the beginning is better than regret later. Attempting to get a parrot to unlearn a word or phrase is even more difficult than getting him to say it in the first place.

While recrossing the river a pretty little parrot fell head-long into our boat, having dropped from a flock which seemed to be fighting in the air. I was surprised to find the bird uninjured. There had probably been a quarrel resulting in our little stranger being temporarily stunned by a blow on the head from the beak of a jealous comrade. It was a Green Conure with a patch of scarlet under the wings and called by the natives Maracana. *All of our efforts to reconcile it to captivity were in vain; it refused food, bit everyone who went near it, and damaged its plumage in its exertions to free itself. My friends said that this kind of parrot never became domesticated so I gave the intractable creature to an old Indian woman who was said to be a skillful bird tamer. In two days she brought it back almost as tame as the familiar Love-Birds of our aviaries. I do not know what arts the old woman used but I believe the chief reason why almost all animals become so wonderfully tame in the house of the natives is their being treated with uniform gentleness.*

Adapted from *The Naturalist On The River Amazon*
By Henry Walter Bates, 1863

Henry Walter Bates traveled through South America collecting and observing for a period of almost eleven years. Bate's journey took place in 1848.

A fully relaxed Hyacinth Macaw. *Photo by author*

6
Training Techniques

EVEN THOUGH PARROTS ARE INTELLIGENT and have the capacity to become tame and learn many tricks, they possess natural protective instincts which may, at first, interfere with training efforts. For this reason the first step in any successful training program is to gain the parrot's confidence.

The greatest problem for most new parrot owners is impatience. They generally choose a parrot as a pet because they have seen how charming and delightful a parrot's behavior is in the home of a friend or perhaps on television. Many people unrealistically expect similar behavior as soon as they purchase a bird of their own, but this kind of behavior takes time to develop. If you can overcome the urge to expect and demand too much too soon, you will have a better chance of successfully training your own parrot.

Gaining a Parrot's Confidence

Once the parrot has been brought home and is located in the room where he will live, he should be allowed to settle down for several hours before being approached. The new owner can, of course, fill his seed and water dishes and provide a few kind words; but an opportunity for him to quietly look around his new cage and his new location is very important.

At this stage, it is best not to clutter up the parrot's cage with too many toys or a swing. As a matter of fact, a swing can wait until the bird is hand-trained—otherwise the swing will be something extra for him to grab as he attempts to avoid an eagerly outstretched hand.

A playful and valuable armful. *Photo by author*

She has him in the palm of her hand. *Photo by author*

There is nothing sadder than a parrot who stays in his cage all the time. These intelligent little creatures not only need and enjoy exercise but also thrive on attention, physical contact and the opportunity to see new sights and hear different sounds. For this reason, the first training efforts should aim towards hand-training the parrot. This is nothing more than training the bird to leave his cage on a person's hand or finger. Unless the newly-purchased parrot was previously trained and is superbly confident, his first reaction when the cage door is opened will probably be to move as far away from the new owner as he can and to avoid looking at this "stranger" in the hope he will go away.

Place your hand in the cage with the palm down and rest it on the perch near your parrot. Try to make some sort of physical contact with his feet or body but be sure to do it slowly, as rapid or abrupt movements will frighten the parrot.

Do not be intimidated by the bird's threatening noises or gestures. In general, a parrot's reaction to danger is to attempt to avoid it. He will make every effort to get away from a hand before he actually bites it. He will also probably fluff up his feathers and raise his wings in an effort to look larger and more threatening. Unless the bird is a "bronco" (a wild, possibly untamable parrot), most of this behavior is pure bluff. Take your hand out of the cage and let him calm down for a few minutes. Leave the door of the cage open and sit in a chair nearby as you talk to the parrot, using a gentle tone and calling him by name. Repeat this procedure five or six times and then let him rest and relax until the next training session.

After a day or two the parrot will realize that your hand is now a familiar object and should react in a calmer fashion when you put it into the cage.

Finger Taming

When you can get this far, the next step is to close your fingers so that only the index finger is extended, and again, with the palm of your hand facing down, place the index finger either under his claws or against his belly. If the parrot intends to climb onto your hand, he will use his beak to steady himself when he places his claws on your extended finger. This is a moment of truth for you and the parrot. Is the beak coming down to bite you, or is he simply using it as a third foot, as parrots do? You will never know unless you take a chance and keep your hand steady. If you jerk your hand away, you will frighten the bird, who might have been getting ready to climb onto your hand. Keep your hand steady and risk his bite. It is worth the risk, as it is the first step toward a future relationship. If you are dealing with a large bird or you are very concerned about being bitten but still wish to test the bird's intentions offer your arm or wrist instead of your finger as the parrot cannot get a really good biting grip on these parts of the body.

Some birds will meet taming efforts only part way. They will place one claw on the proffered hand and keep the other on the bars of the cage. Don't attempt to pull a parrot that does this out of the cage, as it is virtually impossible to do so. As quickly as you unfasten one claw from the bar, he will grip another. Instead, take the opportunity to pet him gently as he sits there with one claw on your hand and holds on to the cage for dear life with his other foot. Do not be concerned or upset if he nibbles you or even squeezes firmly with his beak. It is only actual biting (where blood is drawn) that cannot be tolerated. All other actions with his beak should be considered in the same light as the innocent mouthings of a young puppy.

If you do not get a positive reaction in your efforts to encourage the parrot to climb onto your finger, try pushing gently on his belly with the edge of your open hand (once again with the palm down). If you persist with this gentle pressure, he will either climb onto your hand or be pushed off the perch. Most parrots will choose the former. If either technique works and you now have the parrot on your hand, let him know how pleased you are by praising him and then move him gently to a "T" stand. Sit quietly some distance from the "T" stand while the parrot familiarizes himself with his new location. He will probably engage in a certain amount of wing flapping, but this is just his way of stretching and is not an indication that he is about to fly away. In anticipation of training, ask the bird seller or your veterinarian to clip the flight feathers on one wing so that the parrot's ability to fly will be limited. This is painless and harmless to the bird and saves the new owner a great deal of running and climbing. A parrot who has one wing clipped can fly well enough to break his fall if he leaves his "T" stand, but cannot fly any great distance.

If friend parrot refuses out of his cage with these techniques there are several alternatives left. One is the procedure known as stick training. This is similar to the method described above, but instead of offering the bird his hand, the trainer substitutes a short (about six inches) length of perch. It is astonishing to watch a parrot who has refused any contact with a hand climb amicably upon the stick, which to him represents a familiar object, similar to his own perch. Use the stick to move the parrot to a "T" stand and thereafter keep shortening the stick by holding more of it in your hand. Eventually, the parrot will have one foot on the stick and one on your hand. From that point

Pinky the Moluccan riding her bike. *Parrot Jungle, Miami*

"I think this one goes here." *Parrot Jungle, Miami*

on you should be able to use your hand in place of the stick. Don't wait too long to make the transition from stick to hand because the longer you wait the less the parrot will want to give up his little security blanket.

When you reach the point where you can hold your bird, try to keep him on your index finger so that you can gently but firmly anchor him by placing your thumb over his claws. If he attempts to fly, (which he will probably do if you move or walk with him) it is important that you move your hand to follow the direction of thrust and lift generated by his flapping wings. If you fail to do this, his feet or claws can be injured by the strain placed on them.

If you don't seem to be getting anywhere with hand or stick training, a third technique is to keep the door of the parrot's cage open until he climbs out by himself. It is almost second nature for a parrot to do this and he will undoubtedly end up on top of his cage. Once he has done this, you can try using either your hand or the stick technique. Many people actually prefer to begin at this point, as the bird has fewer places to move on top of the cage when you offer him your hand.

Head Scratching

After a week or two, getting your hookbill in and out of the cage should no longer be a challenge. It is now time to aim your sights a bit higher. Most parrots love to have their heads scratched in the nape (back) of the neck. They also like to have their cheeks and the area below the jaw scratched. The only problem is getting them to permit the first scratch so they can see how delightful it is. Parrots are very wary of movement coming from above them. Therefore, work your way up by touching the parrot's wing and then moving gradually to the cheek or the side of the head. You might try using your little finger to gently scratch his cheek or the back of his head. If he appreciates what you are doing, he will bend his head and ruffle all of his neck feathers. Eventually, parrots become so addicted to head scratching that they may actually pull your finger to them and bend their head down to assist you. Bill, my Yellow Naped Amazon, closes his eyes in ecstasy as I scratch him. Duda, my African Grey, says "Oh, yes," as I scratch her head, since this is what I say to her each time I perform this service.

If your parrot seems unwilling to let you engage in head scratching, try walking into a strange room with him. You will now be the most familiar object in the room and the parrot may permit you many liberties that he would not normally allow on his own territory.

90

A patriotic way to start the day. *Parrot Jungle, Miami*

Proper training can result in amazing displays of confidence. *Kelley*

91

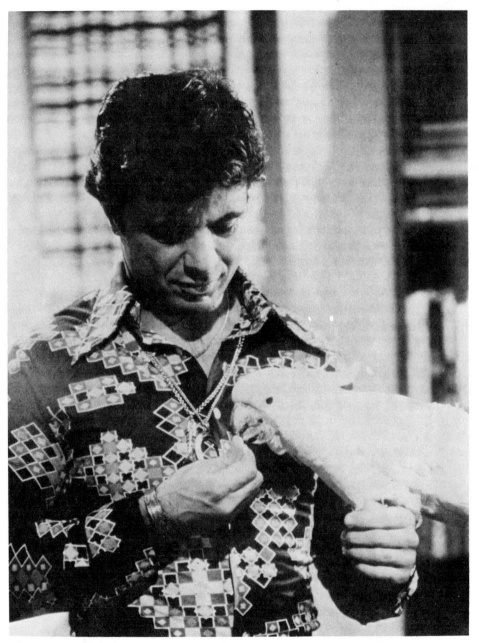

Robert Blake (Baretta) and Fred. *Copyright © Universal City Studios, Inc. All rights reserved.*

92

Developing a Repertoire

From here on you can accomplish as much as you are willing to work for in training your parrot. You can teach the bird to lie on his back in your hand or to ride your shoulder as you walk around the house. Parrots can be trained to push little carts or to throw small objects and to catch them as you throw them back. Some parrots like to walk on the floor while others are fearful of doing so. If you have a floor-walker, there are many interesting activities that he can be taught.

There are a few basic principles of training that will serve you well as you attempt to teach your parrot more tricks or stunts.

Avoid adding to his tasks by demanding that the parrot learn activities which seem frightening or threatening. Parrots do not like change and take time to adjust to anything new in their environment. A simple prop which appears harmless to you may frighten the bird to the extent that he will not be able to concentrate on learning the trick you are attempting to teach him. In such cases, it would be better to give up the prop and perhaps the trick rather than wasting your time and upsetting your parrot.

It is wise to begin training by selecting an action which is part of the bird's normal behavior, and then modifying it into an amusing activity. For example. parrots use their beaks almost as a third claw. If your bird is holding your hand with two claws and his beak, slip his claws off your hand and he can hang by his beak for quite a long time. You can swing him from side to side or in a circle without his letting go of your finger or becoming upset. Many parrots are particularly responsive to music. This natural response to rhythmic sounds can enable you to teach the bird to give the appearance that he is dancing to a catchy little tune.

The best teachers reinforce learning activities with praise and rewards. In the case of your parrot, your exclamations of delight and your laughter at his antics are the best reinforcement. Many birds will even laugh along with you, and I have one parrot who laughs at his tricks even before I do.

Remember that the first step is hand-training and, it is the foundation for all future training. In addition patience is the keynote to success in training. When you see a parrot doing something appealing, like hiding under his owner's sweater, or lying on his back in a totally defenseless position, remember that these feats were not accomplished overnight. Time, common sense and perseverance were all required.

Slight Billed Parakeet. *Lydekker*

Theophile, was a yellow and white cat who had the run of her owner's home. One day a parrot was left to be cared for while his owner went on vacation. The bird knew that it was in a strange place and pulled itself to the top of its perch stand and sat silently with its feathers trembling.

The cat had never seen a parrot before and she studied it intently. Her owner had the feeling that she was thinking that this might be a green hen. After arriving at this delicious conclusion the cat approached the parrot in a semi-crouch with her stomach flat and her back arched like a stalking panther.

The parrot followed these movements with great anxiety. He ruffled his feathers and moved from foot to foot. He realized that the cat was probably thinking, "although it's green, it must be good to eat."

Suddenly the cat landed at the base of the perch with a single bound. Although the parrot was terrified he began to speak (as parrots will sometimes do when frightened or excited). In a deep and solem voice he called out, "Did you lunch well, Jacquot?" The human voice frightened the cat; her thoughts were vividly expressed on her face. "That is not a bird, it is a man. He talks!"

The parrot immediately understood the advantage it had gained and began to sing a familiar song in a deafening voice. The cat threw her mistress a questioning look and left the room. From that moment on and for the remainder of Jacquot's visit she considered the parrot as a person and treated him with respect.

Old French Story

A recommended medicating technique. *Katz*

Poor feathering or plucking may be caused by boredom, improper diet, mites, frustration or low humidity. *Kelley*

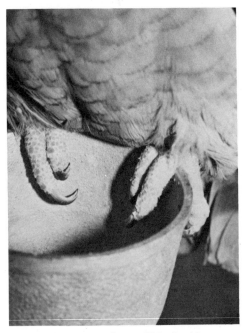

Overgrown claws which should be clipped. *Photo by author*

7

The Well Parrot and the Sick Parrot

FOLLOWING THE PURCHASE of your parrot, select a veterinarian within relatively easy traveling distance of your home. He or she should be willing to treat birds and have some knowledge of parrots and their ailments. With the increase in parrot ownership, more and more veterinarians are familiarizing themselves with current methods of treating birds. However, those living in smaller communities may have to do some research to find such an individual or may not be able to find a local vet with a background in birds at all.

If the latter is true then the next best procedure would be to establish contact with a veterinarian who, while he may not be within traveling distance, would be willing to listen to you or your local vet describe the bird's symptoms via telephone and to make suggestions based on this information. This is not as strange as it sounds and I know a number of people who have successfully used this method to get adequate treatment for their parrots.

Treating Your Own Bird

If the above possibilities are not available, you may have to depend upon yourself to provide medical attention for your bird. Start off by obtaining a current book on the treatment of bird diseases and a selection of medications which ought to be put together in advance as many of the most effective products cannot be obtained on short notice or require a prescription.

Bird owner's are fortunate that the tremendous strides made in pharmacology just after World War II have had a "spin off" effect which has provided veterinarians with new and powerful drugs. The growing use of antibiotics in treating birds can be a mixed blessing. These substances are extremely useful but they can only be effective when used with organisms susceptible to their effect. If used improperly they are dangerous.

Administering Medication

Medications can enter the body in a number of ways. The easiest and most common method is by actually squirting the antibiotic into the parrot's mouth using an eyedropper. For obvious reasons a glass eyedropper must be avoided and care should be taken to be sure that liquid medication goes into the digestive tract and not the lungs. A clever technique described in the *Magazine of the Parrot Society* involves the use of a wooden dowel with a number of holes drilled into it. The dowel is offered to the sick bird who, being a parrot, will almost always grasp it in his beak. One of the holes is then lined up with the open beak and an eyedropper with a rubber extension placed through the hole. The medication can now be administered with ease.

When the injection of antibiotics is called for the injection is generally made into the well developed breast tissues as they offer a suitable target. Many practitioners refer to injecting a bird as "popping" him. Injection has the advantage of getting medication into the bloodstream rapidly but requires more skill than the oral approach.

On occasion I have used an antibiotic designed for opthalmic purposes in humans by lightly packing the bird's nostrils with it. This topical method of application to the nostrils can be used to treat the sinuses. Antibiotics may also be administered through the bird's drinking water but this method is rather passive and its success will depend on how much water the bird drinks.

Antibiotics

It is crucial that the owner always use the proper physical form of antibiotic as injecting something meant to be taken orally can prove fatal.

By its very nature an antibiotic can have a dramatic effect on living organisms. Due to their potency, negative effects are also possible. Many are toxic unless careful attention is paid to the body-weight/dosage relationship. Some can have side effects which damage organs while others are safe if given for several days but can cause damage if extended usage occurs.

Very few people still recommend the use of antibiotics as an anti-stress treatment or simply at the first sign or feeling that the bird is somewhat "off" his normal behavior. I do think, however, that a reasonable case can be made for the use of a broad-spectrum antibiotic when a new bird is introduced into the aviary.

Prevention is Best

Parrot owners are fortunate that the *Psittacidae* (which include all members of the parrot family) are not exceptionally delicate birds. With reasonable care, a nutritious diet and avoiding foolish risks, the owner can expect his parrot to live a long and healthy life.

Reasonable care refers to clean cages and clean water. The microorganisms which can cause disease need a medium in which to develop. You are asking for trouble if you allow your parrot's cage to become food encrusted, or neglect changing his water for days.

A nutritious diet is important and keep in mind that it is important to be consistent. You cannot substitute whatever is at hand when you run out of the parrot's regular mix just because you lack the time to visit the feed store or pet shop to replenish your supply. After all, you wouldn't feed your child candy for lunch just because you lacked milk or vegetables at the time. Vitamins and other supplements should also be a regular part of your bird's diet.

Exercise will also go a long way towards keeping a parrot fit and in good condition. Its importance tends to be underrated and as a result many parrots fail to live out their full life potential. Taking the parrot out of his cage for exercise is also fun for both for owner and bird as well as being therapeutic.

Always be alert to protect your parrot against unecessary dangers. Don't expose your pet to drafts even if it means closing a window on a mild day or giving up his company while the window is open. Discourage people from bringing their birds to visit yours. This may sound overprotective but you don't know what a visiting bird may have been exposed to. You can control your own situation but you have no way of knowing if others have been as careful. If you have other birds and are bringing home a newcomer, fight the impulse to immediately have him join the others. Any new bird should be isolated for several weeks or longer. This is not as difficult as it sounds. Isolation can simply mean keeping the new parrot in another room in your home; preferably on another level if this is possible.

99

While it is true that many microorganisms are airborne, it is at least possible to reduce their concentration around healthy birds. If you have the misfortune of bringing home a parrot who is either ill or incubating a disease, isolation will inhibit disease. Of course, the best protection against bringing home a sick bird is to choose a healthy one in the first place. Don't jump at the chance to purchase a bird who sits quietly and doesn't bother to move away from you if you attempt to pick him up. Such a degree of tameness generally does not exist. You may be dealing with a bird who is sick and who is showing it by sitting very quietly and not responding with normal aggressiveness to the attentions of a stranger.

Know What You're Treating For

Members of the parrot family are susceptible to diseases caused by viruses, rickettsia, bacteria, fungi, protozoa, worms, and mites. Since medications available to you or to your vet range from broad-spectrum medications to substances very specific in their action, it is important to know the organism causing the disease. Without this knowledge you may treat with a medication that is totally ineffective against that particular organism. Parents of young children frequently wonder why the doctor will not give their sick child a "shot" to cure his sore throat or other ailment. The reason, of course, is that if the doctor suspects a virus as the cause of the condition he knows that the various wonder drugs will be useless as they do not affect viruses. We are faced with the same problem in treating a parrot. The best solution is to make use of a diagnostic laboratory that can test fluid from the parrot's nostrils as well as his blood and droppings. Using modern techniques, the laboratory can advise you or your veterinarian which disease-causing organisms are present in the sample you have supplied.

Bacteria absorb stains in different fashions. Some bacteria absorb a stain called Gram's stain while others do not. Those that do absorb it are referred to as Gram-positive, while those that do not are called Gram-negative. This one bit of knowledge might be sufficient to suggest to you or your vet that you use an antibiotic which is specific for the appropriate bacteria. For example, Chloromycetin acts upon many Gram-negative bacteria. Thus, you would not use it if the lab reported the source of disease as a Gram-positive bacteria. Your choice might then be Ampicillin (a newer and more effective member of the penicillin family) which acts upon a wide range of Gram-positive bacteria (as well as others). If both Gram-positive and Gram-negative bacteria are present or if the lab is in doubt or if you have no laboratory facilities available, you or your vet might wish to try a broad-spectrum antibiotic such as Chlortetracycline, which is effective against a wide range of Gram-positive and Gram-negative organisms. If the lab reports a viral condition, then the major value in using an antibiotic would be to fight off the secondary bacterial agents of infection, which may thrive because of the bird's weakened condition.

Other antibiotic possibilities which you can discuss with your vet are the sulfur drugs which are still considered quite useful.

As you can see, proper treatment of your parrot should ideally be left to a veterinarian who can diagnose ailments and identify organisms (or has a lab available to him where correct identification can be made). Since most medications are extremely potent you must use care to follow proper dosages as well as length of treatment. If at all possible, try to get professional help rather then medicating your parrot yourself.

First-Aid

First-aid for your parrot may save his life if you have to wait for the veterinarian to become available. First aid for a parrot involves heat. Heat is a standard treatment for warm-blooded animals which are in shock. Raise the temperature in the bird's room to between 85 and 90 degrees F. If you only want to raise the temperature inside the cage, you can do so by using an infrared lamp or a large wattage light bulb or by making use of a hospital cage. The effect of heat on a sick bird can be dramatic. I have seen birds so ill that they were lying on the floor of their cages regain enough vigor to move back to their perches in a matter of hours. When your parrot's condition is stablized, reduce the heat gradually.

Don't let a sick bird stop eating. A parrot's metabolism is very high. If permitted to go without food for any length of time, he will die. Tempt the sick parrot with the foods that he loves. If necessary, try such things as peanut butter (which he will have to touch with his tongue to remove even if he doesn't intend to eat it). Some birds will eat chewed up food from your mouth even though they will reject regular food.

The problem of bleeding is not uncommon in birds. It may occur because of carelessness in cutting nails or be due to an injury inflicted by another parrot. Sometimes the premature loss of a large feather can also create a situation where help is needed to staunch the flow of blood. Hydrogen peroxide will usually stop bleeding. A ball of cotton makes a good applicator or in the case of a bleeding toe, the toe can be dipped directly into a capful of peroxide. When more heroic measures are required, silver nitrate applicators will generally stop any form of bleeding. Silver nitrate can, however, damage body tissues and therefore must be used with the greatest care. Bleeding from the nails can be avoided by cutting them often (which will cause the blood vessel to recede and by avoiding the temptation to cut more than the sharp tip of the nail. Mounting or hanging a carborundum wheel or block in the cage for parrots who violently oppose any form of pedicure, no matter how gentle, will enable such birds to wear down their nails themselves.

Signs of Health and Illness

It is known that parrots will try to hide their illnesses until they can no longer do so. Note any change in your bird's behavior and keep a close watch on him if you see unusual changes. As a matter of fact, it's a very wise procedure to check the tray of the cage before you dump the papers, droppings, old feathers and empty seed hulls. You can thus get a good idea of what the parrot is eating and the general state of his health each day.

A healthy parrot will show it by eating enthusiastically and engaging in lively parrot games such as climbing and hanging in odd positions during a good part of the day and evening. Of course, even the healthiest parrot will slow down when tired. A cold room will also diminish the activity of parrots who have not been gradually acclimated to lower temperatures.

Common Health Problems

Although parrots are normally hardy birds they are susceptible to certain illnesses and injuries. Your ability to recognize these or to report symptoms promptly to your veterinarian will be an important factor in your bird's recovery. Some common health problems follow.

Aspergillosis — This condition is caused by the spores of a common fungus. It develops when the individual swallows or inhales the spores. The body of a healthy bird will normally not permit the spores to establish themselves but when a bird is run down or in an otherwise weakened state the condition can develop.

Respiratory Ailments — Nasal discharges almost always indicate that something is amiss in some part of the respiratory tract. Many parrots function quite well even when they are suffering from such an infection and even play normally. It is still advisable to have your veterinarian determine the cause and treat for the specific organism. A parrot who is wheezing should also be seen by the vet even if there is no fluid discharge from the nostrils. Sneezing may not be of any significance unless it is repeated frequently and produces a discharge. It is quite normal for a healthy parrot to clear his nostrils of dust or other foreign matter by sneezing.

Enteritis, paratyphoid and salmonellosis — These conditions are all associated with poor sanitation. Bacteria, which cause these diseases, are found in animal wastes and under circumstances where crowding and lack of cleanliness exists. Diarrhea, loss of appetite and loss of weight are among the symptoms for these conditions. Victims should be segregated and treated with heat as well as appropriate medication. Cages and dishes of all birds should be carefully cleaned.

Scaly legs — Generally due to a mite which can also affect the beak. The raised and discolored scales are quite obvious when this condition occurs. In addition to treatment of the bird by your vet you should thoroughly clean the cage with a mite killer and either provide new perches or scrape and clean the old ones.

Worms — Loss of appetite, diarrhea and lack of activity may signal the presence of worms. The various worms which infect birds have different shapes and sizes. In a number of cases they are visible to the naked eye. Worm medications are quite toxic and the dose for a bird is predicated on his body weight. Since the object is to kill the worms without killing the parrot the owner should stick to the dosage the vet prescribes. Worms are much less common in caged birds than they are in birds living in aviaries with dirt floors.

Feather plucking and mutilation — This is one of the most common and aggravating problems which parrot owners are faced with. The condition can stem from boredom, frustration, poor diet or high heat-low humidity settings. A vicious cycle can also occur where moderate feather plucking which stems from boredom is followed by skin irritation which results in still more plucking. In extreme cases birds can pluck to the point where blood is drawn. Prevention is, of course, much better than attempting to cure this ugly condition. Toys, attention, changes of cage and location and spraying with water have all been known to have varying degrees of success. A combination of these along with dietary modifications may also work.

103

Air Sac Mites — This condition is caused by a parasite of the respiratory system, *Sternostoma tracheocolum.* The organism lives within the bird's breathing apparatus and can be spread rapidly throughout the aviary. Symptoms include wheezing, heavy fluids in the respiratory organs, swelling of the tissues of the mouth, fluffed-up feathers, loss of appetite and loss of weight. The affected parrot is also open to infections by other organisms due to the body's lowered resistance. Sometimes the secondary infections may confuse the issue and be taken as the main problem with subsequent inappropriate course of treatment.

In an excellent article on this condition in the November, 1967 issue of *Animal Hospital,* T. J. Lafeber, D. V. M., describes successful treatments of infected birds using a vapor of malathion. Because of the equipment and chemicals involved this technique should only be used by trained individuals.

Egg Binding — A female with this problem will be obvious by her strained efforts to pass the egg. A swollen region near the vent will also be easy to spot. Heat plus the application of a warm oil can help but care must be taken not to break the egg within the body cavity.

Newcastle Virus — Parrots with this disease show a variety of symptoms as resistance to the condition differs widely among birds. Fluffed-up feathers, failure to eat, trembling, abnormal droppings and breathing problems may all indicate Newcastle.

Since birds imported into the U. S. are quarantined for at least thirty days to prevent the importation of diseased birds it is to your disadvantage to buy from sources which deal in smuggled birds.

Special Summer Care

Along with the pleasures of the season, summer also brings special problems and risks. Most people take at least a short summer vacation which frequently involves travel. Your parrot is better off at home or temporarily living with a friendly host than he would be on any lengthy journey with you. Before you make any housing committment for your parrot you should consider certain important aspects of the home in which he will temporarily live.

If possible, try to arrange a reciprocal arrangement with another parrot owner; he takes your bird when you go on vacation and vice versa. Such an individual will have some knowledge of parrots as well as a liking for these unusual birds and this gives your pet an immediate advantage. Food and care in such a household will also be a cut above average (for parrots) and this will help make up for the temporary separation. If you have any doubts about the type of care your bird is going to receive, it would be a good idea to check on the cleanliness of the cage of the resident parrot as well as the contents of the food and water dishes. Needless to say, a home with a parrot or any other bird who has a running nose or a listless appearance should remove that residence from consideration as a summer resort for your bird.

If you are anxious to have your hookbill stay with a parrot owner but you don't know any such person, you may be amazed to find how many contacts you can make in your own area by checking at your local pet shop or seed supply store. The parrot "sub-culture" tends to keep a low profile at present due to the rising incidence of parrot-napping. Thus you may have to expend some energy to find people who share your interest. It is worth the search, however, as parrot people tend to look after their own.

Other possibilities to consider would be pet owners who keep Budgies or other cage birds. These are all individuals who may want to exchange services with you. Of course, you don't have to limit yourself to bird people. Someone who keeps fish, hamsters, or gerbils may also be a likely candidate. Think twice, however, about dog and cat owners. Not every dog or cat is a menace to your parrot as these animals can develop some very amicable relationships with parrots but it is unusual and unlikely to develop during a short summer vacation.

Children in the household are another factor to be taken into consideration before committing your parrot to summer residency. Very young children pose no problems unless the parents object to the usual morning and evening jungle screams at which parrots excel. Any child capable of walking (but not fully capable of reasoning) may prove a danger to your bird. The apparently harmless, inquisitive act of opening a cage door could mean "bye bye birdie" if a window is open in that room. Very few escaped parrots are ever returned to their original owners.

If you feel you know someone well enough, it is much safer, less traumatic to the parrot and generally easier to have the pet-sitter come to your home instead of bringing the parrot to his. Big Beak is then in his own familiar surroundings and you need not worry about any threats to his safety from other animals or from children. A light should be left on and it would also be humane to have a clock radio , if you have one, set to go on and off instead of remaining on, constantly. The light should also be on a timing device as the parrot will not sleep soundly if the light is constantly on.

One approach always open to you is to have your bird boarded by your local pet shop or veterinarian. This has the advantage of generally guaranteeing that the people who care for your pet will be relatively knowledgable and quick to spot any problems. The disadvantage of this approach is the possible exposure to other birds who may be infected with a contagious condition.

Regardless of who cares for your pet when you are on vacation, remember to simplify the routine of care that you pass along to the pet-sitter. A limited variety of seeds which should include the parrot's favorites makes for easy feeding. Remind the host that the seed dish should be emptied and refilled every day even if it looks full. Some parrots eat the seeds on the bottom first and what looks like a full dish really isn't. If your vacation is just a two-or three-week affair, vitamins, and other additives can be omitted and this will prevent the possibility of the parrot's water becoming fouled if the weather turns warm and his host or hostess is a little slow in changing his water. Don't hestitate to caution the people your parrot stays with about the key factors of parrot keeping. These, of course, include food and clean water, absence of drafts and air conditioning and normal safety precautions to prevent harm from children or pets.

Do's and Don'ts of Summer Care

Give your parrot a light spraying with water several times a week. A plant mister filled with tepid water is an ideal instrument for this. If it is the first time you have attempted to shower him, be slow and gentle in your approach (a good general rule for any activity with parrots); and if he shows fright or discomfort, stop and try again later. Most parrots will react with delight and show it by extending their wings and twisting their bodies to provide the largest possible surface so that they can catch the maximum amount of water. Spraying should always be done early in the day so that the bird has a chance to thoroughly dry his feathers before bedtime. If necessary, a quick spray can even be given while the bird is in his cage.

Cleanliness, cleanliness, and more cleanliness is the key word for summer parrot care. That skipped food or water dish wash-up that you can get away with in the middle of winter is really begging for trouble in the hot, humid weather of summer. Use a dish-washing liquid and thoroughly clean and rinse all food dishes every day. Summertime is also a good time for a complete cleaning of the cage and perches. Pay particular attention to the openings for food and water dishes as material tends to accumulate in these areas. The cage tray should be thoroughly scrubbed and this is also a good opportunity to scrape the perches clean and wash and dry them in the sun. If perches are worn or very dirty, replace them.

There are various sprays on the market with which you can "mite proof" the cage. These sprays should be used after the cage has been cleaned and while the bird is out of the cage. A total housecleaning of the birdroom is also in order at this time, and you will probably be amazed at the seeds and bits of fruits and vegetables which have found their way under cabinets and tables.

Your diet changes in the summer and you should be equally considerate regarding your bird's diet. The basic seed mix that you use can be continued although many bird keepers reduce or eliminate the most oily seeds (such as thistle) during the warmer months. Since a greater variety of fruits and vegetables are available, you ought to take advantage of them. The many farm stands which appear during the summer months can provide free or inexpensive sources of highly nutritious vegetables for your parrot. Carrot and beet tops (including stems and leaves) are rich in many vitamins and minerals. Most stands remove these tops and discard them. If you get there early in the day you can pick up a considerable supply before they are thrown away. It is important that you thoroughly wash these vegetables and a good way to store them is in plastic bags in the crisper section of your refrigerator. Two or three carrot and beet tops which have been freshly rinsed make an excellent breakfast and will even provide a wake-up shower if you put them on top of the cage and let the parrot drag them in.

As you will probably have more time to spend with your bird in the summer, you might want to try experimenting with an extremely healthy food. Sprouted seeds (such as the ones which make up a part of Oriental cooking) are highly nutritious and in many respects come very close to the types of foods which parrots select in the wild. When a seed sprouts, the plant embryo, which is within it, begins to develop and a supply of carbohydrates, oils and proteins in an easily digestible form develops. Vitamin content also increases at a remarkable rate. There are many, many seeds which can be sprouted and the procedure is not difficult. Read through Gay Courter's *The Beansprout Book* or similar books for information on the techniques and the simple equipment used.

Don't make too many changes in your pet's lifestyle for the summer. Parrots are extremely conservative creatures and prefer life to follow an unchanged pattern. If you can provide an occasional fresh air outing on a screened porch or in some other secure location, by all means do so. Do not, however, risk taking a bird outdoors even if his wings are clipped.

Emphasize cleanliness, good food and the avoidance of drafts, air conditioning and other obvious dangers. Common sense and forethought will provide your parrot with a pleasant summer and bring him through it prepared for a healthy fall and winter.

Hasday-Marc

My friend . . . possessed an ancient Grey parrot which being addicted to the vice of feather-plucking was nearly bald. The bird answered to the name of Geier which in German means vulture. Geier was certainly no beauty but he redeemed himself by his speaking talents. He said "Good Morning" and "Good Evening" quite aptly and, when a visitor stood up to depart, he said in a benevolent bass voice, "Na, auf wiedersehen." But he only said this if the guest really departed . . . he was tuned in to the finest . . . signs . . . and we never once succeeded in provoking the retort by staging a departure.

Konrad Lorenz, *King Solomon's Ring*, Harper & Row, 1952

The African Grey, one of the most familiar parrot species, is considered by many the most talented talker of all psittacines. The typical scalloped effect of the plumage is produced by the light margins on the feathers. *Photo by author*

8

The African Grey

THE AFRICAN GREY PARROT is one of the best known and most desired parrots in the world. His history probably goes back to biblical times. Dr. Greene believed the Grey Parrot was actually known to the ancient Hebrews and suggests that an error in translation caused an inaccurate report that one of King Solomon's ships was carrying (among other curiosities) "apes and peacocks." Modern sources indicate a better translation might be apes and parrots since the area of travel referred to was that portion of Africa now known as Guinea which was and still is a source for the Grey Parrot.

Bechstein in his classic on cage birds written in 1794 described an African Grey owned by Cardinal Ascanius. The parrot was considered a wonder of the times in that he could recite the Apostles' Creed in a most articulate and uninterrupted manner. Although this bird had the fault of mumbling in its sleep (it apparently dreamed aloud) its owner had paid the princely price of one hundred gold pieces for it.

The Dutchess of Lenox kept an African Grey as a favorite pet. Although several hundred years have passed, one can view his stuffed remains at a museum in London.

The African Grey has the scientific name of *Psittacus erithacus.* He is also frequently referred to as the Jaco. This name may have been given to the parrot by Portuguese sailors because the echo of this bird's natural cry sounds like that word in the Portuguese language.

The original habitat of the African Grey is West and Central Africa. Greene describes a fascinating island off the coast of West Africa called Prince's Island on which is located a 12,000 foot mountain called by the natives *Pico de Papagaio* or Peak of the Parrot. The heavily forested mountain makes passage quite difficult for humans but presented no obstacle to the parrots who would roost in the dense forest at its top. Greene commented on the sunset scene in which parrots approaching in large parties were greeted with loud whistling and screaming by those who were already there. No doubt some of the whistles and screams were to identify a mate to a tardy or slow flyer.

It is interesting to note that the geography of the African continent has more or less isolated the Grey. Thus, one will not find African Greys that have originated anywhere except Africa unless, of course, they are descendants of birds brought by man to a new area and successfully bred there by him.

The Grey parrot is generally ash gray in color. (The name of the bird is traditionally spelled in the British fashion as "African Grey." When describing its color we use the more common American spelling of "gray.") The feathers have light edges and overlap each other in such a fashion as to suggest that he is wearing a suit of gray armor. The wing feathers are a darker gray and lack the light edge. The quill feathers are almost grayish black. When the wings are spread, you can see that the grayish white middle and lower part of the back are visible. After the first molt, the tail becomes bright red. This bird is about the size of a large pigeon with 14 inches a normal length. The beak is black, as are the nails. The eyes are a fine indicator of the age of the bird as young Greys have black eyes. When they are several months old, the eye color changes to an ash gray. At about five or six months the eye is light gray, and when the bird is about one year old, the gray begins to change to a pale yellow. Some indication of the relative age of the parrot can be gotten by examining his feet. Young birds have smoother feet, while the feet of the older ones become more scaly with age.

The sexing of Greys (and other parrots) has always been a topic which is subject to a varied set of opinions and interpretations. Some believe that color is significant but actually the gray of this parrot varies from tattletale through battleship to steel. The depth of color appears to be related to the geographical origin of the parrot (or his ancestors) rather than the bird's sex. Some breeders consider females to have what they call a snaky demeanor. This stems from the belief that African Greys with almond-shaped eyes and a flattened, elon-

112

gated head and beak are females. There may actually be something to this theory but someone would have to do a computer run on the relationship between positively identified females (either through egg laying or autopsy) and a snaky look before we could consider this bit of information as exact. Display behavior (a form of showing-off by changes in posture and spreading of feathers) along with aggressiveness tends to be credited more to males than females. Again, there may be some truth to this but I tend to believe that it is such a vague factor to measure that it cannot really be used by itself. Birds, of course, lack an external sex organ and have also had their internal urinogenital system designed in a rather space-saving manner. Sperm, eggs, and both liquid and solid wastes are excreted from a structure called the cloaca (the Latin term for sewer) from an opening to the outside called the vent. The pelvic bones which are directly in front of the vent must of necessity be spread somewhat apart in females during the egglaying season. The so-called pelvic bone test is a rough measurement of the space between these two bones and is usually done with the finger (unless one is dealing with a parrot who bites at such indignities). The general rule is that if you can feel a space about the width of a pencil then you are probably dealing with a female. In males there is no appreciable space. My own recommendation for sexing would be to use all of these tests and to make a decision based on the pattern they seem to follow. If you are involved in breeding and the sex of the parrot is crucial, one can have a form of minor surgery performed by an expert. This is called laparotomy and involves a small incision in the abdominal wall which permits the investigator to visually note the presence of testes in males and ovaries in females. Still another procedure which was pioneered by researchers at the Zoological Society of San Diego uses a comparison of the ratio between male and female sex hormones in the waste products of birds. By comparing the figure from this calculation against a standard established from a similar bird of known sex, highly accurate results can be achieved. This procedure, however, is less accurate when dealing with very young birds or a bird who may be ill.

An African Grey parrot can be purchased for between $400 and $900. The individuals at the high end of the price scale would be either hand-fed babies (very tame) or extremely talented talkers (who are generally tame, since there is a relationship between responding appropriately to good treatment and intelligence). Although many parrots can be enjoyed for their antics even if they are not talkers, buying an African Grey who will not speak is rather like getting a whistle that doesn't work—there's just not much point to it.

This mature African Grey enjoys being outdoors, so the flight feathers of his right wing have been clipped. In this way the bird can still benefit from the fresh air without risk of escape. *Goyanes*

114

The African Grey manages quite well on a standard parrot diet. Fruits and greens are also eaten by these birds but not to quite the same extent as they are by the Amazons.

I am lucky enough to own two African Greys. Jaco, who I believe is a female, is about five years old. Duda, my friendly male, is just four years of age. My judgement regarding their respective sexes is based on the fact that Duda is larger than Jaco. Additionally, I have closely examined their physical structure (since they permit it) and Duda seems to have a much more narrow pelvic region than Jaco.

Their personalities are quite different. Jaco is shy and cautious. I am able to scratch her head and hold her on my hand, but she always seems anxious for these interludes to be over so that she can return to her perch or cage. She loves her outside perch and pops out of her cage like a jack in the box when she realizes she's going to be allowed out for exercise. Once outside she flaps her wings and plays quite happily. Jaco speaks well and has learned the rather charming trick of saying "good!" when she is given food, water, or a treat. Both birds do a beautiful wolf whistle. I was under the impression that I had taught them this until I read that this and several other whistles are part of the natural cries of the African Grey and can be normally heard in the bird's jungle habitat.

Duda has a totally different personality. He is sweet and lovable and delights at being held and played with. He kisses and rubs his beak against me in a very affectionate manner. Duda is an excellent talker and exhibits in his speech the ability to mimic particular individuals' voices. There are times when I am sure my son is in the bird room talking but when I go down, I find it is really Duda. Duda acts like the little child he is. Before coming out of his cage, he usually hits each toy with his beak to get them swinging. If I do not move fast enough, he holds the door closed with his claw when he realizes that I am getting ready to open it. I then have to walk away and pretend to be interested in something else, and wait for him to let go of the door. He is quite an acrobat—as are all African Greys—and often hangs upside down by one claw for a great length of time.

Duda and Jaco like to sit together and they seem quite friendly. Perhaps you have never realized what "bill" means in the expression "bill and coo." Bill means to touch beaks. Duda does this with Jaco almost as if he were shaking hands with her. Jaco loves this attention and her cooing would impress any pigeon.

These birds are capable of feeling deep affection for their owners and will often show their sorrow if moved from their original homes. In Jaco's case I was asked to adopt her as her owner had

115

planned some extensive and lengthy travel. Jaco was a very depressed bird for several months until I got the bright idea of placing her cage next to that of Duda. Jaco then perked up considerably and to my delight I discovered that when the seed and water dishes were removed for cleaning the two African Greys played with and preened each other through the openings left by the removal of the dishes. Another benefit to this friendship was that Jaco, who had begun to engage in feather plucking, ceased this mischief and became a more contented parrot. She is devoted to Duda and will call loudly to him if either one of them is taken out of the room to visit upstairs.

Many, many stories have been written and told about African Greys. One of my favorites tells of a Grey who sang songs in both German and French. Occasionally he would switch a song from one language into the other and then laugh hysterically at his little trick. This same bird used to murmur in his sweetest voice, "Ah, how lovely Polly is," while he stroked his beak with his claw. Another describes an astonishing African Grey which spoke German and Dutch. If he did not know a word in German he would substitute the appropriate Dutch word. Still another Grey who upon seeing the family sit down to supper, would say, "Give some to the parrot!" He would continue this in a louder and louder voice even after receiving a share of the food until his owners would either have to cover his cage or remove him from the dining room.

Speaking of parrots who talk German brings to mind an incident which occurred on the day that I first brought Duda home. He was silent for much of the evening and then without warning I heard a little voice say, "Bismarck, you vant to go oudt?" Yes, the parrot had a thick German accent and he was repeating what his previous owner usually said to Bismarck, the family dog. Duda has since lost his accent or perhaps I should say he has learned many new words and phrases in unaccented English.

Most people who are familiar with parrots will acknowledge the fact that the African Grey tops all other parrot species in the potential for speech, ability to learn throughout its lifetime and the ability to mimic specific sounds and voices. Occasionally, the owner of an African Grey will get carried away with enthusiasm and make rather broad claims for his bird's range of talents. One English gentleman reported that his African Grey was not only linguistically talented but also extremely polite. This bird presumably would listen to people speak before he would talk so that he could drop his "h's" if they did or pronounce them if the speaker had more refined pronunciation.

116

A mated pair of African Greys. *Kelley*

The Timneh Grey, a subspecies of the African Grey, is distinguished from the more familiar nominate species by its reddish beak and dark ear coverts. *Reusch*

Lorenz describes a Grey parrot whose memory was extraordinary. His owner kept a tamed hoopoe named Hopfchen. The Grey could call the other bird by name. Naturally, the Grey outlived the hoopoe and it was considered forgotten as the parrot did not say its name any longer. Nine years later, another hoopoe was acquired and as the parrot laid eyes upon him for the first time, he said once and then repeatedly, "Hopfchen . . . Hopfchen."

I could go on and on with dozens of stories and experiences about these creatures. Needless to say, people sometimes embellish their stories a bit. In the case of the African Grey the bird is so clever that it is hardly necessary to do so.

You may be fortunate enough to come across a Grey parrot which at first glance seems to be a true African Grey, but is darker than usual. The tail will be a reddish brown and the beak, instead of being black, will be a reddish gray. Such birds were originally thought to be a variety or perhaps even a younger version of the true African Grey parrot. The bird described above, however, is a separate species. It is called the Timneh parrot. They are rather uncommon and perhaps that is because people who own them do not realize that they actually have a separate species. The Timneh parrot generally comes from the northern portions of West Africa. In terms of intelligence and speaking ability, the Timneh is much the same as the African Grey.

African Grey. *Century Dictionary*

Mrs. Proschek, of Vienna, had a favorite Yellow Naped Amazon whom she considered the most charming and delightful creature imaginable. When anyone rang the bell or when the dogs barked he called out, "there is someone there!" When it heard her speaking it flew to her and whispered in the most attractive voice, "where have you been?" If he saw her preparing to leave he would fly on her shoulder and in a most plaintive manner recite, "don't go, stay here." It went to sleep on its mistress's arm after being covered with a handkerchief and its bed time ritual involved saying, "good night, good night," in a little voice which got weaker and weaker.

Dr. W. T. Greene, *Parrots in Captivity*, 1887

The Amazons form a large, popular group with distribution throughout the Caribbean, Central and South America. They are distinguished from one another by the color and placement of their markings and physical size. The St. Vincent Amazon shown here is a typical Amazon species.

New York Zoological Society

9
The Amazons

ALTHOUGH THIS POPULAR GROUP bears the name of a river which flows through the contintent of South America (largely in Brazil) the term Amazon has come to include a large number of New World parrots also found in Central America and certain Caribbean Islands. In most cases their major color is green but size differences as well as a great many variations and combinations of forehead, crown, cheek and nape colors make it possible to identify the different species and subspecies. For obvious geographical reasons the Amazons are more common in the United States than in Europe. The mutual border which the United States shares with Mexico at one time provided a ready access route for these parrots but the strict enforcement of quarantine and customs regulations have effectively put an end to this traffic.

Yellow Fronted Amazon *(Amazona ochrocephala ochrocephala)*

The Yellow Fronted Amazon is a familiar member of a readily available group all classified as *Amazona ochrocephala*. There are enough significant differences between individuals to have them separately categorized into subspecies.

The parrot is referred to by several names. In addition to being called the Yellow Fronted Amazon, it is often referred to as the Single Yellow Head. This is to differentiate it from the Double Yellow Head, who at maturity has a much greater portion of yellow head feathers than does the Single Yellow Head. Some authors use the name Yellow Headed Amazon for this parrot. As with most of the Amazons, the basic color of the Yellow Fronted is green. The forehead is also green and yields to a yellow marking on the crown. While this area may increase somewhat with age, it never completely covers the head nor does it extend down into the region of the cheek. The beak is a dark horn-gray with some variation among different birds. The eye is orange-red with a bare eye ring. A mature specimen is generally about 14 inches long. It is built somewhat along the lines of the Double Yellow Head but not quite as sturdily.

My Single Yellow Head is a plump, timid little fellow named Valentine. (He was a present from my wife on Valentine's Day.) Although Valentine does not bite, he is capable of vigorously pushing me away with his feet when I attempt to get him onto my hand. It took about six months for Valentine to lose his fear of me but he will now hold my finger in his mouth and nibble at my ring. He also plays several cute games with me. One of them involves my swinging his bell back and forth until he decides to catch it. He can do this quite easily by putting out a claw or his beak. Valentine's vocabulary is limited, but I have hopes that it will continue to develop as time goes on. For the first few months that I had him, he would not eat, drink or move around his cage when I was in the room. I took to spying on him to be sure that he was capable of doing these things. Peeking through the doorway reassured me of his love for sunflower seeds and peanuts and the fact that he could hang upside down with the best of them. This period of shyness has long since passed and his beak now hits the seed dish before I finish getting it in place.

Double Yellow Head (*Amazona ochrocephala oratrix*)

The Double Yellow Head meets virtually all the requirements that the true parrot lover finds important in a bird. *Amazona oratrix* is available in good supply and at realistic prices. Birds at the high end of the price range would be particularly handsome specimens; individuals which show a high aptitude for speaking; hand-fed babies; or ideally, a Double Yellow Head showing a combination of all of these traits. An older name for these parrots is LeVaillant's Amazon after the man who first described them.

The general plumage is green with a lighter green under-surface. The forehead and areas around the eyes (called the lores) are bright yellow. The yellow areas increase with each successive yearly molt so that to an experienced observer the amount of yellow which the bird shows can be a fair indication of his age. Very young birds have a yellow forehead while the rest of the head is only dappled with yellow. In older birds the bright yellow marking moves back across the crown and down the nape and neck. I have seen truly magnificent specimens whose yellow markings are so large that they look like they are wearing the hood portion of a child's yellow rain slicker.

A highly sought after, but somewhat rarer subspecies from the Tres Marias Islands (which are off the coast of western Mexico) *Amazona ochrocephala tresmariae* resembles the Double Yellow Head but has a much greater area of yellow extending over the head and neck at an earlier age. This subspecies can also be recognized by its massive head and beak, generally greater length and large red markings on the bend of the wings.

The Double Yellow Head has a characteristic which is typical of many parrots but which has developed to an unusual degree in this species—they strongly desire the attention of their owners, and to gain and keep this attention, they will engage in all sorts of delightfully silly behavior. To an individual who does not know or understand parrots, this behavior may even appear threatening, as it can include rapid dilation and contraction of the bird's pupils as well as a fanning out of the tail feathers and quick and somewhat wild movements of the head. This is usually accompanied by loud renditions of the parrot's vocabulary, or unfortunately, sometimes just the constant repetition of one part of it. Blondi, one of my two Double Yellow Heads, also has the knack of turning her head upside down and peering at me as if I were the one in an unusual position. José, my other Double Yellow Head (a beautiful specimen of *Tres Marias*) engages in very aggressive swipes of his beak. If he does connect, however, he quickly changes over to a kiss.

Although all Double Yellow Heads have a sweet and almost smiling appearance, they do not all behave this way. Before becoming overly familiar with any parrot, ask his owner if it is safe to do so.

The Double Yellow Head has been popular as a pet for several hundred years. There is a portrait in the British Museum of an English noblewoman with her Double Yellow Head next to her. This portrait is more than 300 years old.

Dr. Greene makes references to a very clever Double Yellow Head who could sing several songs as well as give himself a set of soldier's drill commands. This parrot would talk on request and had a preference for people with harsh or rough voices. The author speculated that this might have been because his original owner was a French sailor with a rather guttural voice.

A large, well-fed Mealy Amazon. *Photo by author*

A Mexican Red Head searching for an apple. *Photo by author*

A Double Yellow Head. One bird, two heads? *Photo by author*

124

These parrots are being successfully bred in captivity in the United States, Europe, and England. The average clutch consists of two or three eggs with an incubation period of about three and a half weeks. The young do not generally leave the nest for another two and a half months after hatching, with still another three weeks elapsing before they can be considered independent. Of course, breeders with the time and inclination to do so will remove the young from the nest within a week or so after hatching and hand-feed them until they are capable of eating seed by themselves. While there is risk and effort involved in doing this (because parrot babies, like human babies, need multiple feedings) the tameness of the hand-fed bird makes the effort worthwhile. These parrots make the best pets and fetch the highest price in the marketplace.

Many people believe the term Double Yellow Head refers to the amount of yellow on the bird's head. George Sutton suggests that the name actually stems from the unique way all the feathers of the neck and crown are raised when this bird becomes excited or agitated. The head virtually doubles in size. From personal observation of numerous Yellow Heads, I tend to agree with Mr. Sutton.

In recent years, my correspondence has regularly included letters from people whose "Double Yellow Heads" seem to be undergoing a strange metamorphosis. Within six months to a year after purchasing the bird, green and red feathers began to replace the yellow head marking. In virtually every case that I have investigated, we were dealing with the problem of painted parrots. This is not some exotic disease, but merely another example of man's greed and the extent to which some people will go to gain a few extra dollars. The Green-cheeked Amazon is even more abundant in Mexico than the Double Yellow Head. It is also somewhat easier to trap, and thus, some bird sellers have taken to actually painting the head of the Green-cheeked Amazon and selling him as a Double Yellow Head. As the bird molts, the painted feathers are replaced by the original green and red feathers, leaving the owners with many questions.

Yellow Naped Amazon *(Amazona ochrocephala auropalliata)*

The Yellow Naped Amazon is a fairly large bird and can reach a length of about 16 inches. It is green from head to tail with the tips of the tail feathers a light yellowish-green and the under-surface a much lighter green than the upper-surface. Young birds lack the yellow marking on the nape which in adults takes the form of an irregular bright yellow patch about the size of a 25 cent piece. The marking is not well defined in terms of shape but its location is unique and makes

125

The Double Yellow Head is one the most sought-after of all Amazon species. Compare the head and shoulder markings of this eight-year-old specimen with those of the Tres Marias subspecies below. *Photo by author*

The Tres Marias subspecies of the Double Yellow Head is easily recognized by its distinctive markings. The extensive light markings and large shoulder markings of this relatively young bird are typical of its kind. *Andrews*

it a positive means of identification for this Amazon. The bright nape begins to develop at about one year. Yellow Napes also have a small yellow marking on the forehead but this is not consistent, and I have seen this mark actually diminish in some specimens as they grew older. The cere is covered with dark black hairs and the eye is orange. The upper beak is black except for the sides which are a light horn and the lower beak is a mixture of black and horn. The feet are gray with black nails.

Young specimens may be confused with the Panama Amazon and occasionally with the Yellow Fronted Amazon. The Panama is a shorter and stockier bird with a large yellow marking on the forehead and no yellow marking on the nape. The Yellow Front is also smaller then the Yellow Nape (about 14 inches) and it has a green marking on the forehead followed by a yellow patch. There is no nape marking.

The Yellow Naped Amazon is an excellent pet who is not only a fine talker, but who also has the uncanny ability to relax with his owner to the point where the bird can engage in some truly amazing demonstrations of confidence. I have seen a tame Yellow Nape who let his owner cover him with a handkerchief while he pretended to go to sleep and others who hang limply by beak or claws from the owner's finger.

Some parrot keepers specialize in breeding these birds, and hand-feeding the baby parrots while showing them great affection. They are thus imprinted (a psychological term referring to the implantation of special behavioral patterns early in life) in such a way that they believe themselves to be "little people" rather than little parrots. These birds are the ultimate in affectionate pets and several that I have seen, follow their owners around like puppies. It is hard to understand why a particular Amazon should have such great potential for speech and friendship, but these traits have been praised in the Yellow Nape in literature appearing as early as the mid-nineteenth century.

Dr. Greene gives very high grades to the Yellow Nape. He considered the bird to be, "Delightful . . . clever, gentle, and tractable . . ." He describes one Yellow Nape who would respond to the doorbell by shouting "Someone's there!" This same bird would fly to its owner's shoulder when he entered a room and whisper "Where have you been?" If he saw his owner getting ready to leave the house, his voice would become plaintive and he would say, "Please don't go, stay here." Dr. Greene describes another Yellow Nape whose morning cries alternated between, "Rose, bring the coffee" and "Jaco, bring the coffee." Rose was the family cook but Jaco, unfortunately, could not oblige as he was just another parrot.

Just to give an idea of how the price of parrots has changed over the years, Dr. Greene mentions that the cost of a Yellow Nape who could speak will be about $30.00 or $40.00 dollars. The price today would be at least ten times that.

This parrot has been known to collectors for well over 100 years. It was first fully described in 1842 when Lesson, the ornithologist, mentioned that the Central American Indians kept the Yellow Nape as a pet because of its pleasing personality.

Another early author, Reverend F. G. Dutton, writing at the same time as Dr. Greene, described a rather amusing experience involving a Yellow Nape which he purchased in France. This parrot was apparently mute until Reverend Dutton brought home a Double Yellow Head which also came from France. The two birds then began to chatter away in French as if they were long lost friends.

When I decided to add a Yellow Naped Amazon to my collection, it was very difficult to locate one. This was during the period in the early 1970s when the importation of parrots by individuals was banned in the United States and the quarantine stations were not yet in existence. Any parrots available at that time were birds already in the country. Great caution had to be exercised when buying birds, as after all, why would anyone want to sell a tame and talking parrot? What was usually available were parrots who excelled only in biting.

Surprisingly enough, I was able to locate a very talented Yellow Nape in a pet shop on Bleecker Street, one of the main thoroughfares in that part of lower Manhattan known as Greenwich Village. The Village has been the home of actors, artists, fortune tellers, and other unusual people for many years. A focal point of Bohemian life, it is probably the last place in the world one would go to seek out a Yellow Naped Amazon parrot.

On the day I started my hunt I began to check by phone with all of the large pet shops and bird sellers within driving distance of my home. I was told of Blue Fronted geniuses, Sulfur Crested acrobats and all kinds of Yellow Heads and Red Heads—but no Yellow Napes.

Suddenly I remembered an ad that had appeared in the *Sunday Times* with great regularity. It was for a pet shop and referred to "exquisite birds." The sound of this intrigued me. I called the shop and spoke to a very pleasant lady who assured me that she did have a Yellow Nape available.

Since I had previously made several disappointing trips to shops only to find that the bird for sale was a Panama parrot, I questioned her quite carefully. "What color is his beak? Does he have black feathers across the top of the beak?" I went on and on. "Sir!" she said,

"I have been in this business for over 20 years. The bird is without a doubt a Yellow Naped parrot and truly a very unusual one. Why, when the phone rings, sometimes he answers it!" I got my traveling directions and headed for Greenwich Village.

The trip went quite smoothly and I got to the shop while the staff was still doing morning clean-up chores. I found the disinfectant smell of the scrupulously clean pet shop very pleasant, probably because I associated it with fond memories of birds previously purchased.

The young lady who met me said, "Oh yes, Mr. Freud. Miss Dotty is expecting you. Just go right through to the back." This also impressed me. Her birds were not on display up front for everyone to poke and prod. Serious customers were, of course, invited to the back room to see and examine the birds. I greeted the owner of the shop but it was a rather brief greeting because directly behind her was the object of my interest. There, in a gleaming new cage, was one of the most beautiful parrots I had ever seen. He was a large Yellow Nape (about 16 inches long) without a single feather out of place. I am afraid I ignored Miss Dotty as I quickly walked over to this sleek, green beauty. On his cage was a paper sign. It said, "Bill, Eighteen Months, Tame and Talking."

Bill peered out at me with bright, intelligent eyes, "Hello Bill," I said. To my delight and astonishment, he answered with a deep "Hello." Then he repeated the hello but this time in a sweet little girl's voice. I was amazed as very few talkers will do so on command; in fact many parrots refuse to talk when strangers are present. Miss Dotty was beaming. Cautiously I put my finger into the cage. Bill bent his head and waited for me to scratch him. "I'll take him!" I said.

Since it was a rather cold day I put my overcoat around the cage and carried Bill and his cage to the car. A friend had come with me to do the driving. Because of the size of the cage, I put it in the front seat and I sat behind it in the back. As we proceeded out of lower Manhattan, Bill was extremely attentive to his surroundings and the passing scenery. I looked at him very carefully. His forehead was light green except for a few yellow feathers. At the nape of his neck was the typical lemon colored band for which this parrot is named. His beak was slate colored with a hint of white at the base. Just above the beak were some black, bristly feathers. He was without doubt a Yellow Nape.

My friend, who was driving, asked if I was pleased. I told him that I was delighted and Bill thinking that I was talking to him did an acrobatic turn and twist which brought him face to face with me. I said, "Hello Bill" and he responded with a loud, boisterous laugh. I scratched his beak and he not only permitted this but once again inclined his head to have his neck scratched. I couldn't wait to get him home and into the company of his future companions.

We finally arrived and I quickly got him out of the car and downstairs into the birdroom. I dispossessed my little Beebee parrot and placed Bill's cage next to Blondi, my Double Yellow Head. Blondi began to scream and was joined by Jaco and Duda, the African Greys, while Fogel, the Blue Fronted Amazon, also pitched in. The noise was deafening and Bill seemed bewildred. Up until this time he had been in the company of four quiet, well-behaved Mexican Red Heads. I was so excited at finally getting my Yellow Nape that I did a foolish thing. I offered him a drop of water from my finger. The noise must have really frightened and upset Bill so that instead of taking the drop of water, he bit and bit hard!

Returning with a Band-Aid I decided to be more cautious. After setting Bill up with fresh food, I forced myself to leave the room and stay away for an hour or so. When I returned, I attempted to try to take Bill out. After all, he had proven his tameness in the store and in the car. Putting my hand in the cage brought several quick bites, each of which drew blood. I kept my temper and sat down to puzzle out the change in behavior. Obviously the noise and change of scenery had frightened him, and patience was the answer. I went to the side of the cage and Bill poked his beak through. I rubbed the big beak gently and Bill responded with a clear and distinct, "no bite," as he attempted to nip my finger.

At this point my feelings were mixed. I had paid a lot of money for a tame and talking Yellow Nape. He was talking and he was a Yellow Nape but he didn't seem too tame. I waited another hour and then tried putting my hand in with a glove. This is not always a good idea as many birds are caught by gloved individuals or receive rough treatment at the hands of someone wearing gloves and I have seen birds who become terrified at the sight of gloves. This was not the case with Bill. He was not at all frightened. He did continue to bite, however, and instead of coming out he climbed on his swing. I gave the situation a lot of thought and decided that the next day I would remove the swing and then Bill would have nowhere to go except onto my hand.

I was in the birdroom bright and early the next morning. Bill seemed cheerful and quite receptive to the carrots, grapes and string beans which he and all the other birds got. While he was busy munching, I uncrimped the swing with a pair of pliers and removed

The Yellow Naped Amazon has been the object of the highest praise by bird fanciers for generations. It has excellent potential for speech and makes a most engaging pet. *Photo by author*

The Puerto Rican Amazon is one of a number of presently endangered parrot species.

U.S. Fish and Wild Life Service

131

it. That afternoon I tried again. To my delight after a perfunctory bite Bill climbed onto my finger. During the next hour, I had him on and off my gloved hand dozens of times and finally moved him on to a stand. I was a little nervous at this point and frankly a little afraid of him but he seemed very calm. He looked the room over carefully from this new vantage point. I offered him my hand and he climbed aboard as if he had been doing it for years and then back into the cage he went without any difficulty.

By the next day, I was able to get Bill on my hand without a glove once he was out of the cage, but I was still using the glove to remove him from his cage. By the weekend, I realized I would have to take a chance and uttering cries of, "good Bill, sweet boy!" I offered him my ungloved hand. Down came his beak, but only to steady himself as he grasped my finger and willingly left the cage. You can imagine the tremendous feeling of accomplishment that I had at that moment.

From that point on there was no trouble getting Bill in and out, although I still had reservations about his formidable beak. Bill seemed anxious to climb up my arm and I permitted him to do this. He investigated my arms and neck and then seemed content to remain on my shoulder. This was the pattern that our future relationship was to follow. To this day when Bill comes out he quickly walks up my arm to my shoulder. If we go upstairs to the living room he will stay on my shoulder while I read or if particularly playful, will prevent me from reading by trying to remove my glasses. I can turn him over on his back and he will hang by his beak from my finger. He gives kisses and permits me to caress him. He loves to have his head and cheek scratched either in or out of the cage.

Bill's speech is excellent. Everyone who enters the birdroom is charmed by his little girl's voice saying, "hello." When anyone leaves he will say, "bye-bye." This time, however, his voice is that of a tough longshoreman. He does not really answer the telephone but his vocabulary numbers at least 30 words and phrases. Bill hates to be returned to his cage after he's been out. I virtually have to "peel" him off my neck or shoulder but as quickly as I remove one set of toes, he grabs hold with another. I have worked out a technique which gets him off without hard feelings but it takes so long that I try not to take Bill out of the cage unless I have at least a half hour to spend with him. He gets particularly annoyed if I take him out and try to put him right back in.

Bill has more than exceeded all of my hopes for a tame, talking bird. His behavior and intelligence truly match the enthusiastic description of Yellow Napes given in all the old books and I can recommend the Yellow Naped Amazon as a very satisfying parrot to own.

Puerto Rican Amazon *(Amazona vittata)*

This small but well-proportioned member of *Amazona* has feathers which are the vivid green of new spring grass. The under-surface is a more yellowish-green while touches of black can be noted on the edges of the feathers of the head and neck. A scattering of red feathers is visible in the regions of the cheek and ear. The eye is a reddish-yellow and the beak a light horn color. A scarlet band across the forehead is quite noticeable and is responsible for the bird's alternate name of Red-Fronted Amazon as well as its scientific name *Amazona vittata* which translates from the Latin as "banded or bound with ribbon."

These vivacious creatures are about 12 inches long. They are unique to Puerto Rico although a subspecies once existed on the nearby island of Culebra. It is now extinct with the last specimens (a smaller bird with more delicate feet) reported around the turn of the century.

Amazona vittata is probably destined to follow in the path of the extinct subspecies *(A. v. gracilipes)* as the population of these parrots has declined to a point where they do not constitute a viable breeding group. The decline in numbers appears to have occurred with relative speed as Dr. Russ and other nineteenth century sources considered them to be among the most common parrots in the bird trade. By 1912 only small populations of this Amazon were being observed and reports in the 1950s and 1960s indicate drastic reductions in their numbers with the parrots only being found in their last stronghold, the Luquillo National Forest Reserve in eastern Puerto Rico.

An attempt is being made to establish a breeding colony of these parrots at the United States Fish and Wildlife Service's Research Center which sprawls along the banks of the Patuxent River in Laurel, Maryland. Patuxent is well known for the broad variety of programs in which it engages in an effort to protect and study wildlife with birds being of particular interest. This 4,500 acre facility (the largest of its kind in the world) is probably best known for its endeavors with the Whooping Crane which had all but vanished by the early 1940s but now numbers close to one hundred thanks to the people at Patuxent. Current projects include work with the Bald Eagle, the Screech Owl and Canada Geese. Dr. Ray C. Erickson directs the endangered species program.

Rosemary Low points out that the Puerto Rican Amazon is basically a fruit eater (frugivorous) and mentions that prior to its decline it was so numerous that children were kept out of school during harvest time to keep these greedy birds out of the corn fields

The Yellow Fronted Amazon is closely related to the Panama Amazon and can be distinguished from the latter by its dark beak and dark feathers of the cere. *Kelley*

A light-colored beak and cere help to identify the Panama Amazon. *Hoffman*

where no doubt they engaged in the usual parrot trick of damaging the crop by taking a few bites of an ear of corn and then dropping it for another ear which suddenly looked better.

In a final irony we note that *A. v. gracilipes* (the subspecies originally found on Culebra and Vicques islands) though common in 1899, was extinct by 1912 which was three years before it was even formally named.

Blue Fronted Amazon *(Amazona aestiva)*

The Blue Fronted Amazon has been known to collectors of birds for many years and he appears in literature about parrots written well over one hundred years ago. As with all Amazons, his major coloration is green. There are areas of bright yellow near the crown, around the eyes, and on the cheeks. The amount and exact location of the yellow varies widely from bird to bird. The blue feathers which give this parrot his name are found directly across the area near the base of the beak as well as around the eyes and may extend over a considerable part of the forehead. Once again, the exact location and amount of blue coloration will vary with individuals.

The Blue Front is a medium-sized parrot, about 14 to 15 inches long, with a well-proportioned, graceful appearance. The beak and nails are black and the eye is orange with a dark pupil.

Blue Fronts are extremely clever birds but also quite independent. Some are capable of developing large vocabularies but as with all parrots, talking ability is not something about which one can safely generalize. Some authorities consider the male a much better talker than the female but I have not found any real evidence of this.

Plumage for males and females is the same although females are more petite.

A smaller Amazon which also has blue feathers in the region of its forehead is the Orange Winged Amazon. It is frequently confused with the Blue Front and is sometimes mistakenly sold as a Blue Fronted Amazon. If in doubt check the beak of the bird in question. In the Blue Front the entire beak is black while in the Orange Wing the horn colored beak is black only at the tip.

My own Blue Fronted Amazon is not a great talker. He does, however, make up for this with his remarkable personality. Fogel cannot bear it when any other bird in the room has my attention. When he sees me at another cage, he goes through a whole series of antics which comprise what we have come to call Fogel's routine. He begins by dancing backwards. He then falls off the end of his perch but saves himself by grabbing his bell and swinging from it. Should this fail to attract me, he will hang upside down while pumping his wings and making high-pitched noises. This never fails to get my attention, but when I walk over to congratulate him, he finishes the act by taking a rapid swipe at me with his beak as if he were going to penalize me for my interest in the other birds.

Parrots are known to be extremely conservative individuals. They resist and resent change. (I am sure we all know humans who are the same.) Fogel, and other Blue Fronts which I have known, carry this conservatism to an extreme. He once stopped eating for days because his food container was changed from glass to ceramic. A few months ago I hung a set of Chinese wind chimes in the birdroom. I foolishly put them in the vicinity of Fogel's cage. He refused to come out until I moved them to the other side of the room.

Blue Fronts may be fed with a standard parrot diet. They are, however, particularly fond of fruit. They love to chew and should always be supplied with wood or other safe chewables.

Although I have had Fogel for many years, he has the typical Blue Front fault of nipping when he is excited or very hungry. This should not discourage you from purchasing a Blue Fronted Amazon if you have have the opportunity to do so, although, for some strange reason, they are more common in Europe than in the United States.

St. Vincent Amazon (Amazona guildingi)

This unusually marked Amazon is also known as Guilding's Amazon.

As with many Amazons there is quite a bit of variation in plumage from bird to bird. Generally, the forehead, front of the crown and region around the eyes are white blending into a yellowish-orange moving to the back of the crown, cheeks and throat. This Amazon's personality, general appearance and mannerisms remind me a great deal of the Double Yellow Head. The several which I have observed seem to show a regular progression of the white feathers extending over and down the head as the bird matures. Thus, it is possible that the increase in white on the head of the St. Vincent parallels the movement of yellow feathers on the head of its brother Amazon, the Double Yellow Head. The rear of the cheeks and the ear coverts are a lilac-blue. Its underparts are a mixture of orange and bronze with the abdomen a dull green. There are rich blue feathers in the wings as well as the central region of the tail. The tip of the tail is yellow. The eye is a golden-yellow and the beak is white. This parrot is quite sturdy in its build and is one of the larger Amazons; achieving lengths of 16 to 17 inches.

The Blue Fronted Amazon has been familiar to bird enthusiasts for well over a century. *Reed*

The St. Vincent Amazon can be recognized by its very distinctive white head marking. In this adult, the white feathers have completely covered the head.

New York Zoological Society

These birds are found only on the island of St. Vincent which is one of the Lesser Antilles in the Caribbean. Rutgers and Norris point out that this is the only parrot found on the island. They note that though it has always been rare, the London Zoo possessed a specimen as early as 1874.

Edward J. Boosey who was an artist as well as an author and highly talented ornithologist, mentions that the Duke of Bedford owned two fine examples of this parrot. Boosey was commissioned to paint the portrait of one of them.

A. A. Prestwich provides some background on Lansdown Guilding, for whom N. A. Vigors named *Amazona guildingi* in an article which Vigors wrote in 1836. Guilding was born at Kingstown, St. Vincent in 1797. He was an accomplished naturalist and painter and spent many years on the island of his birth where he held the post of Colonial Chaplain. Guilding made extensive collections of the fauna on St. Vincent as well as other islands of the West Indies. He is as well known for his work on certain forms of sea life as he is birds.

Rosemary Low confirms the hazardous position of the remaining population of these birds on their home island . She cites Keith Frost who in 1959 advised that on his annual visits to St. Vincent the bird could still be purchased for between eight and ten dollars.

Ms. Low also quotes the Duke of Bedford who believed that these large Amazons should only be kept in outdoor aviaries. One member of the Duke's pair was an outstanding pet and a completely fearless bird. It could say some words distinctly and carry on long but garbled conversations. He was an expert at laughing and used laughter to indicate his pleasure when food arrived or if he had been successful at committing some mischief. When the door to his shelter was being closed at night (something he would attempt to prevent by interfering with it every inch of the way) he would rap sharply on it with his beak as a last show of defiance.

W.H. Hudson also discusses the St. Vincent Amazon. He tells of the St. Vincent brought home by Lady Thompson, the wife of an early 20th century Administrator of the island. Hudson advises that the parrot (which he identifies with an older classification as *Chrysotis guilding*) received its name as a compliment to a clergyman who saved bird skins as well as men's souls. He is, of course, referring to Guilding, who as noted earlier was a chaplain on the island. Hudson goes on to describe the arrival of this parrot in England in the month of December. The birds including seven less rare traveling companions were enjoying themselves in a comfortable room in London where they could see the view from a large window. Suddenly they began to emit harsh screams of alarm—a sound which would nor-

138

mally mean the appearance of an enemy in the sky. Lady Thompson noted that large snowflakes had begun to fall and that the birds had apparently mistaken their first view of snow for falling feathers, a universal indication that some bird of prey was attacking birds.

In spite of the fact that the St. Vincent Amazon blends so well with the tropical vegetation of its home island, only a small population of these birds still exists.

Robert J. Berry, Curator of Birds at the Houston Zoo recently described a successful breeding of the St. Vincent which is unique in that it represents the first captive breeding of this species. Another special aspect of the breeding is that it was a cooperative effort by the Brookfield Zoo of Chicago, the Bronx Zoo of New York, the National Zoo of Washington, D.C. and the Houston Zoo. They had pooled their St. Vincent specimens to form a breeding group and should all be given credit for the success.

Mr. Berry's description of the island of St. Vincent makes it sound like a parrot paradise. He tells of the dense growth of many varieties of trees, shrubs and ferns with the area abounding in birds.

One might ask how, in such an ideal setting for parrots, could the falling off of a species that was considered very common only eighty years ago occur. Bob Berry describes a devastating hurricane that occurred in 1898, which resulted in heavy losses among these parrots with the dead and injured being found for days afterward. Two were even driven off course to St. Lucia, an island more than twenty miles to the north. A second disaster struck shortly thereafter when St. Vincent's volcano, *La Soufriere,* erupted, killing many more parrots and destroying much of their habitat. Apparently these successive blows sent them into a decline in numbers from which they have never recovered. (*La Soufriere* erupted again in April, 1979 but fortunately it was a much less violent eruption.)

There are a number of laws which place restrictions on the sale, trade, importation, export or shipment of birds which are listed as endangered species. One of the oldest and best known of these is the Lacey Act of 1900. Another is the Endangered Species Act of 1973 which prohibits any commerce in or the possession of many species of endangered and threatened wildlife and plants. The list is not static. It is constantly being updated with the information appearing in the Federal Register.

The current Federal Register lists the St. Vincent Amazon as being endangered throughout its entire range. The St. Vincent was originally listed as of June 2, 1970 and thus, ownership obtained after that date (with certain exceptions for scientific or propagation purposes) would not be legal.

139

A Grand Cayman Amazon.
National Zoological Park

Finsch's Amazon has a deep lilac crown and maroon lores. These distinguish it from the similar Mexican Red Head.
Kelley

140

Although we all resent restrictions which may interfere with our hobbies and interests, this type of control is long overdue. If the St. Vincent's remaining habitat is not destroyed and export of this parrot is stopped, (by preventing it from being profitable) the species may have a chance to survive.

Finsch's Amazon *(Amazona finschi)*

This fairly small member of the Amazon group is only 13 to 14 inches long. I suspect that rather than being as rare as it appears in the marketplace, when it is available it is frequently offered under the wrong name as there are several other Amazons for which it can be mistaken. This parrot is also known as the Lilac Crowned Amazon.

The Lilac Crowned resembles all other Amazons with its green plumage. Its ventral surface is a lighter green and the feathers of the chest have dark edges giving the bird's underside a scalloped look similar to that of the African Grey. In the African Grey we are dealing with dark feathers tipped with light edges, but the effect is much the same. There is also a deep maroon marking on the forehead and lores. This along with the unusual chest feathers and lilac crown can be used to differentiate it from the Green Cheeked Amazon which it resembles. The cheeks and ear-coverts are a light enough green so that they can be considered a separate marking. The eye is orange and the beak is a light horn color.

This parrot originates in western Mexico and was considered abundant in its range until at least ten years ago. Once again, I can only assume that there are more Lilac Crowned Amazons around than we suspect but that they are not being properly identified.

Rutgers and Norris describe Finsch's as a bird capable of shrill shrieking which it would tend to give up as it became tame.

Cyril Rogers represents Finsch's as being rather squat as compared to the Green Cheeked Amazon. Rogers considers them as good pets and particularly favors the hens which he believes can be identified by their flatter heads. The Duke of Bedford believed the female to have a broader and shorter beak and to be somewhat duller in color than the male.

I would be remiss if I did not mention Dr. Finsch himself, for whom Dr. P.L. Sclater named Finsch's Amazon in 1864. Doctor Finsch has been honored by having his name attached to at least three other parrots that I know of. Aside from his vast number of other accomplishments he was honored by Sclater because Finsch clearly identified the Amazon which bears his name as being distinct from the Green Cheeked Amazon.

Dr. Otto Finsch (1839-1917) published over 400 papers dealing with ornithology as well as a number of other important works. His monograph, *The Parrots,* is considered a classic. Dr. Finsch's study took him from Siberia to the South Seas and you will see his name quite frequently if you read any of the older literature on birds.

Rosemary Low relates interesting details about the Lilac Crowned Amazon and quotes from C.W. Beebe's description of the sighting of flocks of several hundreds of these parrots, "massed together as closely as possible . . . alternately soaring and fluttering. Then the entire flock swung upward in a magnificent loop from wall to wall . . . the delicate lavender edgings of the feathers showing plainly as they swept past with a loud whir of wings, each little foot clenched tightly close to the tail feathers." What a beautiful and perfect description this is of flying parrots!

Mrs. Low indicates that Finsch's Amazon is rarely imported into Britain. She describes several breedings, including one at the San Diego Zoo where the incubation period was 28 days. The infant was virtually hand-reared since the parents ceased feeding it at the age of five days. This may have been because the parents were only three years old which is a bit young for breeding. The hand-fed baby was eating well and quite independent by age four months. Mrs. Low also mentions a 1954 breeding by a Mrs. F. Hubbell, also of San Diego, where the offspring left her nest at eight weeks.

Green Cheeked Amazon *(Amazona viridigenalis)*

This parrot is a medium-sized, stocky bird which is generally only 13 or 14 inches long. It is also referred to as the Mexican Red Head and both names are applicable as it does indeed have a bright red cap along with its green cheeks. It is sometimes confused with Finsch's Amazon (the Lilac Crowned Amazon). Finsch's Amazon, however, has yellowish-green cheeks and a crown of deep lilac color. The beak is horn-yellow and the iris is also yellow.

This parrot is still quite common in northeastern Mexico where large flocks can be a problem to farmers because of the damage done to crops.

Most authorities agree that they are very noisy creatures but make up for this with their ability to become tame and affectionate. The Red Heads which I have seen have been better at imitating sounds than in speaking actual words.

I do not own a Mexican Red Head but I almost did on one occasion. I had been listening to a local radio station which broadcast public service announcements. They indicated that a lady in town a few miles from my home had found a "green parrot" and was anxious to contact the owner. Visions of gaining a parrot leaped into my mind and I called the number that the station had given and asked the woman who answered if she had any plans for the parrot if the owner did not get in touch with her. She explained that she really didn't quite have the parrot. It seems that it had come to roost in her apple tree and had spent several contented days there munching on the little crab apples. She was worried that the diet was bad for him (wise woman) and also feared that a cold night might harm him. "Come and get him if you'd like him," she said, "no one else has responded to the broadcast."

I quickly got my parrot-catching kit together. It consisted of a pair of gloves, a cage and a large sheet. Unfortunately I omitted a net which is a crucial item.

Arriving at the house I was greeted by the lady and her children. They were quite thrilled to see me and obviously expected quite a performance to be put on for them. Up to this point I wasn't really sure that I would be dealing with a full-sized parrot. I had remarked to my wife before I left that it was probably going to be a wasted trip since if it were a parakeet or even a Bee-Bee parrot I was really not interested in pursuing the bird.

One look into the apple tree made me realize that the agile little fellow who was hopping from limb to limb was none other than a Mexican Red Head. The apple tree was not particularly high and I was able to climb it with ease. The parrot sat on his branch and quite calmly ate his apple. As a matter of fact large chunks of apple fell on my head. I had the strange feeling that he was purposely dropping them on me. Getting within reach I put out a gloved hand. Mr. Red Head moved up two branches. I moved up two limbs and he flew to the next tree. The sequence of events was repeated in this tree except that I got a little closer and this time he flew to a large pine tree which put him about 100 feet in the air and completely out of my reach. I climbed down and talked to the lady and her children in the hope that the parrot would come back for the apples which he seemed to like so much. This was not to be. After about an hour I left and asked them to call me if he returned to the smaller tree. I had already decided that I would borrow a net and could catch him easily with that.

I did hear from the woman about two days later. They had borrowed an old cage and placed it in the tree. They had left peanuts and other goodies all around the cage. Yes, you guessed it! The parrot returned and entered the cage and one of the children who had been watching closed the door. This was obviously a tame bird and he was probably glad to get back into a place which looked familiar.

The Green Cheeked Amazon is more familiarly known as the Mexican Red Head. While this species has a reputation for being noisy, it makes up for this with its personable, affectionate disposition. *Goyanes*

The lady of the house told me that she and her husband and children had been so impressed with my raves about parrots as pets (given while I was waiting for the Red Head to return to the apple tree) that they had decided to keep him as a pet for themselves. I could hardly blame them.

Mealy Amazon *(Amazona farinosa)*

This is one of the less popular Amazons, which is unfortunate, as a good specimen can prove to be a delightful pet. The Mealy Amazon can be found in the south of Mexico as well as eastern Brazil and parts of Bolivia. Various subspecies of this parrot are found in Colombia, Ecuador, Costa Rica and Nicaragua.

The Mealy is one of the largest of the Amazons. Some members of this species achieve lengths of 18 to 19 inches. A good-sized, well-fed bird can be quite heavy. The major color of the plumage is green; dark grass green on top and a much paler green underneath. Some specimens show a few yellow feathers in the crown. Others have a crown which has a distinctly violet color. The lower beak and part of the upper beak are yellowish while the tip of the beak is dark grey. The legs are pale grey. The eye is a reddish-brown in color. It is a very large eye and is surrounded by an equally large white eye ring which is quite outstanding. Eye rings of this size are more typical of Conures.

The reason this bird is called the Mealy Amazon is because its feathers appear to be covered with a light dusting of powder. The feathers are not actually covered with powder, it is just the peculiar grey-green color of the feathers which gives this impression. Dr. Greene wrote that he had never seen a Mealy Amazon without wanting to give it a good shaking so as to remove the "powder." He went on to say, however, that this would not be a very judicious thing to do considering the size and strength of the Mealy Amazon's beak. Greene and other authors consider this bird to be an excellent talker.

Both Dr. Greene and Dr. Russ refer to its gentle disposition. They indicate, however, that the bird is capable of the most ear-piercing shrieks and that this should be considered before purchasing such a bird.

Within the nominate species are several well-known subspecies. These include the Plain Colored Amazon *(Amazona f. inorata),* the Blue-Crowned Amazon *(Amazona f. guatemalae),* and the Green-Headed Amazon *(Amazona f. virenticeps).* Variations in size, eye color, and head color provide the distinctions between these subspecies. All Mealy Amazons, however, bear the telltale sign of appearing as if they had been lightly powdered with flour.

Don't try to shake the powder from the feathers of a Mealy Amazon! *Kelley*

The Yellow Shouldered Amazon is very uncommon and strictly protected. *New York Zoological Society*

The beautiful Orange Cheeked Amazon is known by a variety of familiar names, but in scientific nomenclature he is *Amazona autumnalis*.

Photo by author

146

My own Mealy Amazon is actually a Plain Colored Amazon. He is solid green with just a hint of lilac in his crown. He is an immense specimen, easily 18 inches long and so heavy that after a while holding him can be tiring. I purchased him under rather unusual circumstances. My favorite pet shop always calls me whenever they obtain a particularly handsome or clever parrot. Since it is a small shop, they do not purchase birds from importers, but occasionally get them on consignment from someone who has either become unable to care for their bird or who has purchased one and realized the amount of work involved is too much for them.

When the shop owner first called to tell me that he had gotten in this huge Plain Colored Amazon with a fantastic personality, I really wasn't particularly interested but I thanked him for calling me. About two weeks later I called him to see if he had any vitamins in large sizes. He did and he also mentioned the Plain Colored Amazon again. He told me that the bird was talking well and was extremely tame. I decided to take a ride out and to look at the parrot at the same time that I picked up the vitamins. Well, as you might have guessed, it was love at first sight! Birl greeted me with a big hello, and scrambled right out of his cage onto my arm without a moment's hesitation. My fate was sealed, however, when he nestled his big green head into my neck and shrieked, "hi, pretty boy!" in a shrill voice into my ear. Needless to say, I purchased him and he has been a constant source of pleasure to me ever since.

Orange Cheeked Amazon (*Amazona autumnalis*)

Amazona autumnalis is frequently called the Yellow Cheeked Amazon and it is also referred to as the Red Lored Amazon. The lore in a bird refers to that region around the eye and between the beak and the eye. Since even very young Red Lored Amazons show this red marking I have a preference for this name. The yellow or sometimes orange feathers of the cheeks and ear-coverts are just hinted at in young birds and take about a year to become fully obvious.

Some authors choose to refer to this bird as the Scarlet Lored Amazon as well as the Primrose Lored Amazon.

Although this parrot's colors are somewhat muted the Red Lored is a beautiful bird. It bears the typical green color of the Amazons with the upper feathers a darker green than those of the ventral surface. The lores and forehead are red and the area of red coloration increases as the parrot ages. The red forehead blends into a delicate lavender colored crown with some lavender tipped feathers also appearing on the nape. The upper beak is horn colored with a dark tip while the lower beak is somewhat darker. Some authors refer to a yellowish beak but I have not seen this marking. The eye is orange; the legs are dark gray.

The Orange Cheek is about 14 inches long and resembles the Blue Fronted Amazon in size and build. Meyer de Schauensee notes that it is found in Venezuela, northern Columbia and western Ecuador.

Several subspecies are recognized. *Amazona autumnalis salvini* lacks the yellow cheeks and is a bit larger than the nominate form. It also has a distinctive red marking near the tail. Arthur A. Prestwich indicates that this subspecies (which is frequently called Salvin's Amazon) was named in honor of Osbert Salvin, an English ornithologist. Salvin, who died in 1898 held the Curatorship of Ornithology at the University of Cambridge and also wrote extensively on birds with those of the Neotropical region being his field of greatest interest. Salvin authored many papers on birds as well as contributing to a number of important volumes dealing with his specialty. Having his name added to a subspecies of *A. autumnalis* is a fitting tribute to him.

Orange Winged Amazon *(Amazona amazonica)*

These friendly and clever little parrots are often confused with the larger Blue Fronted Amazon. There are some similarities between them but when the two species are viewed together, the differences are quite obvious. I suspect that one reason for the confusion that has always existed between these two birds is that the blue, orange and yellow color configuration in the region of the forehead, crown, cheeks and throat shows considerable variation even among individuals of the same species. Thus, it is necessary to use additional characteristics to make an accurate identification.

The Orange Wing is the smaller of the two species. It is between 11 and 13 inches in length while Blue Fronts are 14 to 15 inches long. The body of the Orange Wing is green but it has a distinctive yellowish-orange crown with cheek feathers that are also yellowish-orange. The Orange Winged Amazon frequently tends to fluff out these yellowish cheek feathers and they look much like old fashioned "mutton-chop" sideburns although I doubt if any Victorian gentleman ever possessed a pair of sideburns of such splendid color. The forehead, lores and the region above the eyes are blue and the ear coverts are a deep green; a marking not found in the Blue Fronted Amazon. The eye of the Orange Winged Amazon is darker than that of the Blue Front with the former having an orange-brown eye and the latter's being yellow-orange. The most marked and obvious difference can be found in the beaks. The seed cracking tool of the Blue Front is black while *Amazona amazonica* has a horn colored beak which becomes black only at the tip. Koko, my own Orange Wing, has been awarded the nickname of "The Maltese Falcon" because he is so timid that when taken out of his cage he will sit as still as a little statue. Koko has grown in confidence and now permits me to pick him up without biting and he will also sit quietly with me and give kisses (although somewhat grudgingly) as well as making use of all of the toys in his cage. He is a fairly quiet bird and his mild disposition and tameness is similar to that described by the owners of other Orange Winged Amazons with whom I have been in touch.

Meyer de Schauensee notes these parrots are distributed through Peru, Brazil and Columbia as well as Trinidad and Tobago. Great quantities of them have entered the United States market during the last few years and they are readily available. I have seen them priced rather moderately and, of course, as with any item offered for sale this is due to the large supply. Rosemary Low notes that the Orange Winged is one of the parrots most consistently imported into Europe. Other reports indicate they have been and still are quite plentiful in the wild.

Yellow Shouldered Amazon *(Amazona barbadensis)*

This uncommon Amazon has a number of characteristics which are reminiscent of the Double Yellow Head. These include his stocky build (although he is an inch or so shorter with his average length being 13 inches) comical manner and a number of similar markings. In terms of supply, however, there is vast difference between the two birds with *Amazona barbadensis* being strictly protected and virtually unobtainable as compared to the Double Yellow which is one of the most commonly imported of all parrots.

The characteristics which identify this parrot include its yellowish-white forehead and lores. The crown, cheeks, ear coverts and occasionally the upper throat are yellow. There is a blue wash in the lower portion of the cheek which continues down the throat. There are bright yellow markings on the tops of the shoulders and their intensity as well as the large area they cover make them highly visible. A particularly attractive marking is found in the bright yellow "stockings" which begin at the claws and extend up the thighs. The flight feathers are quite dark and range from blue to almost black. The eye is a dark orange and the beak a light horn color.

These parrots are found along an arid coastal region of Venezuela as well as on the island of Aruba. Alternate names include Yellow Winged parrot and the rather lengthy Single Yellow Fronted Amazon parrot. By a quirk their current and latest classification (they were once classified as *Psittacus ochropterus*) is based on a geographical error as the Latin barbadensis in the scientific name translates to "of Barbados" and these parrots do not occur on that Caribbean island.

These birds were common early in the century but in the brief span of 30 years there was a decline of such magnitude that by the 1930s the parrot was considered rare.

There is also a subspecies, *Amazona b. rothschildi* which is much like the nominate species but with less yellow on the crown and with the bend of the wing having its yellow mixed with red feathers.

Dr. Ernest Hartert writing in 1892 indicates that the subspecies was named for the Hon. Walter Rothschild who had apparently supported Hartert's expedition to Venezuela and the Caribbean. A.A. Prestwich points out that Rothschild was the British born son of the famous banking family. He was evidently much more devoted to natural history than the family business.

Rothschild became a great collector of birds with the collections ultimately increasing to the point where they became the foundation of the Tring (England) Museum. Dr. Hartert was appointed as Director and through the years the ornithological collections came to rival those in the British Museum. Lord Rothschild (succeeding to his father's title in 1915) wrote hundreds of papers dealing with the exotic birds of the Pacific.

A considerable part of the Tring collection can now be seen at the American Museum of Natural History in New York. When Lord Rothschild died in 1937 the Tring Museum, including an extremely valuable 30,000 volume library was left to the trustees of the British Museum.

Rutgers and Norris confirm the information given by other authors but add that the *A.b. rothschildi* is about an inch smaller than the nominate species and is confined to the islands of Bonaire, Blanquila and Margarita which are off the coast of Venezuela. They believe that the rapid loss of birds on Aruba was largely due to the usual parrot crime of destroying fruit and corn crops with resulting retaliation on the part of the native population.

Rosemary Low also describes how rare this parrot is and makes the interesting point that most of the specimens now available (including the one at the London Zoo) are probably the subspecies which now exists in comparatively greater numbers than the nominate race.

The Spectacled Amazon, smallest of the true Amazons, is a courageous little bird. It is not at all conscious of its size and makes an amusing pet. *Photo by author*

Spectacled Amazon *(Amazona albifrons)*

This rather noisy little parrot is the smallest of the true Amazons with a length of slightly over ten inches. It has the typical green color of the Amazons but its small size and distinctive facial markings make it a very easy bird to identify. *Amazona albifrons* has a forehead which varies from white to yellowish-white. A bright red marking begins where the yellowish-white feathers of the brow end to join the feathers surrounding the eye. This parrot's common name is, of course, derived from this red marking which contrasts so vividly with the other feathers of the face and head. The beak is yellow and the legs are a light gray. In young birds the white forehead tends to be more deeply tinged with yellow and there is a smaller area of red marking on the face. There are several subspecies with the most common one differing from the nominate species by virtue of being slightly smaller.

The Spectacled Amazon is found mainly in Mexico, Guatemala and Costa Rica.

It is also referred to as the White Fronted Amazon. Rosemary Low adds the synonym White Browed Amazon and hints that the male may possibly be identified by his bulkier body. She also notes that they are rather noisy and describes their screams as "ricochet-like." That's an excellent description of this bird's noises and I can attest to just how the parrot's screams ricochet off the walls of a basement birdroom. I would only add that it takes very little to set my Spectacled Amazon off on a binge of screeching.

The Duke of Bedford considered this a very rare Amazon. This may have been the case in England at the time of his writing but it is no longer so as great numbers of these parrots are imported and available throughout the world.

Cyril Rogers adds still another name to the roster when he refers to this Amazon as the Red, White and Blue Parrot. He also confirms their tendency towards screeching but mentions that they are relatively good talkers and good pets.

Dr. Russ indicates that this bird was known as early as 1651. He calls it the White Browed Amazon or the Spectacle Parrot and also uses the older scientific designation *Psittacus albifrons*. Dr. Russ describes a Spectacled owned by a friend, Mr. F. Arnold of Munich, whose bird spoke many words but only a few clearly. Mr. Arnold also complained that while his bird learned quickly it would forget what it learned just as quickly. Apparently it was a delightful companion and permitted the children of the household to do as they liked with it. One of their mutual pleasures was to take the bird for rides in a doll carriage which it enjoyed greatly. This bird was a bit of a tease and it had a little trick where it would climb the curtains to just a high enough point so the children could not reach it. It would then call to them until they stood on a chair to get to it and, of course, at that point it would promptly move out of range again. This particular little parrot apparently had a very strong personality as Russ describes how if its owner failed to satisfy certain simple desires such as scratching its head or "shaking hands" it would become angry and later reject all efforts at reconciliation. Unfortunately, the rejection took the form of sharp nips!

When I purchased a Spectacled Amazon I named him Taco as I have a preference for one or two syllable names (in the hopes that the parrots will learn to say them). Thus, Taco was named after a delicacy of his country of origin. Had I known more about his personality I would have broken my own rule and named him "Tough Guy." He undoubtedly thinks he is at least three times the size that he really is and does not hesitate to cross beaks with any of the larger parrots in the room. Taco is still quite young and he tends to have more yellow than white feathers on his forehead but this is not uncommon in younger Spectacled Amazons. He is just as noisy as all the books indicate but does speak several words quite clearly including a long and drawn out, "Helllooo." He is extremely agile and is also quite a chewer. I have replaced many of his perches because they were at the point where he had almost chewed through one end. Perhaps we'll let him finish the next one off so that he can see what happens when you chew the limb you're perched on.

Black Billed Amazon (*Amazona agilis*)

This parrot provides another example of how the indiscriminate use of names can cause confusion and perpetuate errors. *Amazona agilis* is also referred to as the Active Amazon, All Green Amazon, and Lesser Jamaican parrot. Early authors such as Dr. Greene and Dr. Russ as well as a few modern authors use the name Jamaica parrot for another parrot, *Amazona collaria*, also known as the Red throated Amazon or Yellow Billed Amazon. To add to the confusion both parrots come from Jamaica in the West Indies, and have a number of similarities. Using the Latin name or the Black Billed name clarifies the matter, as *agilis* has a much darker beak than *collaria*. Incidentally, the Latin name *agilis* refers to the quickness and nimbleness of this bird.

Distribution is confined to the island of Jamaica where according to Rutgers and Norris it favors the more heavily forested hill regions.

These authors note that although it was at one time a relatively common parrot with large flocks flying and screeching through the forests it is currently quite rare. The damage they do to the corn crops and their trick of destroying pimento berries to get at the seeds, resulted in counter-attacks by the local population which has reduced their numbers greatly.

This parrot is one of the smaller Amazons and generally does not exceed 11 inches in length. Their plumage is a very bright green on their dorsal surface with the under surface a more yellowish-green. The crown is a much darker green with the flight feathers a mixture of blue and green. The feathers on the nape are edged with black and a few red feathers can be found on the forehead. Some red can also be found on the lower edge of the wing. The beak is gray to black and it becomes much lighter towards the base. Immature birds have colors which are generally duller.

Sidney Porter gave an interesting description of his experiences in Jamaica while trying to track down some specimens of *A. agilis*. From Kingston he traveled 25 miles into the mountains which at that time were still almost virgin forests. The mistress of a local school who was quite familiar with the fauna of the island advised him that although much rarer than the Yellow Billed Amazon the Black Billed did exist in the mountainous district of the island. Porter first saw specimens of the Black Billed Amazon in an aviary at the Jamaica Institute in Kingston. There he compared them with the Yellow Billed Amazon and noted that the Black Billed was larger, more robust and of an unusually deep and rich green color. Porter was eventually able to purchase a specimen which was brought by a native but he described it as being in extremely poor shape. Once he had it aboard ship, hand feeding seemed to strengthen it which pleased him as the natives indicated that these birds were not "very good" as they "always died in captivity." Just before leaving Kingston, Porter was able to secure a true pair of Black Bills in excellent condition and extremely tame. They had been collected deep in the forest. He described them as young birds, six to eight weeks old, and with their plumage a bright glossy green but not so bright or rich as the adults. The hen of the pair was rather selfish and would fly into a fit of rage if any of the other birds he had collected were fed before her. Mr. Porter successfully brought his Black Billed Amazons back to England where they thrived.

Although apparently rare this parrot does not appear on the List of Endangered and Threatened Wildlife which is published by the United States Department of the Interior. I have spoken with officials

154

from this department and there are currently no plans to take such action. During the last several years I have also been surprised to frequently note ads offering these parrots for sale.

Vinaceous Amazon *(Amazona vinacea)*

This moderately-sized parrot is an attractive, colorful member of its genus. *Amazona vinacea* is about 14½ inches long. It is dark green with the feathers of the crown as well as those of the back of the neck and mantle edged in black. The forehead, chin and lores are crimson. It also has a red band across the forehead which blends with the crimson of the lores. The throat and the upper portion of the breast are a dark wine-red or burgundy color. This marking, of course, provides the bird's name. The beak is red with a light tip. The female is duller in color and the beak is not as red as in the male. Immature birds resemble the female.

Wolfgang de Grahl places the habitat of this parrot as southern Brazil and Paraguay. He comments that the Vinaceous seems to appear on the market at only certain seasons. He considers them good house pets although not outstanding talkers.

Rutgers and Norris give a good description of this bird and mention the long feathers which are found on the back of the neck. These feathers are blue-gray and are edged with black. They also comment that the Vinaceous is a common species in its native land and that the flocks of this parrot are large enough to create a serious problem in the orange groves. The natives prefer it as a cage bird and thus, Rutgers is surprised that it is not more commonly exported to Europe or the United States. These authors also mention that the Vinaceous is a particularly gentle parrot which seems to delight in human company and gets along well with other parrot-like birds. They credit Clifford Smith with the first successful breeding of this species in 1971.

Rosemary Low believes this parrot to be one of the most desirable of the Amazons available in Europe. She advises, however, that it is irregularly imported and then only in very small numbers. She describes a most charming member of the species owned by Miss Maude Knobel who purchased it even though it was in poor health. Warmth and good food helped it to regain its health and it soon developed into a very tame individual. It became talkative, lively and loving and enjoyed running around the floor. It squealed with joy when it found a dark corner to hide in.

155

Although current literature seems to stress the fact that this parrot is not frequently imported it does not hint at its being rare or endangered. This bird has, however, been listed in the Federal Register as being endangered throughout its entire range. The initial listing was June 14, 1976.

Perhaps the Vinaceous Amazon has had one of those sudden drops in numbers which have occurred in other parrot species in the past.

The final source, Dr. Russ, reveals that the species was known as early as 1760 and was fully described by Wied in 1820. Russ notes the erectile neck feathers and also quotes a Mr. Petermann's description of the Vinaceous which for me is a perfect description of every Amazon face. ". . . their orange-red eyes gleamed with uncontrollable defiance; yet they are not wicked, but gentle . . ."

The scalloped plumage of Finsch's Amazon is somewhat similar to that of the African Grey. *M. Morrone/S. Rosenblum*

In Georgetown all Macaws are called Robert, just as most parrots in England are called Poll or Polly. When you buy a Macaw in Guiana you can be certain that it will be able to say its own name, as well as deafen you with its screams. The two Macaws would amble across the cage tops, and occasionally one would stop and say, "Robert?" in a pensive sort of way. Another would reply, "Robert!" in outraged tones, while a third would mutter, "Robert, Robert," to itself.

Gerald M. Durell, *Three Tickets to Adventure*

The Macaws are probably the most spectacular members of the entire parrot family. Their exquisite colors and impressive size make them popular favorites in any public or private collection of birds.

Parrot Jungle, Miami

158

10

The Colorful Macaws

MACAWS ARE LARGE AND VIVIDLY HUED members of the Parrot race. A glimpse of their bright and unusual color combinations gives the impression that nature has let her imagination run wild in the arrangement of color in the feathers of these striking birds. Their large size, powerful muscles and formidable beaks earn them a degree of respect of which they do not seem to be unaware. While Macaws are generally not vicious, people tend not to trifle with them and the birds almost seem to expect proper treatment as a result. Their intelligence is obvious in their behavior and studies of Macaw brains indicate that the cerebrum (the site of intelligent behavior) is eight times as heavy in the Macaw as in fowl of comparable body weight.

Most larger Macaws exhibit an exquisite control over their tremendous biting powers and show great care to differentiate between clothes pins or twigs and such delicate structures as fingers.

Loud screams of "Ow wow!" will help get the message across if they err but several of my Macaws use that expression immediately after nipping and although it shows a knowledge of guilt on their part it does little to comfort me.

Macaws originate in Central and South America, and very large numbers have been exported to the United States and Europe in recent years. Some countries now restrict the export of their Macaws as they have realized that their numbers are falling to a dangerously low level. It is still possible, however, to purchase a fairly wide variety of different species.

Interest in these conspicuous parrots has always existed and much has been written about their relationships with men. More than a hundred years ago Brazilian natives learned that if they removed the red feathers from Macaws and then inoculated the site with fluid from a frog or toad, when the feathers next grew they would be a bright yellow or orange until the next molt. Apparently, some temporary damage was done to the feather tract but the bright colors made the feathers more valuable.

Lyndon L. Hargrove notes historic references to Macaws as early as 1536 in a Spanish report which described how Indians living south (of the present states) of New Mexico and Arizona, "traded parrot's feathers for green stones far in the north." A later report by the Spanish priest Padre Velarde written in 1716 states that at San Xavier del Bac (now Tucson, Arizona) there are many Macaws "which the Pima Indians raise because of the beautiful feathers of red and other colors . . . which they strip from the birds in the spring, for their adornment."

Other tribes such as the Pueblo Indians also raised Macaws and made use of their feathers as shown in early tribal paintings. Old documents indicate an almost religious significance in the relationship between the Indian and these birds with the belief that one could not keep a red Macaw if he were an individual of poor moral character or if his household was not maintained in a harmonious fashion.

In August, 1963 *Life* Magazine reported on Louis, a cranky, brandy-drinking Blue and Gold Macaw who lived in Victoria, British Columbia. Louis was said to have been born in 1863 which would have made him 100 years of age at the time the article by Russell Sackett was written. Sometimes a parrot is represented as being older than he actually is because the original bird dies and his replacement is thought by younger members of the family to be grandfather's original Macaw and this may have been the case with Louis. Nevertheless, he was a venerable old bird as well as a pampered recluse whose daily wants were tended to by a personal servant. His financial interests were also protected by one of Victoria's most prominent lawyers.

Louis had been the coddled companion of a prominent spinster, Victoria Wilson. Until her death in 1949, Louis lived with her on a fine piece of real estate on a hill overlooking the provincial parliament and the city's harbor. He had been with Miss Wilson as far back as any contemporary could recall and somewhere in his past had acquired the vocabulary of a longshoreman as well as a thirst for spirits.

160

Louis endeared himself to Miss Wilson to the point that shortly after the turn of the century she purchased an electric automobile just so that she could take Louis for quiet rides as the noise of gasoline engines apparently frayed his already short temper. Louis rasped his displeasure at the electric car and it went into storage with less than one hundred miles on the speedometer.

Miss Wilson decided that Louis might need more than human company and so shortly before her death she bought him his own parrot, a youngster named Morrie who was forty years his junior. Thus Louis, Miss Wilson, Morrie and Yue Wah Wong, her trusted Cantonese gardener, shared the comforts of the huge old house.

Miss Wilson died in 1949 leaving an estate of nearly half a million dollars. The mansion and its spacious grounds were sold to a real estate developer who had plans for a modern, multiple-unit high-rise apartment complex. He had, however, overlooked Louis and an escrow clause tucked away in Miss Wilson's will which stipulated that Louis must live out his days in his original home and that under no circumstances might his environment be disturbed. Thus, the house and its attached aviary had to stand until Louis fell.

Since Louis was a reputed 86 years of age at this time the developer temporarily divided the house into six apartments, intending to wait out the old Macaw. Louis, however, callously recovered from the sorrow of his mistress's passing and to the realtor's rueful astonishment seemed to take a new lease on life. The faithful Wong (accounted for under a seperate provision in the will) continued to serve Louis his daily ration of walnuts, almonds, hard-boiled eggs and a tot of brandy. ("No brandy for Morrie," Wong would chuckle. "Just Louis, very special bird.")

By 1957 Wong was ill although Louis was still in fine shape. Mr. Sackett visited the house to check on local rumors of a melancholy nature regarding its famous occupant. He was reassured by a brilliant blue and yellow view of Louis, looking splendidly indestructible through the dusty, heavily screened window of his private house where he was doing a head stand on his perch. Shortly thereafter the developer gave up on the property and sold it to local businessmen who must have had great patience. Sackett made a second visit which was inspired not only by curiosity but also by vague rumors of Louis' demise. Upon arriving at the Empress Hotel in Victoria one of the locals confided to Mr. Sackett that the house was still standing but that no one saw Louis anymore and if anyone did it was probably because Wong, spurred by self-interest had cornered the local market on Blue and Gold Macaws and schooled a series of stand-ins. As Mr. Sackett

The magnificent Hyacinth Macaw is the largest of all parrot species. This gorgeous bird is much sought after by collectors and makes a gentle pet in spite of its formidable appearance. *Parrot Jungle, Miami*

walked into the gardens next to the aviary he was greeted with a spine-chilling shriek and the commanding voice of a feathered paranoid: "Wong? Wong! Damn you Wong, where are you?" Following Wong's instructions Mr. Sackett walked through the gate to the window of the aviary and tentatively called, "Louis?" There was a shadowy movement far back in the birdhouse, and suddenly there was Louis, jaunty and resplendent as ever, sidestepping deliberately along his perch toward the window. "Wong?" He rasped and eyed Mr. Sackett accusingly.

More than 15 years have elapsed since this description of Louis and Wong was originally written. I hope that wherever Louis is he is being given the respect due a property owner and that whoever is in charge does not forget his daily brandy.

Hyacinth Macaw (*Anodorhynchus hyacinthinus*)

The colors and markings of this huge parrot are so lush and rich that at first glance one might think it is an enormous toy, shaped like a parrot. The Hyacinth (or Hyacinthine as it is sometimes called) is the largest of all the parrots. Mature specimens can exceed three feet in length and its huge, black over-hanging beak adds to its impressive appearance. The over-all plumage is a luxuriant blue. The feathers under the tail are dark grey as are the legs. The eye-ring is a brilliant yellow and the eye itself is dark brown. There is an area at the base of the lower beak which is also bright yellow and which looks as if someone had painted this curved yellow line on this parrot in much the same way a cartoonist does when he wishes to show a smiling face. The first view of a Hyacinth is always impressive and startling. Most Hyacinths originate in the interior of Brazil. This country restricts their export even though they are still relatively common in heavily forested areas. Although they are probably the most expensive of all parrots there is a good number of them in private collections.

It is possible to confuse *Anodorhynchus hyacinthinus* with the Glaucous Macaw and Lear's Macaw. All three have similar coloring but the blue of the Hyacinth is much richer, with the other two birds having plumage that is almost greenish-blue. The Glaucous Macaw and Lear's Macaw are also considerably smaller than the Hyacinth and the yellow marking at the base of the Hyacinth Macaw's beak is longer and thinner. The Glaucous is extremely rare and may already be on the road to extinction. Some authorities have suggested that Lear's Macaw may be a hybrid version of a cross between a Hyacinth and a Glaucous while others believe that it is a separate species which has remained unique because of isolation due to the geography of the region where this parrot originates.

These Hyacinth babies are just as playful and charming as they appear as they cavort about their Brazilian home. *Reed*

164

Dr. Greene makes mention of a Hyacinth in the London Zoo. This bird spoke and seemed to particularly like young children. Greene speculated that perhaps this was because the children shared their cookies with him and he had a "sweet beak." Even at that time (1887) the cost of one of these birds was enormous. Greene quotes a figure of roughly $250.00 for a Hyacinth which is four or five times the price of any other parrot whose cost he mentioned.

Reverend F.G. Dutton, a good friend of Dr. Greene, and a contributor to his book, owned a Hyacinth Macaw who quite easily bent the bars of a cage advertised as "Groom's Indestructible Macaw Cage." Reverend Dutton agrees with other authors that in spite of its huge size and ferocious looking beak, the Hyacinth Macaw is a gentle, friendly bird. Reverend Dutton's Hyacinth (the destroyer of indestructible cages) could cackle like a hen but apparently was so busy with this accomplishment that he never took the time to acquire any other vocabulary.

Dr. Russ notes that this bird was first described in 1790. Russ writes (as do several others) that in the wild these birds are generally found in pairs or families.

The specimens which I have examined have been particularly gentle and friendly. One group of three seemed to delight in each other's company and sat so close to one another on their perch that there was actual physical contact between them. They are not exceptionally noisy Macaws but as noted they require a strongly constructed cage and certainly a large one.

Lear's Macaw *(Anodorhynchus leari)*

A small mystery exists about this member of the Blue Macaw group in terms of the determination of its exact range within the interior of Brazil as well as the most appropriate classification category in which to place it.

Rutgers and Norris note the distribution of *Anodorhynchus leari* as Brazil with the exact range, unknown. They mention that those which are exported to Europe appear to originate in the Brazilian states of Bahia and Santos. Very little is known about these Macaws in the wild. The Dutch ornithologist, K.H. Voous in his 1965 article on specimens of Lear's Macaws in the Amsterdam Zoo, toys with the possibility that it could be a hybrid between the two other members of *Anodorhynchus*, the Hyacinth and Glaucous Macaws. This theory is not commonly accepted because of unique characteristics found in the Hyacinth and absent in Lear's.

Perhaps one reason more is not known about these interesting birds is because for many years Lear's Macaws were combined in shipments with Hyacinths which reached various European importers.

Lear's Macaw is a handsome, well-proportioned member of his race. Measuring only about 28 inches in length, he is considerably shorter than his relative, the Hyacinth. This parrot is also referred to as the Little Hyacinth, Lear's Ara, and the Indigo Macaw. The last designation, of course, being a reference to its color which although almost a cobalt blue is not as rich or intense as in the Hyacinth. The head and neck are a paler blue and the under-surface grayish-blue. The beak is large, black, and formidable. The eye is dark brown and is surrounded by a naked, orange-yellow eye ring which is almost matched by an even more yellowish bare patch at the base of the lower beak. This cheek marking along with size and color can help determine which species of blue Macaw one is observing as the cheek patch in the Hyacinth is long and narrow and rather like a crescent moon. To carry the analogy a bit further the cheek patch in the Lear's Macaw is larger and rounder and similar to a ¾ moon. The lovely and life-like portrait of a Hyacinth done by Edward Lear in 1832 actually looks more like a Lear's Macaw since it has the larger cheek patch marking.

The Duke of Bedford was familiar with this species and considered them "excessively hardy." Perhaps he was referring to the fact that one of his Lear's, when first imported, flew to the top of an oak tree and resided there for more than 48 hours during the month of January. He did not seem at all the worse for this exposure. The Duke was a pioneer in the technique of inducing parrots to remain at liberty without straying. A pair of his Lear's were kept in this fashion with the hen daily flying three miles to town to indulge herself in her taste for city companions. Her activities there included stealing clothes pins from people's lines and playing with the local dogs.

Karl Plath, writing as a curator of birds for the Chicago Zoo in October, 1937, described the Zoo's magnificent Lear's which lived near a Hyacinth in a cage which was surrounded by a most appropriate setting of rubber trees and palms. Almost ten years later Plath noted the presence of the same Lear's Macaw when he listed some old timers at the Chicago Zoo. In 1939 Dr. Jean Delacour wrote of his Macaws at Clères, France. He described the chain and perch arrangement which he used for Macaws with each of these large parrots being fixed by a length of chain to a long concrete fence with a space of about three feet between each Macaw. Their chains were lengthy enough to permit them to play with and preen one another. Seven

Lear's and four Hyacinths were part of the collection of 34 Macaws who were delighted to spend their time on this concrete fence which was in the shade of very high trees. How sad to think that this beautiful sight was destroyed only a year later when World War II reached the area.

Lear's Macaw is named for the English author and artist, Edward Lear who lived from 1812-1888. Lear was born in London and was the youngest of 21 children! A. A. Prestwich advises us that Lear's family was Danish and originally spelled the name Lor. Lear's father, Jeremiah Lear, was a stock broker in London who entered bankruptcy five years before his son began his greatest work. The father was eventually imprisoned in King's Bench Prison because of his debts.

A talented older sister instructed Lear in the basic elements of drawing but he was truly self-taught as a painter and lithographer. When he was only 15 he earned small fees or sometimes just food for coloring prints, decorating ladies' fans and providing drawings for doctors and medical students.

Lear began his efforts on the monumental undertaking *Illustrations of the Family of Psittacidae or Parrots* in 1830. It was quite a task for an 18-year-old who lacked influence, formal training and funds. His goal was to produce a complete portrait of the parrot genera and most of the parrots who were residents of the London Zoo at that time were represented in his work. In writing to a friend at the height of his labors in 1831 he commented that he was so involved with parrots that if he were to return in a new form after his death he would be uncomfortable as anything but a parrot. He advised this same friend that he was so occupied with his lithography tasks that he doubted that he would be able to offer the friend a comfortable seat should he visit, "seeing that of the six chairs I possess five are at the present occupied with lithographic prints . . ."

Although fourteen sections of the work were projected only twelve were completed. The twelve-part work was finished by 1832. It was in the form of a large folio and contained 42 hand-colored lithographs. It gained immediate recognition for Lear including membership in the Linnean Society. His election to the Society occurred on the day following his presentation of a copy of the first folio to them. In a letter commending him, N. A. Vigors, Thomas Bell and Edward T. Bennett wrote that he was highly deserving of the honor of becoming an associate of the Society.

Lear agreed to provide copies of each folio to the Linneans and obviously he chose material which best represented his work when selecting a presentation folio.

The Glaucous Macaw is a seldom seen relative of the Hyacinth. It differs from the latter in its smaller size, less intense color and the shape of the cheek patch. *Buttstead*

The Spix Macaw is another interesting rarity in the blue Macaw group.
New York Zoological Society

168

The artist became associated with John Gould and traveled with him in Europe where they studied rare birds in a number of collections. Some of the plates in Gould's *Birds of Europe* were done by Lear. Lear also worked with Gould on the latter's book on toucans which was completed in 1835. A. A. Prestwich indicates that the relationship was not a particularly happy one. Prestwich notes that the illustrations for the parrot volume of *Jardine's Naturalist's Library* were also done by Lear. He further points out that Lear gave lessons in drawing to Queen Victoria in 1845 and also painted the birds and animals in Lord Stanley's private zoo. While at the home of Lord Stanley, Lear produced the famous *Book of Nonsense* and other limericks for the amusement of his patron's grandchildren. It is strange that so many people remember Edward Lear more for his nonsense verse than for his art.

Brian Reade described Lear's final visit to London and his beloved Regent's Park Zoo in 1880. Reade points out that the bustling city with its heavy traffic was too much for Lear who left for Italy with Foss, his cat, where he spent the final eight years of his life. His health began to fail and his eyesight was no longer capable of handling the close, exacting work of painting birds. Reade comments that Lear wrote to Gould, "My eyes are so sadly worse, that no bird under an ostrich shall I soon be able to do."

Not many copies of Lear's masterpiece are available today although the American Museum of Natural History Library is in possession of an original copy. In October, 1978 Johnson Reprint corporation and Pion Limited of New York and London produced a facsimile volume of *Illustrations of the Family of Psittacidae or Parrots* with 500 copies of this ambitious undertaking being printed.

Glaucous Macaw *(Anodorhynchus glaucus)*

This is a rare species of the blue Macaws. A specimen viewed at Busch Gardens in Florida confirms the usual description that they are a less rich blue than the Hyacinth. They are also smaller, about 28 inches long, and have yellow facial markings more similar to the Lear's Macaw than to the Hyacinth. They originate in Brazil, Paraguay and Uruguay.

Spix's Macaw *(Cyanopsitta spixii)*

Many historians credit Christopher Columbus with having brought the first Macaws from the New World back to Spain. These noisy creatures were called "Aras" by the natives since their screams

169

(and loud ones they are) sound somewhat like that word if one goes to the trouble of spelling out the screams of a Macaw. It is unfortunate that some of the Macaws that Columbus saw or might have seen during his voyages are now extinct and others appear to be traveling that same unhappy road.

Spix's Macaw which is classified as *Cyanopsitta spixii* by some authors and *Ara spixii* by others is not extinct but is becoming rare and reports of sightings of this interesting bird are rather limited.

This parrot, which is also known as the Little Blue Macaw, has facial markings which are somewhat unusual for members of the Macaw family. It lacks feathers around the top of the beak (cere) and eyes (lores) and these naked areas are almost black in color. The yellowish eye set in this black mask gives this parrot an almost forbidding appearance. It has no bare facial cheek patch.

Spix's are relatively small Macaws, only about 20 to 23 inches long. Their over-all plumage is blue to dark blue with the feathers of the head being more silvery or grayish-blue. The undersurface is a less intense blue with tints ranging from greenish on the chest and abdomen to dark gray under the tail. The beak is a deep black. There is a superficial resemblance to the other blue Macaws such as the Hyacinth and the Glaucous but one glance at its silvery-blue as opposed to the rich cobalt of other members of the genus *Anodorhynchus* and its lack of a yellow cheek patch indicate some of the reasons we agree with its separate species classification.

Rutgers and Norris locate this parrot in the eastern Brazilian states of Piauhy and Bahia. They note that the Macaw is seldom imported but indicates that specimens which they have seen kept as pets have become tame and gentle. In an earlier work Rutgers gives the information that Spix's hens are somewhat smaller and have a narrower and shorter beak than males.

The rather odd name of this Macaw can be traced through A.A. Prestwich who credits Johann G. Wagler with the earliest description of the Little Blue Macaw which he named in honor of his friend Johannes B. von Spix. Herr Spix who died in 1826 was a Bavarian doctor who was also a philosopher and a taxidermist. Dr. Spix was an indefatigable traveller whose work on the birds of Brazil is considered a classic. Both Spix and Wagler shared an interest in reptiles along with birds and they wrote many papers on scaly creatures as well as feathered ones.

Wagler, who is probably best known for the Red-Fronted Conure, often referred to as Wagler's Conure, was lost to science and died of blood poisoning resulting from an accidental gunshot wound while out on a collecting mission. The incident bears a sad resemblance to the way in which parrot lovers all over the world lost a good friend when the Duke of Bedford also died from an accidental shotgun wound.

Rosemary Low mentions this parrot's interesting habit of often erecting its elongated head and neck feathers. Mrs. Low also mentions a female Spix belonging to Mrs. Dalton Burgess. This bird laid an egg but unfortunately lacked a mate. She points out that currently there are a pair of Spix's Macaws in Ireland which were imported in 1965, and that the female laid eggs in 1971. She also tells the sad tale of a Spix which belonged to Karl Plath, formerly of the Chicago Zoo. This bird spoke in a beautiful feminine voice and could repeat several sentences. She was a very tame bird and had been in Mr. Plath's possession from 1928 until 1946 when unfortunately, she met an untimely end at the beaks of two pugnacious Amazons.

Since so little exists in the literature about Spix's Macaw, anyone fortunate enough to own one or more of these parrots would be doing a valuable service to all by sharing information about their treasures.

Scarlet Macaw *(Ara macao)*

These birds are among the largest and most vividly marked members of the parrot family. The head, neck and shoulders are bright red. The head has the deepest color and there is a little, curly fringe of bright crimson feathers just above the cere. The red feathers continue down the wings where they gradually change into a broad band of yellow. These extend for several inches and then a third band of feathers is seen which is a lush blue. The extremely long tail feathers are a mixture of red and blue and this beautiful tail makes up almost half the length of the Scarlet Macaw. A good-sized Scarlet can easily reach forty inches in length. Their colors are really quite startling with one almost getting the impression that he is looking at a winged, red, yellow and blue flag.

The huge, sharply tipped upper beak is ivory while the lower beak is jet black. The eye is yellow with a large naked area around it. This bare cheek, typical of Macaws, is rather pink from the blood supply running through it, but it lacks the delicate tracing of feather lines which one can see in the Blue and Gold as well as other large Macaws.

Ara macao is widely distributed throughout Mexico and Brazil. It is sometimes called the Red and Yellow Macaw or the Red, Yellow and Blue Macaw. The latter name would be a good choice as it would help

171

to avoid the confusion which occurs when people confuse a Green Winged Macaw *(Ara chloroptera)* with a Scarlet. The Green Winged Macaw lacks the yellow feathers of the Scarlet and as the name implies, has a considerable amount of green feathers in the wing. In addition, the cheeks of the Green Winged Macaw have an obvious tracing of red feathers. Seeing the two birds together will make the difference quite obvious. Green Winged Macaws always look a little top-heavy to me and do not seem to be nearly as gracefully proportioned as the Scarlet.

People who keep them generally agree that they tame nicely and have a fair capacity for speech. They are quite loud but their spoken words are also very distinct. A description of a trio of Scarlet Macaws written by Thomas Belt in 1875 is as beautiful as it is accurate.

Belt describes "three gaudy Macaws . . . wheeling round and round in playful flight now showing all red on the under surface then turning around all together, as if they were one body and exhibiting the gorgeous blue, yellow, and red of the upper side, gleaming in the sunshine; screaming meanwhile as they flew with harsh, discordant cries. This gaudy colored and noisy bird seems to proclaim aloud that it fears no foe."

Most authors recommend a diet heavy in sunflower seeds and peanuts for the Macaw. I find that mine are quite capable of handling smaller seeds such as hemp, oats, safflower and even canary. Fruit and greens are a must and you can find out by experimenting which particular ones your large-beaked friends prefer.

Dr. Greene considers the Scarlet Macaw as the king of all the Macaws. His references to hand-feeding young babies to produce tame birds are as accurate today as they were 100 years ago. Greene did consider them to be very destructive birds and described the experience of a friend whose Scarlet Macaw destroyed several cages and perches before a proper one of hard wood and mahogany was tried. This new perch lasted several days but when the bird destroyed the leg of a billiard table his owner quickly sold him.

A recent breeding of these parrots was described by D. F. Norman of Hertford, England.

The hen was about nine years old when she laid her eggs. The eggs were incubated for about nine weeks but, unfortunately, the first batch was not fertile. Early in the following year a six-year-old cock became very attentive to the nine-year-old hen. This pair produced two eggs in April. The hen incubated for about eight weeks but once again the eggs were infertile. In July, two more eggs were laid and these were incubated with great diligence. In addition, the male spent

172

The Scarlet Macaw (left) and the Blue and Gold Macaw are the most familiar members of the Macaw family, and, to many, the most splendid. Both species have been kept as pets for centuries and are still held in the highest esteem by bird lovers around the world. *Parrot Jungle, Miami*

most of his time guarding the entrance into the nest box. There was a successful hatching in August with one baby born but the other was dead in the shell. By the end of November, the baby had made it to the end of the nest box but the parents continued to feed it until after Christmas with the hen doing most of the feeding. This bird is now fully grown and in fine feather.

The same pair has had other successful breedings. The aviary in which the breedings occurred is fifteen feet by ten feet by eight feet. Some heating was supplied and the nest box which was a 40-gallon wooden beer barrel (hung fairly high), was filled with wet, decayed wood. These birds were at liberty during the day but would return each night and were then shut into their aviary.

The same breeder has a pair of Blue and Golds who have never been at liberty and who have never produced fertile eggs. He seems to believe that being at liberty is a definite plus in encouraging the larger parrots to breed.

My own Scarlet Macaws include a colorful character named Frodo. His name comes from the Tolkien book, *The Hobbit.* He can say his name as well as eight or nine other words and while this is not a particularly large vocabulary, his speech is extremely clear (as is the speech of most Macaws). Frodo's time is divided between being in a four foot by four foot by three foot cage and climbing about a series of empty cages in the bird room. He loves to investigate these empty cages even though they are much too small for him to enter. Of course, Frodo also spends time on a Macaw stand. He is a tremendously strong bird and has the interesting habit of hanging "no hands" by his beak. This sharp and powerful beak easily opens walnuts. Frodo does this by making a small entry hole with the point of his beak and then enlarging the opening until he has enough room to extract the nut meat. Frodo's method of eating grapes is also quite interesting. He loves grapes and will crush them in his beak with his head tipped back so the juices run down his throat. He is very neat about this and seldom misses a drop. When he finishes he says, "wuk!" which he repeats whenever something particularly pleases him.

Frodo will sit on my shoulder as well as come on my hand. He loves to take my fingers in his beak and exert a strong but gentle pressure on them. If the pressure gets too great, I say, "ouch" and Frodo repeats "ouch" and eases up on the pressure. When Frodo rides on my shoulder, he occasionally rubs his cheek against mine. It is startling to feel the warmth of the bare facial patch when he does this, since one does not normally come into direct contact with the skin of a bird.

All of Frodo's toys are hung from chains. This was a neccessity as he is quite capable of snipping even the heaviest leather thongs into several pieces.

My second Scarlet Macaw, Fiorello, has been with me since he was only a few months old. He originally considered himself the brother of Bluebell, a Blue and Gold Macaw, with whom he arrived several years ago. Although their games have gotten progressively more violent they still play together when given their freedom at the same time. Fiorello is markedly smaller and more gentle than Frodo and will never approach him in size or strength. Frodo appears to harbor strong feelings of resentment and jealousy towards this relative newcomer and when I have attempted to bring Fiorello close to "Uncle Frodo's cage" the older parrot's eyes dilate wildly as he screams and smashes his bell against the bars.

Blue And Gold Macaw *(Ara ararauna)*

The rich blue of the head, neck and wings of these Macaws forms a beautiful contrast to the gold of their chests. Ear coverts and undersurface are an orange-yellow and the bold, commanding eye is also yellow. The lores and cheek are a startling white. This creamy whiteness is emphasized by the greenish black feathers which trace lines across the cheek.

Ara ararauna differs sufficiently from a slightly smaller version of Blue and Gold Macaws, so that the smaller parrot could be considered a subspecies. The lesser Macaw resembles the larger in most respects. The differences are a less extensive bare facial area and a large, broad, blue band on the throat extending up to the ear-coverts. The tracings on the cheek in the subspecies are also somewhat broader than in the nominate race. The subspecies is called *Ara a. caninde* and is also referred to as Wagler's Macaw.

These remarkably attractive parrots can be found distributed through the jungles of Panama and Columbia as well as portions of Ecuador, Peru, Venezuela and Brazil. This wide distribution would indicate that the Blue and Gold Macaw is a highly adaptable bird as compared to others of its brethren whose apportionment is more restricted.

These birds still exist in large numbers in those regions which have not as yet been heavily settled by the natives of the country with resulting damage to their habitat. In the wild they fly at great heights, often engaging in a variety of acrobatics, particularly just before alighting which is generally at the top of the highest tree in the area.

175

Selby describes a very fine specimen of a Blue and Gold Macaw which belonged to a Dr. Neill, who lived near Edinburgh. This bird was allowed the freedom of several rooms and when it was anxious to get its master's attention, it would call out the name, "Robert!" very loudly and distinctly. This may have been the name of its earliest master and it appeared not to have forgotten it. This was the only word the bird could speak.

Dr. Greene rates the Blue and Gold Macaw as a strong rival to the Scarlet Macaw for the seat of honor upon the "throne of Parrotdom." Frankly, I would give the crown to the Scarlet Macaw or suggest that it at least be shared.

Greene considered the Blue and Gold an amiable and desirable pet. He believed that these parrots possessed an aptitude for learning to speak a great number of words with a high percentage of them being very distinct in their pronunciation. Again, I do not totally agree with the good doctor. I have sat and played with many Scarlets and Blue and Golds and find them equally talented in terms of vocabulary and would say without hesitation that both species speak with a notable distinctness when they are capable of speech.

Dr. Greene also makes an interesting reference to the Macaw mentioned earlier who belonged to Dr. Neill and who could distinctly say the name "Robert." Green notes that he has heard many Blue and Gold Macaws say the word "Robert" and he believes it to be one of their natural sounds and not a word taught to them by man. This is similar to the "wolf whistle" which African Greys used in the jungle even before they have had any contact with man. Greene, as with all other writers, cautions about the loud voices of these birds. He suggests not keeping them if noise is a problem. Fortunately, most Macaws do not scream all day long. Instead they generally tend to exercise their vocal cords in the morning and the evening.

The Blue and Gold is not a difficult bird to breed. As a matter of fact, successful breedings have been described in articles written as early as 1818. In one of these the description of the nestbox could come from any contemporary article on the breeding of parrots. It is portrayed as a "small beer barrel, pierced towards a third of its height with a hole of about six inches in diameter and the bottom of which contained a bed of sawdust three inches thick, on which the eggs were laid and hatched."

Reverend F. G. Dutton, a 19th century collector and an avid student of the parrot race owned four Blue and Gold Macaws. One of them was an excellent speaker but he parted with it because it had an uncertain temper. In addition, once it flew to the limb of a tree (his birds were kept at liberty) only force could induce it to leave the tree branch and return to the aviary. Reverend Dutton believed the bird would have starved to death sitting on the tree branch if he didn't take the trouble to climb the tree and rescue it. Since the tree limb was invariably a high one and since the Macaw made its displeasure at being rescued quite evident (with its beak and claws) Reverend Dutton eventually sold it. At the time of his writing (1887) he put a value of about $25.00 on a tame and healthy Blue and Gold Macaw.

Contemporary authors such as Boosey and the Duke of Bedford speak well of this colorful bird. Boosey considered it one of the best talkers among the Macaws, as did the late Duke. I believe Blue and Golds and Scarlets to be equally talented as talkers but, of course, most of us make our judgements based on relatively small samples so it would be foolish to take a hard and fast stand on something like this. Both authors indicate the interesting fact that this Macaw blushes when it is agitated. The blushing can be seen in the naked area of the cheeks. Rosemary Low mentions that blushing may be seen more often in the male than in the female. This, along with the shorter, thinner beak that some authors believe to be typical of the female might help those who are attempting to sex these beautiful parrots.

The Blue and Gold Macaw is capable of being lordly and dignified.
M. Morrone/S. Rosenblum

177

When the mood strikes it, *Ara ararauna* can resemble a "disgruntled blue and gold ape," as it hangs from the bars of its cage. *Photo by author*

A word of caution should be interjected about permitting any child or adult to tease these normally gentle creatures in an effort to stir them into activity. Teasing Macaws can be a dangerous and wasteful affair. Teasing can turn a naturally gentle, friendly bird into a dangerous enemy. In the case of the Macaw, an angry bite can be a serious matter. As a matter of fact, early writers used the term *Macrocerci* for the Macaw which was, of course, a reference to the large beak.

Bluebell, my own Blue and Gold Macaw, considers herself a sister to the tough little Scarlet Macaw with whom she arrived. Bluebell is extremely active and in spite of the fact that her cage is four feet square engages in such a variety of wild activities that her tail feathers are usually frayed. When not occupied with damaging her tail feathers she frequently hangs from the top of her cage by one claw looking much like a disgruntled blue and gold ape as she screams impotent challenges to all who enter the room. It is sometimes hard to link this large, powerful bird with the baby of several years ago who (as with all baby Macaws) had an old and wrinkled face but also the deep, soulful eyes of an innocent.

Green Winged Macaw (*Ara chloroptera*)

For many years confusion existed regarding the proper identification and name of two large members of the genus *Ara* who have both red and blue feathers. *Ara macao* has been variously referred to as

178

the Red and Yellow Macaw, the Red, Yellow and Blue Macaw and the Scarlet Macaw. Sticking to the name Scarlet for this large parrot will help to avoid perpetuating the confusion. The Green Winged Macaw, has also been referred to as the Crimson Macaw, the Maroon Macaw, the Red and Blue Macaw and the Red and Green Macaw. When someone as expert as Dr. Greene uses the term Red and Blue Macaw for the Scarlet while others are using it for the Green Wing you can see the need for clarification of the problem. In 1949 Dr. Osmond Hill, after a careful search of all available literature, recommended that we restrict ourselves to the names Scarlet Macaw when referring to *Ara macao* and Green Winged Macaw when the bird concerned is *Ara chloroptera*.

The Green Winged Macaw is widely distributed throughout South and Central America, and may still be one of the most common Macaws in southeastern Brazil.

Ara chloroptera has a deep red head, chest and tail. The red feathers of his mantle blend into a row or two of green feathers and the green then yields to the light blue feathers which make up the rump. Upon careful examination it will be noted that in the Green Wing the upper coverts are green while the same region is marked with yellow in the Scarlet. The large, bare cheek patch of the Green Winged Macaw has the typical "war paint" decoration which in this parrot is made up of six lines of small red feathers. The upper beak is largely a light horn color except for the tip and base which are black. The lower beak is also black. The eye is yellow except in immature birds which show a brownish iris. These are well built, heavily muscled birds which average three feet in length.

Rosemary Low mentions that the Green Wing is frequently imported into Britain but that it is not as common there as the Scarlet Macaw. I fully agree with her concept that although it is not particularly popular in Europe as a pet, it is still better known there than in the United States. Mrs. Low considers these parrots top-heavy in appearance, and indeed the photograph of the Green Wing in her book shows a parrot with such a massive head and beak that he does give this impression. Others that I have seen, however, are better proportioned although in general their tails are a bit short for their overall length.

Dr. Russ notes the history of this parrot and indicates that it was first described by Gessner and Brisson as early as 1760. Dr. Russ credits the naming of the bird in 1859 to Gray. He is referring to George R. Gray, the younger son of a family of famous English naturalists. In addition to describing and naming the Green-Wing,

The Green Winged Macaw closely resembles the Scarlet and the two species are often confused. There are some obvious differences in color, markings and body shape by which one can tell them apart easily. *Kelley*

The Severe Macaw probably takes his name from his subdued coloring. He is typical of the "dwarf" Macaws and is a good choice for one who admires full-sized Macaws but has limited space for keeping one.

The Military Macaw does not carry the spectacular colors of some of the other Macaw species, but it makes a readily tamed, friendly pet. *Egbert*

Gray, who lived from 1808-1872, wrote numerous works on ornithology and was an assistant in the Department of Zoology in the British Museum. Gray's older brother, John Edward Gray, was honored by having a subspecies of the Short Tailed Parrot named for him. He published more than a thousand works in the field of zoology. The father of these talented sons, Samuel F. Gray, was a botanist.

A.A. Prestwich devotes several pages to the problem of the confusion between *A. macao* and *A. chloroptera*. When early reports on breeding were made the names "Red and Blue" and "Red and Yellow" were often misused. Since Mr. Prestwich is an extremely careful reporter, he qualifies many of his breeding reports by indicating the possibility that the bird being referred to may have been confused with the similar species. An extremely large number of hybrid crosses between the larger Macaws are listed by Prestwich. It is interesting to speculate on this abundance of hybrids as they appear to be much more common among *Ara* than any other genus of full-sized parrots.

Rutgers and Norris record a successful breeding of a Green-Wing which was not hybrid by J.S. Rigg of England. Mr. Rigg won the Avicultural Society's medal in 1962 for the first breeding of this species. His original pair were quite prolific and by 1968 had reared a total of thirteen offspring.

Although it may be difficult to accept, different cultures have different needs and values. At about the same time that Mr. Rigg was striving with difficulty, to breed the Green Wing, individuals in the Matto Grosso of Brazil were hunting the same species for food. The quills of the long feathers would be used to fletch arrows while the colorful breast and wing feathers would be made into personal decorations.

Military Macaw *(Ara militaris)*

This member of the Macaw genus lacks the brilliant mixture of colors which makes many of his other relatives so eye-catching. *Ara militaris* has a plumage which is largely green. The feathers of the head are a lighter green than the rest of the body while the forehead is dark red with these red feathers rather bristly in appearance. The large bare cheek patch has a delicate outline of greenish-black feathers. The beak is large and black, the eye yellow and the legs dark gray. The average Military is about 30 inches long. This would make it somewhat smaller than the more popular Scarlet Macaw but still quite a large bird. Several subspecies are usually acknowledged (one somewhat larger than the main species and the other with minor color

181

variations and found further south than *Ara militaris*). *Ara ambigua* a close relative of the Military, commonly known as Buffon's Macaw, is sometimes considered as a separate species due to its consistently larger size, different countries of origin and variations in colors and markings. I have seen large numbers of Buffon's and also believe they should be considered as a separate species.

The Military Macaw is the most northward ranging of the larger New World parrots. George M. Sutton advises that these parrots can be found in Mexico, Venezuela and Argentina. Mr. Sutton describes several sightings of large flocks that he made in 1938 and 1941 near the Rio Sabinas in southwestern Tamaulipas. At that time he saw groups of 60 to 80 birds. When he and his friends were alerted by the fearsome call of the *guacomayos* (as the Mexicans refer to Macaws) they would leave their breakfast table to watch the impressive, majestic, slow-moving and powerful flight of these parrots. He remarks that he would never return to the house until the last Macaw had passed out of sight and compared this to watching long freight trains as a child and never leaving for home until the caboose was out of sight. Sutton indicates that in Mexico these birds did not go to nest until late in August. He also had opportunities to examine the reproductive structures of specimens obtained in March and April and noted that they were not at all enlarged.

Although the Military Macaw has never been a particularly popular pet it has been known to parrot keepers and writers for many years. P.J. Selby writing in the early 19th century refers to this bird as the Great Green Macaw or *Macrocercus militaris*. He considered it a beautiful bird and described its color as a "fine and lively green." Although writing well over one hundred years ago, Selby correctly locates the Macaw's countries of origin and, except for his usual crude drawing, does a fine job of describing the bird and its characteristics.

C. P. Arthur raises a question which has bothered many other students of parrots. He does not understand why this bird is called Military and as he puts it, "I do not know of any nation which favors grass green as a uniform." The closest I have ever come to an answer to this question was in another old book on parrots which indicated that this Macaw first became well known to Europeans at the time of an invasion of Mexico by a foreign military power. Thus, if one chooses to believe this relationship, the time of a military action, coinciding with the popularization of the bird, yielded its name.

Dr. Greene did not consider this a common parrot and also questioned the soldierly designation in its name. He did not credit the Military with a great capacity for learning to speak but indicated that those he was familiar with had become quite tame and friendly. Dr. Greene quotes an earlier author who indicated that the ancient Incas considered the bird quite valuable and to have someone present one to you was a mark of great respect.

Dr. Russ offers an interesting if somewhat strained possible origin for this bird's name. Russ speculated that the feathers on the bare cheek patches of the parrot bore a resemblance to a pointed moustache of the type popular among soldiers at the time that the bird was becoming well known. Dr. Russ cites some very early references to the Green Macaw. Two of these were as early as 1609 and 1747. Russ tells of a hardy specimen which he had known to be an inhabitant of the Frankfurt Zoo for over fifteen years and a second in the Zoological Gardens at Hamburg which was also a long-lived bird. Dr. Russ alludes to the possibility of subspecies when he points out that scientists of his day had noted the extraordinary variation in size which occured between mature members of this species.

Very little information is available on the breeding of these Macaws. Arthur A. Prestwich mentions a possible first breeding by Emile Dupont of France in 1887. Prestwich also describes several cross-breedings between Military Macaws and Scarlets including one by F. S. Scherr of the Parrot Jungle in Miami in 1950.

Within the genus *Ara* there is a group of small Macaws which are all largely green. The different species of these dwarf Macaws have red, yellow, blue or black markings. They have an area of bare skin around the eye but lack the large naked cheek patch possessed by full-sized Macaws. Their wings are also comparatively shorter than those of the larger species.

Yellow Naped Macaw *(Ara auricollis)*

For those who are anxious to own a bird that looks like a Macaw and has all the spirit and playful personality associated with these super-beaked parrots but who have a space problem which precludes the oversized cage or large perch-cage combinations necessary for the great hookbills, I highly recommend the Yellow Naped Macaw, a member of the attractive group of smaller green Macaws within the genus *Ara*. Another, and not inconsiderable inducement, is that the price of these pocket-sized versions is generally several hundred dollars less than that of the full-sized Macaw.

Ara auricollis is also referred to as the Yellow Collared Macaw, (which is actually a partial translation of his Latin name) the Golden-Naped Macaw and Cassin's Macaw. They are colorful birds and average 16 to 18 inches in length although occasional good-sized

The Noble Macaw is the smallest of the Macaw family. These birds breed readily in captivity, have good talking potential and are easily trained. *Kelley*

The Yellow Naped Macaw combines convenient size with very attractive color and markings. The distinctive collar increases in size on intensity as the bird matures. *Grudin*

184

specimens reach 20 inches. Their area of distribution includes eastern Bolivia, Paraguay, several of the north western provinces of Argentina and the State of Matto Grosso in Brazil.

This parrot's overall plumage is green but its forehead and cheeks are so dark as to almost approach black. The feathers of the crown (particularly towards the rear) blend from black to blue and the nape is adorned with a yellow collar which in mature birds is so vivid that it almost appears as if a shaft of sunlight has struck the parrot's neck. The collar is evident as soon as the bird is feathered, reaching its maximum size rapidly (unlike the Yellow Naped Amazon) increasing in intensity of color with successive molts. The collar also appears to extend for a greater distance around the neck as the bird ages.

The wings are blue on their lower edge with the flight feathers a slate-blue. The feathers toward the tail are a reddish-brown. The beak is black with a lighter tip and the iris varies from red to brown. There is a good sized, creamy white, bare patch surrounding the eye and extending into the cheek region.

Most sources have very little if anything to say about this Macaw as it has not been widely imported until fairly recently. They are currently being imported in fairly large numbers which has resulted in realistic prices. Attempts at captive breeding (including hybridizing) have also been successful.

Rutgers and Norris remark that these parrots get along quite well with each other even during the breeding season. Mr. Rutgers comments on their clumsy and awkward waddle when they are on the ground, but I find that all Macaws move like this and consider it to be more comical than clumsy. As a matter of fact, I rather suspect that the Macaws accentuate their funny walk to please their owners (but then I always think the best of parrots).

Rutgers and Norris note a pair of Yellow Naped Macaws which could be seen in the Parrot House of the London Zoo as early as 1920. They indicate that these were the first of the species to be seen in England.

Rosemary Low credits the pair in the London Zoo to a Mr. Goodfellow and she advises that one of the pair was still at the zoo in 1937. She mentions three of these birds at the Wassenaar Zoo in Holland (with two of them having been added as recently as 1970) and advises that several other British zoos are exhibiting them. Ms. Low also points out that Busch Gardens (Florida) has reared at least nine young Yellow Napes.

More recently, Don and Pat Mathews of Allison Park, Pennsylvania have had fine results in repeated attempts to breed these

Macaws. In 1978 they also achieved a hybrid cross with an Illiger's Macaw and a Yellow Nape which I believe is a first captive breeding of this nature.

Severe Macaw *(Ara severa)*

This member of the dwarf Macaws is not especially colorful which may have been the reason for the origin of its name. Those which I have seen have ranged in length between 15 and 19 inches which makes them close in size to the Yellow Naped Macaw. Some collectors refer to these birds as the Chestnut Fronted Macaw. This, of course, is because of the chestnut-brown feathers adorning the forehead, cheeks and chin. The general coloration of *Ara severa* is green although some specimens have light blue feathers in the crown. There is a bare area on the face which is white with just a hint of black to give the typical facial markings which Macaws possess. The beak is grayish-black, the iris is yellow and the legs are gray. The Severe Macaw can be found in Panama, Bolivia and parts of Brazil. Large numbers still live in the tropical forests of Panama. This is probably why importers have been offering these Macaws in recent years for less than $200.00 each on a wholesale basis.

They eat the standard parrot diet but are very fond of fruits. They are not especially noisy and their owners speak well of their temperament.

The Duke of Bedford considered them to be intelligent and affectionate birds. He described one who was quite tame and who had fair talking abilities but poor diction.

Dr. Russ refers to this parrot as the Brown Fronted Macaw and notes that it was first described in 1684. Russ considered it a gentle, endearing bird, better at imitating cries and whistles than speech. In reading Dr. Russ, it is apparent that the Severe Macaw was quite popular among collectors in the nineteenth century.

In recent years many individuals have successfully bred these parrots.

Illiger's Macaw *(Ara maracana)*

This bird is a less common member of the dwarf Macaws of South America. It is most commonly found in eastern Brazil, Paraguay, and parts of Argentina. As with all of the small Macaws, its main color is green. The head and cheeks are a bluish-green with a red marking on the forehead which matches a similar red band across the abdomen. Illiger's strongly resembles the Severe Macaw but the marking on the forehead is a quick and excellent means of distinguishing between them. The flights and edges of the wings are blue-gray. The tail feathers are a reddish-brown with blue tips. The bare cheek patch has a yellow cast to it while the same area in the Severe is creamy white. The beak is black and the eye is reddish-brown. These Macaws are about 16 inches long. The red on the forehead of young birds is less intense and not as extensive as in adults. The red on the abdomen of immatures is also less deep and more yellowish.

Rutgers and Norris observe that the adult female may have less red on the forehead. They do not give too much credence to this as a sexing technique, however, and wisely point out that this marking can vary among individuals of either sex. They note that in the wild these birds exist in large flocks, except during the breeding season, when they pair off. These authors do not consider the Illiger's a popular bird and indicate that this may be because of its rather dull colors. Since it is actually just as colorful as most of the smaller Macaws, I would suspect that what we have is not a lack of popularity but a lack of correct identification with a good number of these birds being owned and thought of as Severe Macaws. Rutger's and Norris indicate that they are affectionate pets who enjoy stroking and petting but who sometimes lose their tempers and then bite. (This sounds like a description of every parrot I know.)

Ara maracana was described and given its name by the ornithologist Viellot in 1816. Viellot named the parrot in honor of the biologist Illiger. The term *Maracana* is from the Spanish and is imitative of the parrot's cry. A. A. Prestwich advises that this bird is also known as the Blue Winged Macaw and the Red and Blue Macaw. The second and probably both names should be avoided to prevent confusion.

Cyril Rogers tells of a number of successful breedings of this species including some second generation results. He confirms the gentleness of these birds and describes a breeding success which a friend of his had with an Illiger's given to him as a gift and a bird he just happened to buy. Mr. Rogers' description makes it sound as if these birds were free breeders but I suspect a lot of effort went into the three healthy chicks bred in his friend's aviary.

The Duke of Bedford discusses an affectionate and playful Illiger's who loved to amuse himself by emptying the wastepaper basket and strewing the contents over the floor. His only fault was that he was an ankle nipper.

A headstudy of a young Red
Fronted Macaw. *Photo by author*

The Red Fronted Macaw is an extremely rare species and is seldom seen, even in large collections. This pair was photographed at Walsrode Vogel Park in Germany.

Crimmson Star

188

Rosemary Low also makes reference to this same Macaw. She mentions that he was extremely fond of bathing and would actually lie down in the water in a large basin; turning from one side to the other to fully wet himself. He often got so wet that his owner would have to dry him with a towel. Ms. Low indicates quite a difference in character between the Illiger's and the Severe.

Dr. Russ reports that these birds are "common in the trade" and could be seen at zoos and exhibitions. He refers to one which lived for fifteen years in the zoo at Frankfurt and a pair which belonged to a Dr. Frenzel of Freiburg which bred but, unfortunately, failed to rear the young.

Dr. Greene tells of two fine Illiger's specimens living in the Parrot House of the London Zoo of his day. He describes the poor location of their cage on the upper shelf of the stand in the center of the Parrot House. Greene was unhappy about this arrangement as he felt that it resulted in the birds not being noticed by the majority of visitors. He also sorrowed over the small size of the cages that these and other parrots had to occupy and expressed the hope that a Parrot House would be built where each species could have a cage of sufficient size so that it could use its wings. Dr. Greene would be very happy if he could see the Parrot House which currently exists in London as the birds are all well tended and in large cages. Reverend Dutton, a colleague and contemporary of Dr. Greene, noted that in 1884 these Macaws sold for between $10.00 and $15.00 a pair.

A. A. Prestwich reports on the extensive number of breeding successes which people have achieved with this small Macaw. The London Zoo receives credit for young Illiger's bred in 1931, 1932, 1934, 1935, 1937, and 1938. He also tells of the efforts of Dr. Frenzel mentioned earlier. There have also been more recent successful breeding attempts.

Red Fronted Macaw (*Ara rubro-genys*)

Several years ago I had the opportunity to photograph a rare parrot. Needless to say it only took me a day or two to make the time needed as the parrot was the seldom seen, Red Fronted Macaw. The visit taught me a useful lesson. The strobe for my camera seemed to be working normally but I vaguely recalled that when I had last used it, it had cycled rather slowly. This is generally an indication of weak batteries and when the Macaw prints arrived about ten days after I had sent them to be developed I knew I had wasted my time. Fortunately, a second trip wtih fresh batteries resulted in good photos.

Ara rubro-genys is one of the largest of the dwarf Macaws. The specimen I examined was about 20 inches long which is a bit smaller than the measurement given by other authors but I suspect I was viewing a young bird who would probably be adding several inches as it matured. The Red Fronted is also known as the Red Cheeked Macaw and Lafresnaye's Macaw.

The Red Fronted Macaw is a fairly light green. The feathers of the head and neck are a more intense green with the forehead, crown, and cheek bright scarlet. The typical cheek feather tracings are present but they are limited to an area just below the eye. This marking is made of dark brown feathers. The beak is black and the eye is an orange-brown. This parrot occurs in a fairly restricted area of Bolivia and is probably confined to the provinces of Cochabamba and Santa Cruz. It is one of the least known of all South American parrots with little in the literature on their habits.

Rutgers and Norris report that the Red Cheeked Macaw inhabits dense forest and that they are generally found in the tree tops where they seek fruits and nuts. These authors advise that the Macaws nest in holes in the trees and lay three to four eggs which hatch in about 25 days. The same authors remark that Red Fronted Macaws can become quite tame and are very intelligent. They consider them ideal pets and good mimics. They caution, however, that they are very active birds and should be taken out of their cages for regular exercise. It would be foolish for me to make a judgment based on one observation but the specimen that I saw was quite friendly and gentle and matched Rutger's description. It had a stocky build and relatively short wing feathers.

Dr. Rolando Romero of Bolivia has studied this parrot in depth. According to Dr. Romero this unique Macaw was first caught in 1973 and he attributes its rarity to the fact that it is found only in a small valley in Cochabamba. Dr. Romero first observed the bird in 1970 but at the time thought it was simply a hybrid between a Blue and Gold and a Military. On a visit to the London Natural History Museum in December, 1970 he noted a skin of one of these Macaws and was advised just how rare this bird was. He then spent almost three years attempting to discover its natural habitat which was quite difficult due to the narrow and dangerous roads involved. Dr. Romero finally located a few of these Macaws and observed them in flight as well as while feeding. Their diet was mainly corn, cactus fruits and several native fruits.

Males and females seemed identical in color with size (the male appeared larger) being the only apparent difference. The younger birds lacked the orange and red markings which develop after they are at least a year old.

Dr. Romero indicated that there were a very limited number of these Macaws in captivity throughout the world.

Noble Macaw (*Ara nobilis cumanensis*)

Ara n. nobilis is the smallest of the dwarf Macaws with a length of only 13 to 14 inches. Because of its small size it is occasionally confused with the Conures of the genus *Aratinga,* particularly the Blue Crowned Conure. This is not as strange as it may sound as *Ara* and *Aratinga* have a close morphological relationship and as a matter of fact the Blue Crowned Conure is actually an inch or two larger than the Noble Macaw.

This parrot is also referred to as the Red Shouldered Macaw. De Schauensee indicates that it originates in Guyana, Surinam, Venezuela and parts of Brazil. It is still fairly widespread in Guyana and Surinam with noisy flocks being frequently seen.

The Noble is a small, green Macaw which has a blue crown as well as a tinge of blue on the lower edge of the wing. The bends of the wings are clearly marked with scarlet and thus the origin of the alternate name. The naked, white patch around the eye does not extend fully into the cheek region as it does so commonly in the larger Macaws and the eyes themselves are yellow.

There are three recognized subspecies: *A. n. nobilis,* frequently referred to as Hahn's Macaw, *A. n. cumanensis,* the bird we refer to as the Noble Macaw and *A. n. longipennis,* whose name refers to the extra length in its wing. *Cumanensis* is simply a reference to the Bay of Cuman in the Brazilian State of Maranhao which is one of the places where this subspecies is found. E. A. Dracup, points out the best way to differentiate between subspecies. In *A. n. nobilis* (Hahn's Macaw) the upper beak is black while in the other two it is almost white.

Rutgers and Norris mention that the most obvious difference between the sexes is that the female is more petite. They consider these Macaws to be affectionate pets as well as clever mimics. These authors note a Noble Macaw owned by a Mrs. von Proschek of Vienna which had a vocabulary of more than fifty words. They also indicate that the first successful British breeding of these birds occurred in 1949 and was the accomplishment of the well known E. N. T. Vane.

Rosemary Low gives full details on Mr. Vane's breeding of the Noble Macaw including the interesting tidbit that the breeding group was actually a trio consisting of two males and a female. She also reports on how prolific these parrots were with the group having eight young by 1951 and almost thirty by 1956.

A. A. Prestwich describes several earlier breedings including the work of a Mr. and Mrs. Vance Wright who achieved success (in the United States) both in 1939 and 1940. Prestwich also notes Vane's work and points out that Vane received the Avicultural Society's first breeding medal for his accomplishment with the Noble Macaw. Mr. Prestwich also comments on a report that a pair belonging to the aforementioned Mrs. von Proschek hatched eggs but failed to rear the young.

In a more recent breeding report T. H. Alston of England tells of excellent results with a pair of *A. n. nobilis*. Mr. and Mrs. Alston set the pair up in a 15 foot by three foot by seven foot flight. Due to a cold, wet January both birds became ill and had to spend time in a hospital cage. Fortunately, they recovered and in April, 1968 they were placed in an outside flight and given a nest box which was four feet deep by ten inches square. Five eggs were laid in May but all were clear. The second round was also infertile but in the third round there were two fertile eggs. The two chicks which hatched from the eggs were still in the nest at the age of six and one half weeks, looking exactly like their parents except that their lower beaks were not completely black.

In a final breeding report, John Halford of Hampshire, England described his reversal of the normal way in which birds are usually routed. Mr. Halford, who has been breeding these Macaws since 1969, has also been shipping the birds to Tobago where he believes they are being gradually released in an effort to repopulate the island with Hahn's Macaws.

John Selby, refers to this bird as the Noble Parrot-Macaw. His description of the parrot is excellent as is the designation of the geography of its origin. Selby notes the upper beak as being yellowish-white which could mean that the specimen he observed was *A. n. nobilis.*

Dr. Russ believed the Noble Macaw to be the best known and greatest favorite among the small Macaws. He advises that it was first described in 1764.

From all the reports the Noble Macaw should really be given more attention as it appears to possess such major virtues as being a free breeder, a good talker and a most readily-tamed pet.

One of the nicest Cockatoo-tricks . . . arose from the ardent love of the bird for my mother who knitted without stopping. The Cockatoo seemed to understand exactly how the soft skeins worked and what the wool was for. He always seized the free end of the wool with his beak and then flew lustily into the air, unravelling the ball behind him . . . Once when nobody was there to stop him he encircled the tree, right up to its summit, with brightly colored woolen strands . . . our visitors . . . were unable to understand how and why it had been thus decorated.

Konrad Lorenz, *King Solomon's Ring,* Harper & Row, 1952

The Cockatoos are indigenous to Australia, New Zealand and surrounding islands of the South Pacific. As a group they seem aware of their conspicuous beauty and delight in displaying for any audience. The bird shown here is a Greater Sulphur Crested, one of the most familiar Cockatoo species.

Australian Information Service

194

11

The Cockatoos

MOST PEOPLE equate the ability to speak with intelligence in parrots. Although there is truth to this within specific species where, for example, an African Grey with an excellent vocabulary is brighter than one with a limited vocabulary, the relationship does not always completely follow within the entire parrot race.

Individuals who specialize in studies of parrot behavior agree that Cockatoos exhibit the most intelligent behavior of the entire parrot family even though their talking ability is far from outstanding. The Cockatoos more than make up for this lack by their other pleasing ways and their aptitude for activities which require an enormous amount of dexterity. Their great sense of curiosity also makes it most amusing to watch a Cockatoo examine any new object placed in his cage. Although wary of such objects they will approach them with stealth and observe them from all directions until they are sure they are harmless. Once this is done the new toy is accepted and played with. An additional characteristic which attracts people to this parrot is its vanity. Cockatoos seem to know just what a beautiful picture they present and they will display their wings and toss their heads to achieve positions designed to give an observer the most beautiful possible view. At such moments their crests are usually raised and displayed for the edification of admirers. If one should fail to notice this display or if his back is turned, a loud scream to attract his attention is sure to ensue.

The Cockatoos are the most long-lived parrots with a life expectancy comparable to humans. Stories of these birds living a century or more are probably exaggerated but there are documented cases of Cockatoos who although ragged and rather shrunken have lived into their 80s.

They are powerful flyers and their wings must either be clipped or they should be trained not to fly within the house. Unlike the Macaws, their short tails makes it difficult for them to stop rapidly. Thus, several wing flaps can bring a Cockatoo across the room and into a wall or window.

Konrad Lorenz describes an incident which followed his purchase of a Greater Sulphur Crested Cockatoo who developed a strong love for him. This bird would seek him out wherever he was in the house and if he could not find his master would extend his search over a greater distance. On a beautiful June day Lorenz got off the train in Vienna and noticed a crowd staring into the sky at a huge bird which was flying with slow but powerful wing-beats and occasionally resting by taking long glides. It might have been a buzzard or a stork but then the bird suddenly swerved so that the sun fully illuminated its plumage and Lorenz could see that it was his white Cockatoo who was apparently searching for him at the train station.

Greater Sulphur Crested Cockatoo *(Cacatua galerita)*

This large bird can exceed 20 inches in length. The wing-spread is tremendous and this coupled with the bird's length means that it requires a large cage. *Cacatua galerita* is mostly white in color. The feathers of the crest which are bent back and then upwards at a sharp angle (when not erected) are yellow. There are yellowish-white spots on the cheek and some yellow feathers underneath the tail. The beak is dark black with a white cere. Frequently the fluffy feathers of the face cover the cere. The eyes are black with white lores and the eye of the female is lighter than that of the male.

Cockatoos have been known to ornithologists for many years. The Sulphur Crested Cockatoo was collected as a specimen as early as 1790. This was done by the famous explorer, Captain Cook, on one of his voyages to Australia.

The Greater Sulphur Crested does not usually develop a large vocabulary but it can learn several words and phrases. They become devoted to their owners and are capable of showing great affection.

This Cockatoo poses a problem to Australian farmers. The birds' appetite and size enable flocks of them to do wholesale damage to crops. It is ironic that while the farmers make every effort to destroy these birds the Australian government places rigorous export restrictions on them. Fortunately, there are a number of talented, hard-working breeders in the United States and Europe who are successfully raising these and other Cockatoos so that it is possible to own a domestically-bred specimen.

Barrett tells of a Greater known as Cocky Bennett owned by a Mrs. S. Bennett of the Sea Breeze Hotel in a town with the rather intriguing name of Tom Ugly Point (near Sydney, Australia). Cocky Bennett was believed to be 120 years old when he died. Although his complete history could not be traced, about 100 years of his life have been authenticated. He really looked his age as he was naked except for one or two rather ragged head feathers and as with all old beings, he was also physically shrunken. He was a great source of entertainment to guests at the hotel as his favorite saying was purported to be "I'll fly! I'll fly! One more feather and I'll fly!" Barrett also writes about an authenticated case of an 84-year-old white Cockatoo who unlike Cocky Bennett was well-feathered and still active and playful.

My own Greater Sulphur Crested Cockatoo is a delightful, sweet-tempered bird who has been with me from the time she was three months old. Tutu was hand-fed from an early age. This has resulted in her having a lovely disposition. She is friendly, gentle and affectionate and will freely go to just about any of my visitors. I will never forget how excited she used to get when I opened her jar of baby food which supplemented her regular seed diet. I suspect that she enjoyed the extra attention as much as she did the baby food.

Although Tutu eats all of the seeds in her mix she shows definite preference for pine nuts (sometimes called Indian nuts) and has the bad habit of sweeping the contents of her seed dish to look for the pine nuts. When she does this, naturally all the other seeds land on the floor. In self defense I had to put up a large sheet of plexiglass on the side of the cage near her seed dish. Now at least when the seeds fall they land on the bottom of the cage. When Tutu is not sitting on my shoulder or swinging from her trapeze she resides in a cage which is 35 inches wide, 28 inches deep and 50 inches high. I perfer height rather than length in cages for Cockatoos as they spend a lot of time hanging and swinging.

In recent years there has been some rather careless use of the term "medium Greaters" for Cockatoos who are smaller than the average Greater and who are larger then the typical Lesser Cockatoo. Joseph M. Forshaw responded to my request for clarification on the use of this terminology by pointing out that technically the Greater Sulphur Crested Cockatoo and the Lesser are what is referred to as a

Greater Sulphur Crested Cockatoo in "full display." *Parrot Jungle, Miami*

The Lesser Sulphur Crested Cockatoo has a smaller crest and a thicker beak than the Greater. *Gilliland*

superspecies. This is a reference to two similar species that are geographically separated. Mr. Forshaw noted that since the largest subspecies of Greaters is so much larger than the smallest subspecies of Lessers that an impression is generated (if one sees only the largest and smallest members) that there is a vast difference in size between these birds. Forshaw recommends that rather than using size as a criteria that beak, crest structure and skin color around the eyes can be used as a guide to proper identification. Thus, as a rule, all members of *Cacatua sulphurea* (Lessers) have a heavier, wider and less protruding beak than *Cacatua galerita* (Greaters) while the crest in Lessers is usually narrower and the bare skin around the eye is much whiter.

Birds which are termed "Medium" are probably large individuals of Lesser Sulphur Crested Cockatoos.

Lesser Sulphur Crested Cockatoo *(Cacatua sulphurea)*

This pretty little Cockatoo is about 14 inches long. In many respects it resembles the Greater Sulphur Crested Cockatoo, and because of its size many people refer to it as an "apartment-sized Cockatoo." The over-all color of this parrot is white. The ear-coverts are bright yellow and there are also yellow feathers on its undersurface. The forward-curving crest is yellow, the eye ring is whitish and the beak is black. Males have a dark brown eye while the eye in the female is reddish brown. Young birds are similar to the adults except that the eye is grey. These beauties are found in Indonesia as well as the Celebes, Sumba and other islands.

We can divide *Cacatua sulphurea* into six subspecies. The features which separate them include the islands on which they are found, wing spread and length, size of beak and degree of yellow coloration. One subspecies, *Cacatua sulphurea citrinocristata*, is found only on the island of Sumba and has an orange crest instead of a yellow one. It also has orange ear-coverts. It is somewhat larger than most Lesser Sulphur Crested Cockatoos and is referred to as the Citron Crested Cockatoo. Earlier writers considered it as a separate species.

Dr. Greene speaks well of the Lessers and mentions that they had been imported into England for many years. Apparently Dr. Greene was not too fortunate with the bird which he owned but friends of his are mentioned who indicated that the Lesser is quite docile and can learn to speak. Greene also quotes the famous naturalist Bechstein as saying that this parrot is "fond of caresses and returns them with pleasure. Its motions are full of grace, delicacy and beauty."

The Umbrella Cockatoo is similar to the Moluccan, but lacks the typical wash of pink and salmon crest of the latter. *Kelley*

The Moluccan Cockatoo is highly prized for its beauty as well as its affectionate personality. *Photo by author*

Umbrella skaters. *Parrot Jungle, Miami*

Dr. Russ indicates that the Lesser Sulphur Crested Cockatoo was described as early as 1760. He reports its behavior as droll and tells of one Lesser Sulphur Crested Cockatoo who danced quite well and who when finished performing, would bow as it screamed, "good-bye! good-bye!"

There are individuals successfully breeding Citron Crested and Lesser Sulphur Crested Cockatoos in several parts of the country. Europeans and Canadians have also been quite successful in breeding these birds in recent years. The birds who were successfully bred were generally at least four or five years old and were kept in fairly long flights. Two eggs seem to be the standard clutch for this parrot and incubation takes about 28 days. Both parents take turns in incubating. Both parents also participate in the feeding of the young and babies are able to leave the nest at about ten weeks. Parental feeding can continue for quite a while after that if the birds are not separated from the parent in an attempt to hand feed them.

Moluccan Cockatoo *(Cacatua moluccenis)*

This splendid Cockatoo was first sketched and described in 1751. It originates on Ceram, Saparua, Haruku and Amboina which are all islands in the southern Moluccas. Thus, its scientific name *Cacatua Moluccensis* is particularly apt. This parrot has been referred to by a wide variety of names including Salmon Crested Cockatoo, Rose Breasted Cockatoo, and Great Salmon Crested Cockatoo. I favor the Salmon Crested title, which is popular in Europe, as it properly identifies the bird in terms of the distinctive crest marking which differentiates it from the Umbrella Cockatoo, its neighbor in the central and northern Moluccas. In observing a number of Umbrellas and Moluccans over a period of time I find the crest in the Umbrella to be broader, fuller and higher. Another obvious difference is that the Umbrella is a snowy white while the lovely white feathers of the Moluccan are delicately suffused with pink. The underside of the tail feathers (in *moluccensis*) are marked with a yellowish pink. The beak is black and the eye is quite dark.

Rutgers considers this one of the best talkers among the Cockatoos. He comments on their ability to scream which he also believes to be outstanding. Since virtually every source which I checked makes mention of this characteristic it is something to keep in mind if one plans to own a Moluccan. Rutgers is of the opinion that hens can be recognized by their dark brown iris but this may require some practice as the pairs I have looked at have shown only a shade of difference in intensity of eye color between males and females.

E. J. Boosey along with the Duke of Bedford notes that these birds acclimate quite well to outdoor conditions. Boosey felt they were extremely hardy and that there would be a good chance for success in breeding them in an outdoor aviary. The breeding results available to us have not fulfilled this hopeful forecast. A. A. Prestwich lists a single achievement at the San Diego Zoo in 1951 where a sole chick was removed from the nest at ten days and hand fed. Rutgers and Norris also note the blessed event in San Diego as well as a more recent breeding by Neil O'Connor in England in 1971. An interesting opportunity for research would be available for someone who wished to pursue the problem of why we have had a comparatively large number of successful Umbrella breedings and so few with the closely related Moluccan.

Dr. Russ comments on the longevity of these Cockatoos. He quotes a Mr. Fiedler whose Moluccan followed him "like a shadow." Another friend, Dr. Lazarus, gives a description which any Cockatoo owner will immediately recognize. His bird when on a stand would pose with ". . . erect flaming crest, bristling peach-coloured feathers on the chin, throat and neck . . . with outspread wings and tail . . . it was indeed a beautiful sight . . ." Dr. Russ notes that this beautiful picture was accompanied by ear-piercing shrieks which were unbearable.

Rosie, my own Moluccan, is a gentle, slow-moving bird. She has the most affectionate personality of any parrot I've ever seen and although she does not speak I consider her a treasure.

Dr. Greene describes a Moluccan who would bow its head while lifting its crest and then whisper in the softest and sweetest feminine voice, "Oh, you pretty, pretty Cocky, how I love you." Greene concurs with later writers on this bird's hardiness and its ability to acclimate to cold weather. He is also in agreement about the difficulty of breeding them.

Dr. Greene reports prices of approximately $25.00 to $30.00 for the Moluccans of his time. He tells of an outstanding member of the race who more than earned his price by loud shouts of "Who are you? What do you want?" in the middle of the night. When his owner rushed downstairs he found an open window and a Cockatoo with every feather lifted. The gentleman shut and locked the window, rewarded the watchbird with a delicacy and went back to bed.

Umbrella Cockatoo (*Cacatua alba*)

This is another example of a parrot with so many names in different parts of the world that the use of its scientific classification is a necessity if confusion is to be avoided. *Cacatua alba* is as frequently called the Great White Cockatoo or White Crested Cockatoo as it is called the Umbrella Cockatoo. Some authors combine names and even refer to it as the Greater White Crested Cockatoo or the Umbrella Crested Cockatoo.

One look at its beautiful crest will indicate why all of these names are quite appropriate in describing this native of the various islands which make up the northern Moluccas of Indonesia. Do not let this reference to the Moluccas cause you to confuse this parrot with the Moluccan Cockatoo which it resembles. The Great White Cockatoo is a somewhat smaller bird and, of course, lacks the salmon crest as well as the suffusion of pink in its feathers which immediately identify the Moluccan or Salmon Crested Cockatoo.

Cacatua alba has snowy white plumage. The crest is of the backward-curving type and the only color to the feathers is a light hint of yellow on the underside of the flights and a tinge of yellow near the tail. The beak is black and the naked eye-ring in the birds which I have seen shows a faint hint of blue. As with most of the white Cockatoos the eye of the male is quite dark as compared to that of the female. Although only 16 or 17 inches in length these parrots give an impression of being somewhat larger because of their tendency to fluff out their feathers.

Dr. Greene also warns readers against confusing this bird with the Moluccan. He pointed out that (at the time of his writing) Indonesia being a Dutch possession, these Cockatoos generally arrived in England via Holland. The price asked for an Umbrella during this period was between $15.00 and $20.00. Today, a good specimen can command fifty times the price Greene mentions.

Dr. Greene believed these birds to be easily tamed, particularly if taken from the nest at a tender age. He recommends bringing such young up, "by hand, or rather by mouth . . ." and goes on to explain that chewing a mixture of corn and oats and then letting the young feed themselves from the owner's mouth will produce an exceptionally tame bird. Most of the breeders I know do not go to this extreme but I must confess that if Tutu (my Greater) is with me when I'm eating peanuts that she reverts to this type of feeding even though she is no longer a baby.

Dr. Greene describes an Umbrella named Cocky who was so tame that he had the free run of the house and yard. He seemed to take a particular delight in sitting on a fence a few feet out of range of the household dog who was chained to his doghouse. Cocky took great pleasure in teasing the dog by swooping over him and then flying straight up to escape.

Buffon, the famous naturalist wrote of a pair of Umbrellas exhibited at a fair in Paris in 1775. They were extremely tame and according to Buffon's description would open their wings or bend their heads on command. They could also answer questions asked by their master with appropriate shakes of their heads. People unfamilar with Cockatoos may think Buffon's description an exaggeration but I have seen this type of clever behavior demonstrated by other Cockatoos of this genus.

A description of breeding these birds was written in 1972 by Mr. J. ter Horst. The breeding took place in Holland where the owner of the birds has created a parrot paradise with a huge flight which is 66 feet by 46 feet by 13 feet. The flight encloses part of an orchard and the apples, pears, etc. delight the inhibitants. Mr. ter Horst also left the natural undergrowth which provides a wide selection of greens for his birds. He has many nest boxes of different sizes scattered throughout the flight.

In March, 1972 the birds started displaying for one another. The hen seemed to take the initiative and she chose a nest box approximately 20 inches by 18 inches by 20 inches. Both members of the pair tended the eggs. Unfortunately, these first eggs were broken but the pair chose a similar nest box and were sitting on eggs by the first of June. The sound of a newly hatched bird was heard after 33 days. The parents made good use of the abundant greens growing in the flight as well as fresh twigs. They fed the baby for eight weeks and then Mr. ter Horst took him into his home where the bird thrived.

Ralph Small of Brookfield, Illinois successfully bred Umbrellas in 1976 and hand-fed them from the time they hatched.

Blue Eyed Cockatoo *(Cacatua opthalmica)*

The length of the Blue-Eyed Cockatoo is between 18 and 21 inches. It is a white parrot with a distinctly yellow crest. There is also a wash of yellow on the cheeks, ear-coverts and the under feathers. The eye-ring is light blue. This, of course, is how the parrot derives its name. (The Little Corella or Bare-Eyed Cockatoo is also referred to as the Blue-Eyed Cockatoo and it would be well to discourage the use of this name to avoid confusion.) The eyes in mature specimens tend to be darker in the male than in the female. *Cacatua opthalmica* is closely related to the Greater Sulphur Crested Cockatoo but it should not be confused with the Triton subspecies of Greaters which also have a blue eye-ring. A marked difference between the two is the fact that the crest in *opthalmica* is of the recumbent or backward curving type.

A recumbent crest helps distinguish this Blue Eyed Cockatoo from the Greater Sulphur Crested species. *New York Zoological Society*

Leadbeater's Cockatoo is one of the most beautiful members the genus *Cacatua*. Its white plumage is touched with various shadings of pink and its crest is strikingly marked with alternating bands of red, yellow and red with white tips. The Leadbeater's lovely crest is like a feathered parfait.

Parrot Jungle, Miami

The Blue-Eyed Cockatoo is found on the islands of New Britain and New Ireland off the coast of New Guinea. These names will be quite familar to veterans of the Pacific Island campaigns of World War II. Once again, geography has isolated a parrot by separating it with large bodies of water from the mainlands of Australia and New Guinea. Thus, nature preserves unique qualities.

These handsome birds are not common but their behavior and intelligence matches that of other members of *Cacatua* and makes them highly desirable as pets.

Leadbeater's Cockatoo *(Cacatua leadbeateri)*

This Cockatoo was first fully described following its exhibition at a meeting of the Zoological Society of London in April, 1831. Mr. Vigors, an officer of the Society, identified the colorful beauty as a specimen from the collection of Mr. Benjamin Leadbeater, owner of a natural history firm in London who was well known and admired by the ornithologists of his day.

Selby also describes this debut in his early 19th century parrot volume which was part of *Jardine's Naturalist's Library*. Selby refers to this Cockatoo with the rather awkward title of Tricolor-Crested Cockatoo. His illustration is not particularly attractive but the distinctive crest makes it clear that he is writing about a Leadbeater's. Some of the other names bestowed upon this unusual parrot are Major Mitchell's Cockatoo, Pink Cockatoo, Desert Cockatoo, and Wee Juggler. Actually the Australians and English almost invariably refer to it as Major Mitchell's Cockatoo and use Leadbeater's as an alternate name.

Sir Thomas Mitchell, who made several voyages of exploration to Australia in the early 19th century has had his name associated with the parrot because of the fine account he gave of this bird when he wrote about his expeditions into the interior of eastern Australia in 1838. Mitchell observed that: "Few birds more enliven the monotonous hues of the Australian forest than this beautiful species whose pink-coloured wings and glowing crest might have embellished the air of a more voluptuous region."

History frequently tends to become somewhat distorted as the years pass. A number of accounts imply that it was the Leadbeater's Cockatoo which helped keep up the spirits of Major Mitchell and his crew during their expedition. I am sure that this colorful hookbill provided some diversion for them but I doubt if it was quite the hero of the voyage that some tales imply it was.

The Leadbeater's is a medium-sized Cockatoo ranging in length between 14 and 16 inches. Its main color is white but delicate shades of pink can be noted on the head, nape, upper abdomen and under surfaces. The flight feathers are an even deeper pink. The beak is horn colored while the legs are gray. The eyes are dark brown in the male and reddish in the female. Its unusual crest is what makes the appearance of this Cockatoo so outstanding. To quote Cyril Roger's pun "no other Cockatoo can top the Leadbeater's crest." When the crest is fanned out in all its glory the bands of yellow, red and white which have always made this bird an oject of interest and attention become visible. The base of the crest is red, then yellow, then red again with the final decoration a snowy white tip. It is as if nature has created a feathered parfait in the form of the Leadbeater's crest.

Neville W. Cayley refers to this bird as the Pink Cockatoo. He points out that since the Leadbeater's was an inhabitant of the interior of Australia, early voyagers tended to miss the birds as their journeys barely touched the fringes of this huge continent. Cayley considered this parrot to be the most beautiful of all the Australian Cockatoos and even in 1938 was alarmed that its numbers were declining so rapidly. He suggested rigid protection (which, of course, now exists) to avoid its becoming extinct. Cayley agrees with most writers that Leadbeater's most outstanding attribute was its good looks and that its reputation for speaking is quite far down the list. I would add to this that those I have examined, although attractive, are generally not particularly playful or clever. Mr. Cayley quotes Kendall Bennett as noting that these birds are very destructive of the trees in which they rest. They tear the bark and destroy the branches as a pastime, rather than as a feeding activity. This seems to be particularly evident during breeding periods and prospective breeders of Leadbeater's may wish to make note of this. Cayley speaks of clutches of three to four eggs which are white and oval shaped with the breeding season in Australia running from September through December. Mr. Cayley notes a successful breeding of the Leadbeater's by F. B. Bellchambers of Humbug Scrub, South Australia in 1935. Four eggs were laid and both parents helped with the incubation. The young hatched out in about eight weeks and both parents fed them. It was almost another eight weeks before these babies left the nest.

Edward J. Boosey is another author who would give the Lead-beater's points for beauty but not for cleverness. Boosey mentions the excruciating screams that the Leadbeater's are capable of and rec-ommends an outdoor aviary where possible. Boosey confirms the destruction that the bird can work upon wood and cautions that aviaries or cages built for them must be of heavy gauge mesh. He considered them fairly hardy parrots which I can confirm. A pair I know have managed to thrive under extremely adverse conditions for a number of years. This pair which appear to be male and female (judging by mutual preening and eye-color) live in a huge display cage in a large shopping center. This is a mall type center with a year-round controlled temperature in the low 70s. This may be one reason the birds have survived the cigarette smoke, cooking fumes, dirt, dust and noise as well as general teasing by children and adults who do not seem to realize that they cannot attract a bird by rapping smartly on his cage. Fortunately for this pair the dimensions of their cage provides a dome of over 30 feet. A dead tree which has been firmly mounted in cement plus their typical parrot-like ability to climb the sides of the cage generally result in their being at the highest point and well out of reach of those who would like to poke or prod them.

Charles Barrett points out that the Leadbeater's is among the least plentiful members of the parrot species inhabiting the Australian Commonwealth. On the bright side he states that in areas where it was protected such as Wyperfield National Park in Victoria, its numbers appeared to be increasing. Leadbeater's can always be found in the park and if you visit Australia, Wyperfield in northwestern Victoria should be a must on your places to see list.

Arthur Prestwich credits the first breeding of this bird to a Mrs. Johnstone who accomplished the feat in England in 1901. Since then the London Zoo has been successful a number of times and other individuals including the Duke of Bedford have bred these exotics. The record for the most consistent breeding pair probably belongs to Mr. C. J. Faudell who between 1943 and 1950 bred and successfully reared 14 young! Mr. Prestwich gives credit for the first breeding of a Leadbeater's in the United States to W. H. Browning whose pair bred in 1930.

Rose Breasted Cockatoo *(Eolophus roseicapillus)*

This small Cockatoo is only about 14 inches long. It is widely distributed throughout the interior of Australia. This is another parrot with many names. *Eolophus roseicapillus* is frequently referred to as the Galah (an Australian aboriginal name) the Roseate Cockatoo, and the Willock Cockatoo. Earlier authors such as Dr. Russ used the rather cheerful name Rosy Cockatoo for this bird and Charles N. Page, who wrote a small but delightful little book on parrots in 1906, referred to it as the Rosa Cockatoo. In the case of this particular

The Rose Breasted Cockatoo is also often called by its
aboriginal name, Galah. *Australian Information Service*

A baby Rose Breasted Cockatoo
learning about fingers. *Kelley*

Australian parrot the aboriginal name is quite commonly used and most people refer to this bird as the Galah or the Rose Breasted Cockatoo.

These hookbills are not especially graceful in appearance. Their build could be described as short and squat. The feathers of the forehead, crown and back of the head are white although some pink shows through at the base of the feathers. The wing, tail and back feathers are a silvery gray with the flight feathers a somewhat darker gray. The neck, face and most of the under feathers are a deep pink and thus the name, Rose Breasted or Roseate Cockatoo. The crest is small and similar to that of the Bare Eyed Cockatoo in shape and size. There is a faint suffusion of pink feathers in the crest. The legs and feet are dark and the color of the beak is white to horn. Mature Roseates are easy to sex as the eye of the male is a dark brown while the female's iris is pinkish-red. Some authorities also believe that the female's crest has a deeper pink tinge.

There are several subspecies which can be identified by the intensity of rose color in the plumage as well as the color of the naked eye ring.

The Galah is the most widespread and one of the most abundant Australian parrots. It actually appears to be increasing in numbers as well as extending its range. This rather unusual turn of events may be due to the Galah taking advantage of the expansion of farming to newly cleared areas as well as the establishment of drinking places for livestock. Although they do a considerable amount of damage to crops their innate cleverness and prolific breeding habits have permitted this increase in numbers even though Australian farmers are attempting to achieve an opposite result.

Cyril Rogers advises that young Roseate Cockatoos can be easily trained to become playful and loving pets. He observes that as with most parrots, older specimens are more difficult to train. Mr. Rogers does not speak highly of their talking ability and this opinion is shared by most writers. In spite of this Rogers indicates that the Galah is probably the most commonly kept species of Cockatoo. This is due to their convenient size, good nature, and availability.

Edward J. Boosey indicates how detested these parrots are by the Australian farmers. He describes how one bird (which is periodically replaced by another) will keep watch on a high tree limb while the others feed. Should the farmer or other hunters arrive, the watchbird gives the alarm and the flock will flee, screaming derisively at their antagonists.

Bare Eyed Cockatoo *(Cacatua sanguinea)*

This Cockatoo is found in northern Australia. It is another of the white Cockatoos although it has areas of pink around the cere and on the crown, cheeks and throat. The under surfaces of the tail feathers are bright yellow. The lores are light blue which results in this bird sometimes being called the Blue Eyed Cockatoo. The Australians refer to it as the Little Corella and it is, of course, a different parrot than the Long Billed Corella which is a similar bird with a much longer upper beak.

The Bare Eyed Cockatoo is not a particularly attractive bird and its white crest in no way compares with the magnificent crest of many other Cockatoos. The crest is small and hardly noticable when it is not erect.

It is only fair to point out, however, that this bird is one of the most intelligent parrots. It is among the best talkers of all the Cockatoos and is capable of showing great affection as well as clever behavior.

Charles Barrett comments on the intelligence of *Cacatua sanguinea*. Barrett goes so far as to claim that the Corellas rival the African Grey and even the most talented Mynah birds in their ability to speak.

Those which I have seen have been tame, friendly and playful and these traits are generally associated with intelligence in parrots.

W. T. Greene tells of a Bare Eyed Cockatoo named Toby. Toby belonged to a friend of his and could speak about twenty sentences. His greatest skill, however, was in mimicry. What was unusual about Toby was that in addition to mimicking sounds, he also performed physical actions to accompany the sounds which appealed to him. He loved to imitate the sound and performance of pouring out tea and then putting sugar in it (his beak representing the spout of the tea pot). He could also pretend to be the gardener clipping the shrubbery. He would give his head a little jerk with each snap of the pruning shears with his ever-useful beak again serving as a prop.

Goffin's Cockatoo *(Cacatua goffini)*

This parrot is frequently treated as simply a subspecies of the Little Corella (Bare Eyed Cockatoo) and identified as *Cacatua sanguinea goffini*. Since it is virtually isolated on the Indonesian Islands of Tenimber while its close relatives are for the most part found in Australia, the separate species classification used by some taxonomists appears to be a valid one.

These young birds are Bare Eyed Cockatoos, considered by many as one of the most intelligent of all parrots and one of the best talkers among the Cockatoos. *Photo by author*

This breeding pair of Goffin's Cockatoos shows the eye marking that earned the species its earlier name of "Blood Stained" Cockatoo. *Kelley*

An early and rather crude name for the entire group was the Blood Stained Cockatoo. This is apparently a reference to the light red feathers around the eyes and forehead. The Goffin is somewhat smaller than its close relatives and at 13 inches is one of the smallest of all the Cockatoos. The white feathers which are its main color give the impression of having been freshly cleaned. This clean appearance is enhanced by the special powder down feathers which Cockatoos possess. These break down into a fine, white powder when the bird preens itself and the powder is then distributed by the parrot's beak.

The Goffin has a very short crest which is orange at its base. The shape of the crest can help to distinguish it from another close relative, Ducorp's Cockatoo. The relatively small crest of the Ducorp's (which is made of broad feathers with rounded tips) gradually extends from the forehead to the nape with the feathers of the crest getting progressively smaller and the whole arrangement producing an effect almost like the sharp incline of a roller coaster. The Goffin crest, however, is much more like a spike or horn which ends abruptly at the middle of the crown.

The naked eye ring is white which is another quick means of helping identify this bird as in the Bare Eyed Cockatoo and Ducorp's Cockatoo the eye ring is blue. The iris itself is brown in both males and females although experts claim the ability to see a darker brown in males, particularly in sunlight or bright artificial light. In young birds, both sexes have dark eyes but the eyes turn brown as the bird matures. The Marquess of Tavistock (later the Duke of Bedford) comments on an error by Dr. Greene on distinguishing sex in Goffins via eye color. Greene kept a pair of Goffins and they were apparently among his favorite parrots. Perhaps the fact that he knew the sexes of his birds helped him to see a darker brown eye color in the male than was actually there (Greene wrote that the eye of the male was almost black) or perhaps in this pair the difference truly existed. The Marquess also questioned Dr. Greene's varied insect menu for Goffins but it produced a plump and healthy bird for Greene.

This parrot has a large, bulging eye and as in all of the Cockatoos the eye moves freely in all directions (without the head being moved) giving the impression that the owner of the eye is both inquisitive and suspicious.

Goffin, for whom Otto Finsch named this parrot, was a Dutch infantry officer who in addition to his military career was interested in ornithology. He published important papers on a number of West African birds. Dr. Finsch, of course, has had his name attached to many subspecies.

214

One of Dr. Greene's Goffins used to have access to the family dining room while meals were being eaten. The bird was obsessed with potatoes and became so clamorous for them that his owners knew no peace until he was provided with a serving. After taking just one tiny bite from the morsel he would drop it (like a hot potato) to the bottom of his cage and then wildly shout for "more!"

Greene noted that the screams became so monotonous and unpleasant (covering the parrot only caused them to grow louder) that after a while his owner truly wished that the Cockatoo was back on his native island. Eventually Greene's Goffin, who was named Paul, shouted "more potato!" once too loudly and once too incessantly while the bottom of his cage was littered with that vegetable. In a moment of irritation, Greene presented Paul to the London Zoo where he survived for only two years, perhaps, because he was deprived of potato. Paul knew and answered to his name but was extremely mischievous and thus had to be kept under lock and key or else he would open any type of cage fastening. He worked on his cage padlock for quite some time but obviously it baffled him. If he did get out of his cage, he damaged whatever furniture he could reach and defied everyone except Dr. Greene who could get him to go back into the cage by shouting "Go to bed, Paul!" Paul would then scuttle away and climb to the topmost perch of his cage from which vantage point he would shout, "Oh you bad, wicked bird!" over and over again. It is obvious that Paul had a real talent for repeating himself.

R. K. Day recently described his breeding of these Cockatoos. Day purchased a pair in 1976 after being quite taken with the clever behavior of some he had seen. He successfully bred his birds in a nine foot by six foot flight, using a ten gallon barrel which hung from the roof as a nestbox. Although the birds appeared to cooperate, it wasn't until a year after their purchase that their mating games, which began in March, resulted in two fertile eggs. These appeared three days apart, early in May. The first chick hatched out 32 days later with its sibling appearing on the very next day. Unfortunately, only one of these survived but he was so hearty that by the time he was five weeks old he attended a Parrot Society meeting and met many members.

These parrots are currently readily available at realistic prices and are an excellent choice if you wish to own a Cockatoo.

Red Vented Cockatoo *(Cacatua haematuropygia)*

Until 1977 these Cockatoos were rare in the United States. Large numbers then began to pass through quarantine and thus they have gained in popularity as pets.

The striking, bizarre appearance of the Palm Cockatoo entirely belies its gentle, friendly nature. *Photo by author*

The Red Vented Cockatoo is one of the smaller Cockatoos with a length of only about 13 inches. It is frequently called the Philippine Red Vented Cockatoo since the Philippines are its country of origin. It does not have a particularly prominent crest and thus bears some resemblance to the Bare Eyed Cockatoo.

As with many of the white Cockatoos, eye color can be a help in sex determination. The hen possesses a red eye while the eye of the male is jet black. The basic color is white with yellowish-pink ear coverts. There is also a wash of yellow on the underside of the flight feathers. The under-tail coverts are reddish giving rise to the species' common name.

The beak is white and the legs are grey. Young birds resemble the adults but the eye in the immature Red Vented Cockatoo is brown.

These parrots are quite common in the Philippines and can be found in any bird shop in Manila. Their reputation as being delicate is not deserved. These exotic white beauties (when acclimated) can winter outdoors with no ill effects. The concept of their delicacy may have stemmed from the large number of post-quarantine deaths which unfortunately occur in parrots who cannot tolerate 30 days of constant medication plus crowding.

They are fantastic chewers and will demolish any wood within reach and some that is not. They are not noisy birds, and are rather shy.

Their diet includes sunflower seeds, carrots, apples, corn, peanuts and pigeon scratch. To get them to eat apples one owner had to put the fruit on a nail. How typical of the stubborn parrot! His birds would ignore a cut up apple in a dish but would greedily demolish one stuck on a nail in their aviary.

Palm Cockatoo (*Probosciger aterrimus*)

This remarkable bird has been known by a bewildering variety of names. One of the earliest sources, John Selby calls the bird the Goliath Aratoo. Selby, an early 19th century author, was making reference to the giant beak of the Palm Cockatoo and was combining the Ara from the Latin name for Macaw with the suffix of the name, Cockatoo. Many early writers assumed an erroneous close relationship between Cockatoos and Macaws. Since the drawing which Selby provided was a poor likeness of the Palm Cockatoo I would have missed his reference to the bird completely if I had not spotted his use of the alternate name *Microglossus aterrimus* which was an early Latin classification for this Cockatoo. Selby makes reference to the huge size of this bird as do several others. In actuality it is the head and beak which are large while the total length of the bird is only about 25 inches making it somewhat smaller than the larger Macaws. Although Selby's drawing does not faithfully represent the Palm Cockatoo, his description is a good one and comes quite close to that of modern authors. Selby advises us that the bird was first described as early as 1707.

Dr. Greene updates the name to the Goliath Aratoo and also uses the alternate name, Great Black Cockatoo. His color engraving is beautifully done and is unmistakably that of a Palm Cockatoo. Greene believed this parrot to be the most extraordinary looking member of the entire parrot race. He also confirms 1707 as the original discovery date.

The general coloration of the Palm Cockatoo is black with a steel-gray tinge. The feathers at the base of the forehead and the lores are quite short and look almost like black velvet. There is a large, red, bare facial patch whose intensity of redness undergoes obvious changes when the bird is angry, frightened or agitated. This color change is similar to blushing in humans although it is doubtful it is ever caused by shame or modesty. Some zoologists believe that color changes of this sort are a protective device with the intensification of color being a mechanism to frighten off prospective enemies. The beak is shiny black and truly enormous. The shape of the upper beak is peculiar as it is heavily notched. Because of this irregularity the upper and lower mandibles do not quite fit together when closed so that the bird's tongue is always visible. The tongue is rather small as parrot tongues go with the tip black and the rest of it pink. The legs and feet are black and the eye is brown. The female has a smaller upper beak as well as a smaller bare facial patch. The crest is black and quite large with the crest feathers erect and distinctly separate from each other.

This Cockatoo originates in northern Australia and New Guinea.

Neville Cayley adds two additional names to the collection which this bird has accumulated. He indicates that it is sometimes referred to as the Macaw Cockatoo as well as the Great Palm Cockatoo. He describes a Palm taken from its nest when only about eight weeks old and hand raised by a Dr. D'Ombrain. It turned out to be a fine pet who would go through many comical antics for its owner. Tom, as the bird was named, was 26 years old and in excellent health. Dr. D'Ombrain should really have changed Tom's name as she laid her first egg in her eighteenth year. The doctor is quoted at length about the way in which the Palm Cockatoo uses its powder gland. He

218

describes how she would throw her head completely back at the same time she raised her spine to meet the back of her head. The powder thus collected was used to dust her entire body. The doctor pictures Tom as a very gentle bird and one who was particularly fond of being petted. One of her greatest pleasures was to have her cheek patches gently rubbed.

Charles Barrett makes note of the odd proportions of this Cockatoo. He goes a bit further than my earlier reference to the head being out of proportion to the rest of the body and indicates that the pectoral muscles are rather small for a bird of this size and thus it is a weak flyer in comparison to other large parrots.

Cayley informs us that the Goliath is the only bird capable of opening the hard-shelled kanari nut. He mentions that this nut is the Palm's principal source of food in New Guinea. (Australian members of the species subsist on other types of nuts.)

The Duke of Bedford was also familiar with this giant species. His Palm Cockatoo was so gentle that when it was angry it merely scratched with the tip of its beak instead of biting. I found this reference quite interesting because this is just how Frodo, one of my Scarlet Macaws behaves. If he is really angry he rubs the point of his beak on my hand in the way one uses the eraser on a pencil. Perhaps Frodo knew a Palm Cockatoo when he was younger.

Arthur Prestwich credits a first breeding of the Palm Cockatoo to a Mr. I. D. Putnam of the United States. This breeding occurred in 1944 and Mr. Prestwich mentions several additional successful breedings by Mr. Sheffler of Arizona in 1949.

I have had several opportunities to photograph and observe these large-headed parrots and find their personalities much kinder and more gentle than would be assumed from the bold eye and oversized beak. One of the Palm Cockatoos which I held offered kisses but I resisted the temptation with ease. Another invariably pounded his brazil nut (which his owner substituted for Kanari nuts) against the floor of his cage. Perhaps he was angry at the switch.

Banksian Cockatoo *(Calyptorhynchus magnificus)*

This large, black bird's very impressive appearance is implied in its scientific name. It is sometimes called the Red Tailed Black Cockatoo. Older writers group the Banksians in a category which they called the Long Tailed Cockatoos but this classification is no longer used.

The elegant Red Vented Cockatoo, a native of the Philippines, is one of the smaller members of the Cockatoo family. *Kelley*

The Gang-Gang Cockatoo is, happily, maintaining its numbers in its native habitat at the present time and is protected under Australian law. In this species, only the male (right) has the elaborate topknot. *Australian Information Service*

The Banksian Cockatoo's "Roman helmet" is its outstanding identifying hallmark.
Australian Information Service

Dr. Russ has nothing but praise for these parrots and talks of their great curiosity and the degree of interest they show in whatever their owner is doing. I think the good doctor may have gone a little far when he indicated that this was a "thinking and philosophising bird."

The Banksian Cockatoo is almost 2½ feet long. Its predominant color is black with the feathers of the breast appearing gray. The tail has a band of red feathers and the female gives the appearance of being speckled with yellow spots on the head and neck. Its beak is grayish-black. Young Banksians all tend to look like females but by the second or third molt the males lose their yellow spots and by four years of age the sexual differences are quite evident.

Several observers have noted that when erected, the crest of these dignified looking Cockatoos makes the bird look as if he were wearing a Roman helmet.

Some authors place the Banksians, with other somberly colored members of their race, into a group which they refer to as the Black Cockatoos. The members of this grouping include the Funereal Cockatoo and the White-Tailed Black Cockatoo. They are all impressive looking birds which are seldom seen in private collections.

Gang-Gang Cockatoo *(Callocephalon fimbriatum)*

Australia, New Zealand, and Oceania are so deeply isolated and widely separated from other land masses by their island nature that their bird life has a large number of unusual species. As pointed out by Jean Dorst, "These islands have had no continental connections during the evolution of modern birds, hence the great faunal peculiarity of the area." The Gang-Gang aptly illustrates Dorst's point.

Callocephalon fimbriatum is also known as the Red Crowned Cockatoo, Helmeted Cockatoo and Red Headed Parrot. A free translation of its most appropriate Latin name would be "beautifully fringed head." A glance at a male Gang-Gang will demonstrate just how accurate the Latin designation is.

These Cockatoos are natives of Australia with most being found in the southeast of the island continent. Occasional visits are made by the Gang-Gang to King Island and Tasmania which are off the southern coast. Although this parrot is not frequently advertised for sale, good specimens are available and their beauty, tameness and talking ability make them well worth owning. They still exist in good numbers within their range and they are maintaining their numbers well which is helped by the fact that the Gang-Gang is fully protected by Australian law in all parts of its range.

These are comparatively small Cockatoos with males measuring about 13 inches and females about 14 inches. The basic color is gray but the pale edges of the feathers (which are most pronounced on the back of the bird) give it a scalloped look which reminds one of the African Grey. Adult males have a bright red head and crest. The feathers which make up the crest are quite delicate in appearance. The beak is horn colored with an unusually well-developed lower mandible. The eye is deep brown in both sexes. The female, in addition to being larger, lacks the red topknot. She has a gray crest and head. Immature birds resemble their mothers.

Neville W. Cayley advises that this Cockatoo was first described by the ornithologist Lathan in 1801, Mr. Cayley reminisces about seeing flocks of as many as 50 of these birds feeding on the seeds of the eucalyptus tree when he was a child. They would congregate in small groups on the upper branches of trees and when not feeding, would lazily preen one another's feathers. Cayley remembers one bird lying along a branch with its wings spread while its neighbor carefully went over its feathers like one monkey cleaning another. He further recalls a Gang-Gang owned by his father who used to say, "Poor Cocky has one eye." This was quite accurate as it had been shot and wounded when younger, but in spite of its infirmity it lived as a cherished family pet for many years.

Charles Barrett mentions that the earliest portrait of the Gang-Gang appeared as a color plate in Grant's *Narrative of a Voyage of Discovery in the Lady Nelson* written in 1803. Lieutenant Grant unforunately shot the specimen who then had no choice about serving as a model for the historic portrait. A black and white reproduction of the original painting of the victim appears in Neville Cayley's book which was quoted earlier. It is an excellent portrait with the beak, crest, and light margins to the feathers making it evident that Lieutenant Grant was dealing with the Gang-Gang although he refers to it as a Red Crowned Parrot. Barrett indicates that Gang-Gang is the aboriginal name for these Cockatoos. He felt they were too trusting of many and could easily be approached until they became good, close-range targets for hunters.

Rutgers and Norris caution that older females may show red markings on the head. Thus if there were any doubt about the sex of one of these birds, the age of the parrot would be improtant in helping make a determination. These authors (along with many others) warn that although the Gang-Gang is a beautiful and desirable pet, it is also prone to plucking when in captivity. Margaret W. Neal describes her efforts to persuade a small Gang-Gang to stop destroying her feathers. Ms. Neal believes that there are more theories about the cause of feather loss in hen Gang-Gangs then there are hen Gang-Gangs in Britain. Tilly (short for Waltzing Matilda) although tame had plucked herself to the down. A few days after she arrived, Ms. Neal had occasion to manhandle her back into her cage and an outraged and scolding Tilly simply pecked at Ms. Neal's hands with an open beak. Her basic diet of safflower and canary seed, along with dandelion leaves and grapes was continued; however, a great deal of new chewing material was also supplied. Green pine branches with the bark on and pine cones were very popular. Feathers began to replace down and even a rather ratty-looking tail began to fill out.

On at least two occasions Ms. Neal neglected to replenish the supply of chewing materials and Tilly immediately returned to her destructive ways. Success appeared highly possible for Ms. Neal at the time that she wrote her article. Tilly had added empty walnut shells to her list of chewing toys and although she was still somewhat ragged, it was hoped that following her next molt she would be a more attractive bird.

Ms. Neal points out that perhaps frustration could be the cause of plucking problems; not merely boredom but an actual need to behave in a manner which owner or circumstances prevent. Thus, the owner of a bird who is plucking should research its natural habits and then try to provide opportunities for the bird to duplicate (as much as possible) this behavior in captivity.

Dr. Greene refers to this bird with the early nomenclature, *Psittacus galeatus* and also uses the name Ganga Cockatoo. The perfect portrait which accompanies the chapter leaves no doubt as to whom he is referring. Dr. Greene notes that Captain Cook makes mention of the Gang-Gang in his journal which would be an earlier reference than the one noted previously. Greene points out that the London Zoo obtained its first specimen in 1859 and four more thereafter. They were apparently not long-lived as none existed at the time of his writing.

A. A. Prestwich lists several successful breedings of these birds. Reference is made to the Duke of Bedford's success with two young being bred in both 1951 and 1952. Prestwich also notes a medal awarded to a Miss S. Merrifield of South Australia as her work with Gang-Gangs was considered the Outstanding Breeding Achievement of the 1945 season. Surprisingly, a large number of other breedings were listed with the first success being credited in 1921 to a Mme. Lecallier of France. Prestwich also confirms a successful cross between a Gang-Gang and a Rose Breasted Cockatoo which adds weight to speculation that the two genera may be closely allied.

J. E. Robertson reported a successful breeding (after a five-year wait) of Gang-Gangs in 1976. He writes that his birds have never plucked (they have, however, been well supplied with pine cones and pine needles). Their main nest box was a hollow tree, four feet high by three feet in diameter with a natural hole in the side. It is hard to visualize the fantastic chewing ability of these small Cockatoos but they proceeded to destroy the top of the nest box which was made out of an aluminum sheet and Mr. Robertson had to replace it with a large cinderblock. The hen started to inspect the trunk in April, and in typical parrot fashion, rejected this beautiful natural nest box and laid her eggs in a nest she had ignored for five previous years. This was a standard-shaped nest box about fifteen inches deep. The pair took turns sitting on the eggs; the male in the daytime and the hen at night. A chick was first heard on July 2nd and Mr. Robertson was able to resist looking in the nest box until it was five weeks old. The baby was fully feathered and resembled his mother except for a beak which was much lighter in color. He left the nest on August 25, at which time he still resembled his mother except for a darker head and breast.

Greater (left) and Lesser Sulphur Crested Cockatoos.
M. Morrone/S. Rosenblum

The parrot was called Loulou. His body was green, the tip of his wings pink, his forehead blue, and his throat golden.

But he had the tiresome habit of biting his perch, plucking his feathers scattering his mess about, and spattering the water of his bath. Mme. Aubain thought the bird was a nuisance and gave him to Felicite to keep.

She set out to train the parrot; soon he could repeat "Nice boy," "Your servant, sir," "Hello, Mary!" He was placed next to the door, and people were surprised that he would not answer to Jacquot, for weren't all parrots called Jacquot? They likened him to a turkey, to a log of wood; and each time they did so Felicite was hurt to the quick! But Loulou was curiously stubborn! He stopped talking when one looked at him!

Gustave Flaubert, *A Simple Heart*

A basket of Half Moon babies. *Udall*

12

The Conures

PEOPLE ARE FREQUENTLY CONFUSED by the fact that the same parrot is sometimes referred to as a Conure while at other times it is called a Parakeet. This confusion is not limited to laymen and, in fact, results from the fact that many writers refer to these long tailed, New World birds as Conures while others prefer the term Parakeet. Some authors resolve the problem by discussing the Conures under the heading South American Parakeets even though they range as far north as Central America and Mexico. A more straightforward approach is to note that there is really no difference and that "Conure" is the name given to some Parakeets from South and Central America: particularly those of the genera *Aratinga* and *Pyrrhura*. An alternate solution to the problem is to refer to these birds as Conurine Parakeets. Although the Conures are often referred to as Parakeets they are not at all like the Australian Parakeets or Budgies in personality or temperament. They are much more like the true parrot.

When this sort of problem crops up, it is wise to remember that classification is, after all, a very inexact science. It is man who feels the need to arrange animals into neat categories. Nature, on the other hand, has no compunctions about overlapping so it is best to keep an open mind about problems of classification. In fact, it has happened that through the years various classifications have been modified. For the sake of this discussion we will refer to these birds as Conures.

The Conures represent a very large group of birds which are divided into a number of different genera. There is a great deal of variation in characteristics as well as in prices and availability among them.

Conures may be related to the Macaws and one genus, *Aratinga* is made up of parrots who look very much like small Macaws. Obvious differences, of course, would be the lesser size of Conures; the fact that their lores are feathered and the rather swollen appearance of the beak as compared to the thin and graceful Macaw beak.

These parrots vary greatly in color, markings and size and show a wide geographic range throughout Mexico as well as Central and South America.

They have a limited potential for speech but make clever, loving and readily tamed pets.

Petz's Conure *(Aratinga canicularis)*

This bird is just as frequently called the Half Moon Conure as Petz's Conure.

It is one of the most popular and commonly available pet parrots in the United States. They are small greeen birds and seldom exceed nine or ten inches in length. More than a third of this length is made up by their tail. The nickname "Half Moon" was given to this Conure because of the crescent shaped orange area which covers their foreheads.

In their native land, Half Moons delight in eating the fruit of a tree called *Jacaratia mexicana,* which has the popular name, "Parrot Fruit Tree." Anne Graham notes that this tree also provides protective coloration for these birds and that from a distance of 50 feet it is almost impossible to distinguish the bird from the fruit.

If obtained young, the Half Moon can become a charming and lovable pet. Before buying or accepting an older bird, be sure to check on its friendliness. A Half Moon can administer a nasty bite—despite its small size—if its normally good personality has been ruined.

Golden Crowned Conure *(Aratinga aurea)*

It is unfortunate that the constant repetition of an error will sometimes serve to further spread and propagate the mistake as truth. This has frequently happened in the case of parrots with similar appearances and although it is not done with malice, it does create problems of identification.

228

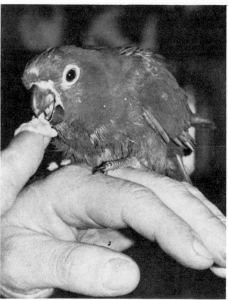

The exquisitely beautiful Queen of Bavaria Conure, a living golden treasure. *Photo by author*

A baby Sun Conure being hand-fed. *Photo by author*

The Golden Crowned Conure is often confused with Petz's Conure. Observing the color of the beak in either species will provide a quick, positive identification. *Hermanson*

The Golden Crowned Conure is also sometimes correctly referred to as the Peach Fronted Conure, the Orange Crowned Conure, the Golden Headed Conure, and the Peach Fronted Parakeet. A few authors sometimes incorrectly refer to the Golden Crowned as the Half Moon Conure, but this is not accurate. Half Moon, as indicated previously, is an alternate name for Petz's Conure *(Aratinga canicularis)*. There is a resemblance between both birds but the error can be easily avoided by checking the colors of the beaks. In the Half Moon, the upper beak is a light horn color with the lower beak a mixture of horn and black. The beak of the Golden-Crowned Conure is a deep, solid black.

Members of the genus *Aratinga* include those Conures which bear a resemblance to the Macaws. Of course, they are much smaller birds; however, their large beaks and prominent eye rings make one think "little Macaw" when viewing members of this genus.

This parrot is found in Brazil, Bolivia, Paraguay, and the north of Argentina.

The general plumage is green with a well-marked yellow forehead. This yellow marking also extends to the front of the crown. The rest of the crown and the region around the upper portion of the eye is blue. The feathers around the eye ring are bright yellowish-orange.

These Conures are nine or ten inches long but a subspecies *A.a. major* is slightly larger.

Dr. Russ has much to say of this attractive bird. Russ was probably describing the larger subspecies as he indicated that the bird was about 11 inches long. He pointed out that this parrot was first described as early at 1648 with further and more detailed references in important works in 1760 and 1788. Russ notes that the Golden Crowned was among the earliest of the parrots brought into Europe. At the time of his writing he described how abundant it was in the market place which leads me to believe that he was simply making no distinction between the relatively common Petz's Conure and the true Golden Crowned. Dr. Russ describes a Golden Crowned owned by the headmaster of a grammar school which could whistle, sneeze and say "Papa." He describes another member of the race who was obtained by his owner in very sad condition. After making a splendid recovery, this Conure learned to obtain treats by screaming "Please! Please!" and adding "good, very good!" when satisfied.

The Duke of Bedford and Cyril Rogers properly differentiate between the Golden Crowned and the Half Moon. Although brief, their descriptions are useful and match quite well those of the other authors quoted herein.

230

Rosemary Low also warns against confusing the Golden Crowned with Petz's Conure. She makes the point that this parrot is little known in the United States where Petz's Conure predominates. She notes that in Britain the situation is practically reversed. Ms. Low describes an early breeding which took place in Germany in 1880 as well as more current successful efforts in South Africa in 1958 and Sweden in 1959.

A.A. Prestwich notes quite a few other breeding successes as well as some hybrid results between a Golden Crowned and a Yellow Headed Conure.

A more recent breeding of the Golden Crowned was achieved by David Derrett in 1973. Since he described his birds as being larger than 11 inches, he probably was working with the subspecies.

Queen of Bavaria Conure (Aratinga guarouba)

This parrot is generally considered the most attractive and desirable member of its genus. It is also frequently referred to as the Golden Conure. Its species name is derived from the Spanish word Guarajuba which means yellow bird.

The Golden Conure bears a marked resemblance to a small Macaw. There is a patch of bare skin around the eye although it is not too extensive. The beak and head are quite large and with its relatively short tail this bird appears somewhat top-heavy.

The Golden Conure occurs only in a remote area of northeastern Brazil, which is a factor in its rarity.

The Queen of Bavaria's plumage is bright yellow which is dramatically set-off by its dark green primaries, secondaries and outer wing-coverts. The beak is almost white and the eye is brown. Young birds have some green on the head. They are good-sized Conures, growing to about 14 inches in length.

Some authors believe that they can identify the female by her smaller size and more delicate head and beak. A successful breeder of the Queen of Bavaria, Dr. Osman Hill, felt there was no obvious visible difference between the sexes. Only their behavior during copulation and subsequent egg-laying indicated their sex to Dr. Hill.

This Conure is a rather noisy bird although I would put their screams down to high spirits as they are also quite playful and friendly. Dr. Greene, writing about this bird in 1887, occasionally refers to it as the Golden Parrot. He confirms its skill at screaming but also notes its gentleness, tameness and droll behavior. It was an expensive parrot even in Dr. Greene's day as he makes reference to prices of about $125 and more if one were fortunate enough to be

231

able to find an available specimen. Greene indicates that this bird was known to early naturalists and was accurately described by Buffon. He also advises that there had been a specimen in the London Zoo since 1871.

I recently observed a large group of Golden Conures which were tamer than any described in the literature quoted above. Although I was a total stranger to the parrots they readily came to my hand and then were more than willing to perch on the young daughter of their owner. These Conures are actually larger than some of the medium-sized Amazon Parrots and have a strong, stocky build.

Sun Conure *(Aratinga solstitialis)*

As with many of the parrots the Sun Conure has been known by several names during its long history. This warmly colored member of its genus has also been referred to as the Sun Parakeet and Yellow Conure. While it does not have quite the same imposing appearance as the Queen of Bavaria Conure, its colors are very attractive and most authors rate it as one of the most beautiful of all Conures.

The Sun Conure's general plumage is yellow which is mixed with orange on the forehead, sides of the head, lower abdomen, rump and lower back. The yellow-orange mixture varies from bird to bird (much as the head and shoulder markings do in the Amazons). The wing and tail feathers are a mixture of yellow, green, and blue. The eye is a dark brown and the beak gray to black. The beak is lighter-colored in immature birds. These Conures are about 12 inches long and are beautifully proportioned.

This parrot shares a number of characteristics with the Jenday Conure and the Golden Capped Conure and it is possible that revisions of classification may link them as subspecies.

Rutgers and Norris note that this parrot is distributed throughout the Guianas and northwestern Brazil. They comment on its beauty and remark that it is a great favorite among the natives who hand-feed the young and then keep the birds at liberty in large flocks. Rutgers mentions that this parrot is seldom imported but notes a first record of it being kept by Mme. de Kerville of France who had several of these birds starting as early as 1872. She is credited with the first breeding of this species and her description of their immature plumage as being "green, lightly marked with yellow, with the under surface greenish-yellow" is quite accurate.

Rosemary Low speaks very highly of these birds. She also comments on their beauty and considers them quite rare. Ms. Low reports on two Sun Conures which were part of a group of four

The branch of the parrot family consisting of Cockatoos includes many outstandingly beautiful species. The Leadbeater's Cockatoo, with delicate shadings of pink in his plumage and exquisitely banded crest must be considered one of the most splendid. *Parrot Jungle, Miami*

Probably the most familiar Cockatoo species is the Greater Sulphur Crested. This large, white bird is the object of admiration wherever it is seen. The Greater seems to know just how stunning it is too, as it delights in displaying for any audience. *Parrot Jungle, Miami*

234

Umbrella Cockatoo. *Kelley*

Moluccan Cockatoo. *Freud*

Red Vented Cockatoo. *Kelley*

Jenday Conure. *Evans*

Patagonian Conures. *Kelley*

Queen of Bavaria Conure. *Freud*

236

An early painting of Budgies, showing their natural color. *Greene*

A pearly Cockatiel, a mutation of
the bird's natural color. *Kelley*

Purple Capped Lory. *New York Zoological Society*

Black Headed Caique. *Evans*

Carolina Conure portrait. *Greene*

The voluptuously-colored Eclectus parrot. The striking differences in color mark the sexes. In this photo the female is at the left. *Freud*

238

Indian Ringneck Parakeet. *Vazquez*

Alexandrine Ringneck Parakeet. *Kelley*

Lutino mutation Indian Ringneck. *Buttstead*

239

Pesquet's parrot, a rare species from the mountains of New Guinea, is also known as the Vulturine parrot. *Kinnach*

imported into England in 1971 and which were apparently scarce enough to create a stir in avicultural circles. She notes, however, that about 30 more were imported the following year.

Dr. Russ adds his plaudits regarding this parrot's beauty. He refers to the name "Kessi-Kessi" used for these Conures by the Venezuelan natives and which apparently comes from the cry of the bird. A Sun Conure with which Russ was familiar was extremely tame and could chatter a few words.

Dr. Greene comments on how greatly these Conures vary in appearance and indicates that "no two of them are . . . exactly alike." He advises that they are painfully noisy at times with piercing and shrill voices. Greene also remarks on the Sun Conure's similarity to the Jendays and the Golden Capped Conure.

Greene mentions the arrival of this parrot at the London Zoo as early as 1862. He points out that the young have more red in their plumage than adults and that they mature rather slowly. They do not fully assume the adult plumage until they reach about three years of age. He considered them rather high priced in 1887 at about $10.00 to $15.00 dollars each.

A.A. Prestwich cites a large number of successful breedings including full details on the success of Mme. de Kerville mentioned earlier. Prestwich notes that the young remain in the nest box for about three months. He also mentions successful breedings in the United States starting as early as 1932.

More current breeding information is provided by N. Ramen of Gox Hill, England who describes his achievement with a pair of Sun Conures which he purchased in October, 1974. Although the birds appeared identical in form and color they attempted to copulate in February, 1975. They were in an indoor three foot by six foot flight with a grandfather clock nest box. In April they were placed in an 11 foot long by three foot wide by nine foot high outside flight with an enclosed shelter. A new nest box (they had destroyed the old one) 18 inches square by 4½ feet long was provided. It had about six inches of peat and dried grass in it. By the sixth of July, the first egg had been laid and three more followed at two day intervals. Incubation took 27 days with the first chick hatching out on August 3rd. The other eggs hatched at two day intervals. Only the female incubated but the father did help with feeding the young. During the week of September 22nd all of the young left the nest box and Mr. Ramen indicates that the young were quite similar to the parents with the major differences being that the wings were mostly green whereas adults had deep orange wings with only the tips green. Writing in October, 1975 his description of the young is every aviculturist's dream. "They are beautiful, strong, and healthy . . ."

Patagonian Conures. *Kelley*

Jenday Conure. *Evans*

242

Patagonian Conure *(Cyanoliseus patagonus)*

The Patagonian is a bird with a rather long, tapering tail. Members of the genus *Cyanoliseus* look less like Macaws than those which belong to the genus *Aratinga*. This parrot is about 18 inches long with the adults having basic olive-brown coloration on the head, neck and back. Its underparts are yellow with an olive tinge while the throat and breast are grayish-brown. It also has a distinctive whitish marking on each side of the upper breast. The beak is dark gray while the eye is yellowish. In immature birds the upper beak is almost white and the eye is pale gray.

Patagonia is a large region near the southern tip of South America. The name comes from the Spanish word, *patagones* which means, "big feet" as the Indians of that region were quite tall and wore large boots. The region was divided between Chile and Argentina under a treaty written in 1881. Thus, the origin of this parrot's name is obvious although it is also found in central Chile as well as northern and central Argentina.

The subspecies *Cyanoliseus patagonus byroni* is the bird frequently referred to as the Greater Patagonian Conure. It is about two inches larger than the nominate species and can be identified by the brighter and more extensive yellow underparts as well as having the whitish marking on the upper breast more obvious and more frequently forming a complete band. This subspecies is currently found only in central Chile.

Arthur A. Prestwich gives some fascinating background on how the subspecies was named. He make reference to an early report written by J.E. Grey in 1831. Mr. Grey added the Latinized version of the name of Captain Lord Byron of the Royal Navy to identify the subspecies. Captain Byron was so honored because it was during one of his voyages that the new subspecies was discovered and identified by the Chaplain of the vessel Byron commanded. Incidentally, the purpose of the voyage was not exploration. Lord Byron was returning the bodies of Kamehameha II and Kamehanelu, King and Queen of the Sandwich Islands who had unfortunately died of measles while on a state visit to England. A further interesting note is that Byron was the cousin of the celebrated poet and succeeded to the title when Byron, the poet, died in 1824.

Rosemary Low indicates that this bird was abundant in southern Argentina many years ago. She quotes earlier authors who describe immense flocks. She further mentions that these Conures are quite friendly to each other (even during the breeding season) and nest quite close together by digging three-to four-foot burrows on the sides of cliffs or high banks. Ms. Low reports that the bird has been readily available in Britain and, while attractive, has a loud and harsh voice. She tells of one Patagonian Conure who was an accomplished mimic and could imitate all types of sounds from the squeak of the stove lid to the sawing of wood.

The Duke of Bedford also confirms this species' skill at mimicry. He considered it a very intelligent bird and a good talker. He notes one individual that was quiet and well-behaved in the company of the family. This same parrot would raise quite an uproar if someone whose appearance displeased him came to the door. I suspect he could have been considered a "watch parrot".

Cyril Rogers describes the Patagonian as well-proportioned with pleasing coloring. His reference is to the subspecies *C.p. byroni* (Greater Patagonian Conure) and Rogers points out that the larger bird is becoming scarce in Argentina and suggests that owners of pairs attempt to breed them in an early effort to avoid having the bird become an endangered species.

In 1971, Paolo Bertagnolio, one of Italy's best known and most successful parrot breeders, was presented with four Patagonian Conures which had been purchased in a shop in Santiago, Chile. He knew his birds were still quite young on arrival as their upper beaks were partly white. There was no attempt at breeding until May 1973 when two eggs plus pieces of shell from at least one other egg were discovered. Two more eggs were noted at the end of May and early in June the first chicks appeared. A third chick hatched out on June 7th and the birds developed rapidly from that point on. Since the last chick to hatch did not seem to be progressing as well as the others Sr. Bertagnolio decided to hand-feed him. Within a month the birds were well feathered and already demonstrating their vocal abilities. The two older chicks left the nest between the end of July and the begining of August and showed great skill at flying. The hand-fed Conure did quite well and gained weight steadily on a diet of baby cereal, banana, apple, spinach and carrot to which vitamins and minerals were also added. This bird is now at the Naples Zoo and you can see him if you have the good fortune to visit that beautiful city.

Sr. Bertagnolio remarks on the similarity between Patagonian nestlings and those of the Macaws. He makes particular reference to the large, fleshy, forehead with its short, bristly feathers.

Carolina Conure *(Conuropsis carolinensis)*

The Carolina Conure lived in huge numbers in the great cypress forests of Florida and the Carolinas. He also lived in smaller numbers in other southern states and was sighted as far north as Ohio.

Although they were strong enough flyers to come even further north, they preferred the southern clime and in particular, loved the fruit of the cypress tree (a heavily seeded fruit in the form of a ball which was a natural object of delight for any hungry, fun loving parrot). They also found the hollow trunks of dead cypress trees to be snug nests and were known to winter in them in a state resembling hibernation.

John and William Bartram, contemporaries and friends of Benjamin Franklin, as well as founders of the first Botanical Gardens in the western hemisphere, explored what was then the wilderness of the western United States during the 18th centruy. Part of their travels took them through Georgia and Florida in the year 1773. At that time the Carolina Conure existed in tremendous numbers and the Bartrams noted how easily tamed and how docile and friendly these birds would become.

The story of their loss to the world is a typical example of man's foolishness and greed. They were hunted by both farmers and sportsmen. The farmers had a more legitimate reason for their actions as this Conure, like most of his race, was a great destroyer of crops. Members of the parrot family particularly aggravate farmers in that they do not finish off the fruit or vegetable they pick up. Instead, for some peculiar reason, after a few bites they will drop it and select another choice morsel.

Hunters killed these attractive birds for their plumage and just for the fun of killing. This parrot along with a number of other animals tended to stay with its neighbors who were killed or injured. Thus, a hunter who had killed several birds would have an easy target in the many others who would be swooping around their fallen fellows.

When birds and other animals become endangered, we finally begin to closely watch their numbers and, generally much too late in the game, attempt to protect them and encourage their breeding. Unfortunately, when the population passes below a certain number of specimens it is virtually impossible to save a species from extinction and at that point zoologists begin what might be called a death watch on the last few members of a species nearing extinction. A rather well known example of this was the death of Martha, the last Passenger Pigeon who died in the Cincinnati Zoo. Interest in this poor little bird was so intense that the actual hour of her death has been recorded.

The photograph of the Carolina Conure which illustrates this book is that of a bird who lived in the Bronx Zoo until its death on May 25, 1913. This photo was taken more than a year before the parrot died. Unfortunately, because of the film used at that time (ortho) all of the shades of black and gray have been shifted to a much darker hue.

This Carolina Conure was a lonely resident at the Bronx Zoo until its death in 1913. Because the (ortho) film used at the time shifted to a much darker hue, the bird's markings are virtually indistinguishable in this photograph. Compare to the illustration below. *New York Zoological Society-*

The Carolina Conure was a bright-colored, attractive bird. The species' sad history among the fauna of the United States is an unfortunate reflection on the human greed and thoughtlessness that caused its extinction. *Greene*

George Laycock decided to investigate the death of the last Carolina Conure, as he felt it a mystery that the final member of the entire race of North American parrots could have been allowed to disappear without records being kept of its passing. Laycock's initial investigation seemed to indicate that the last captive Carolina Conure died on September 1, 1914 in the same Cincinnati Zoo where Martha (the Passenger Pigeon) ended her days, and by coincidence, only two weeks before Martha died. With help of John Ruthven, an artist from Cincinnati, who was also quite interested in this bird, they carried their search to a Dr. Stephan, who was the son of the general manager of the Zoo in 1914. Dr. Stephan, had saved and stored a considerable amount of old materials and records from the zoo and he permitted Laycock and Ruthven to examine them. They included old scrapbooks, photos, and various souvenirs. Their research bore immediate fruit. A clipping from the Cincinnati *Times-Star* of November 29, 1916 indicated that the London Zoo wanted to purchase the two Carolina Conures belonging to the Cincinnati Zoo. Dr. Stephan's father (the general manager of the zoo) was quoted as refusing to make the sale as the pair were about 35 years old and were not only quite scarce, but beyond breeding age. The elder Stephan indicated that the pair had been with the zoo for 32 years.

Laycock speculated on the tantalizing possibility that unknown to zoo keepers there might have been Carolina Conures living deep within some swamp or heavily forested area. As a matter of fact, reports of sightings were sometimes received but generally merely dismissed. He mentions, however, that in the spring of 1926, Charles E. Doe, curator of birds at the University of Florida, actually located three pairs of Carolina Conures in Okeechobee County, Florida. He did not collect any of the birds, but he took five of their eggs, which are currently in a museum collection in Gainesville, Florida.

Mr. Laycock next discovered that in the spring of 1934, a gentleman named George Malamphy, who had worked with the famous Dr. Arthur A. Allen at Cornell, made a journey to South Carolina for the purpose of studying the Wild Turkey. Malamphy leased 12,000 acres of the heavily timbered swamp land along the Santee River. During his observations of the Turkeys, he spotted an Ivory-Billed Woodpecker which was then widely believed to be extinct. He actually viewed this bird 33 times and sometimes saw several at one time. Ornithologists who heard of his reports were extremely doubtful about their validity, but when Malamphy announced that he had also seen Carolina Conures on eight or nine occasions (as many as seven at one time in one instance) two ornithologists from Charleston visited his camp and after intensive questioning and an opportunity to view the wilderness he had leased, decided that there was at least a chance that he was correct in his sightings.

Based on the possibility that Malamphy might have been right the National Audubon Society leased a large area in the same vicinity and in 1936, established a base camp on the property so that they could make a determined effort to spot the parrot.

In the official reports, they indicated the sighting of at least one definite Carolina Conure and a number of other sightings which appeared to be Carolina Conures. These were not simply escaped parakeets and the investigators indicated that they had no hesitation in identifying the birds they saw as *Psittacus carolinensis*. (The current nomenclature is *Conuropsis carolinensis*.) In June, 1938, a game warden in the area spotted two of the Conures who were apparently flying with their young.

Very little was done after 1938 in searching for the Carolina Conures and the Audubon study was unfortunately never published. The report plus dozens of communications from game wardens and other individuals about the sighting of Conures were left to gather dust in the files of the National Audubon Society.

In 1949, Alexander Sprunt, supervisor of southern sanctuaries for the Audubon Society, (who was one of the people who made the sightings in November and December, 1936) discussed what he had seen in his book on the bird life of South Carolina. Sprunt indicated that it was his firm and considered belief that the Carolina Conure, "was in the Santee Swamp in 1936–1938," a remnant of a population which probably had always lived there. The report written by other members of the Audubon staff was equally as positive in identifying the birds they had seen as Carolina Conures.

After completing all of their research, Mr. Malamphy and Mr. Ruthven made a final search of the old records of the Cincinnati newspaper. In the volume for 1918, they found the news story dealing with the death of the last Carolina Conure known to exist. As far as the Cincinnati Zoo is concerned, the last Carolina Conure in captivity was a male named Incas, and he died on February 21, 1918. The Zoo director felt he had died of grief, as his mate of 32 years, Lady Jane, had died late the previous summer.

Dr. Greene and Dr. Russ writing late in the last century speak very highly of the Carolina Parrot, as they refer to it. Naturally they speak of it as a living species but even in 1884, Dr. Greene noted the reduction in their numbers. In a copy of the portrait from his book the ever-present cockle-burrs beneath the claw of the smiling Conure are visible.

I wonder if somewhere in the depths of the Florida and South Carolina swamps there exists today a few Carolina Conures who chuckle as they eat and play with the fruits of their cypress trees while flying gleefully from branch to branch.

Carolina Conures. *Animate Creations*

All-Green Parakeet. *Lydekker*

The Parrot

The deep affections of the breast
That Heaven to living things imparts
Are not exclusively possessed
By human hearts.

To Spicy groves where he had won
His plumage of resplendent hue;
His native fruits, and skies, and suns,
He bade adieu.

For these he changed the smoky turf,
A heatherly land and misty sky,
And turned on rocks and raging surf
His golden eye.

But petted in our climate cold
He lived and chattered many a day,
Until with age, from green and gold,
His wings grew gray.

At last, when seeming blind and dumb,
He scolded, laughed, and spoke no more,
A Spanish stranger chanced to come
To Mulla's shore.

He hailed the bird in Spanish speech,
The bird in Spanish replied,
Flapped round his cage with joyous screech
Dropped down and died!

Thomas Campbell, 18th century Scottish poet

Budgies, the favorite parrot pet of millions, is probably the world's most popular pet bird. Its small size, bright colors, easy care and trainability are some of the factors that have contributed to its universal appeal. *Australian Information Service*

13
Budgies and Cockatiels

THE BUDGIE OR BUDGERIGAR is probably the most popular pet bird in the world. Literally millions have been taken into the hearts and homes of people all over the world.

This small, clever and brightly colored bird was originally a native of the interior of Australia. It has been known to students of ornithology since 1805, although it was not until 1840 that live specimens arrived in England through the efforts of the famous naturalist, John Gould.

To avoid confusion it is necessary to impose on you with a bit of scientific jargon so that we can properly identify just who and what the Budgie is.

Living things are divided into specific groupings which are referred to as their classification. The steps in classification involve the categories Kingdom, Phylum, Class, Order, Family, Genus and Species. The groups are given in order ranging from the largest to the smallest. Thus, all birds (and all other animal life) are in the animal kingdom. As we proceed through the groupings they become smaller and more specific until we reach the genus and species which will actually identify a particular kind of bird. The colorful little Budgie is a member of a large group of Parakeets and is the only member of the genus *Melopsittacus*. His full scientific name is *Melopsittacus undulatus*. The Latin terminology may seem formidable but it serves a very important purpose. Since there are so many languages in the world, the use of the scientific classification makes certain that an individual in one country will know exactly which animal he is reading about when he reads the technical journals of another country. The use of scientific classification (and good descriptions) also helps avoid giving the same bird different names when more than one individual discovers a new specimen. As an example of the confusion which could exist without the help of classification, the Budgie is referred to as the Budgerygah, Shell Parrot, Warbling Grass Parakeet, Zebra Parrot, Canary Parrot and Love Bird. The first of these names, Budgerygah, is the aboriginal (original Australian native) term and I really prefer this name to some of the others because if you say it exactly the way it reads, it gives you the correct pronunciation—Budgery-gah.

Budgies are relatively easy birds to breed. It was not very long after the first of these charming little creatures were brought to England that the hobby of keeping and breeding them spread to other European countries. As larger and larger numbers of this basically green-colored bird were bred, mutations began to appear. A mutation is physical change caused by a change in the gene structure of the individual. When genetic material has been altered in an animal, the change can be passed on to the offspring.

As their numbers increased throughout Europe and the United States, the originally high prices for these birds dropped and they became available to virtually anyone who wanted a clean, friendly and clever pet or anyone who actually wanted to try his or her hand at breeding.

As interest in raising and breeding small parrots increased, people felt a desire to be able to meet and exchange information (as well as livestock) with other Budgie breeders. As early as 1925, a group of British Budgerigar enthusiasts formed one of the first of many clubs. Among the activities of this early group were the formulation of standards for showing birds, the designation of color mutations, and the publication of material which would help keep their members aware of new ideas in this rapidly growing hobby.

At the present time there are numerous active clubs which exist for anyone interested in keeping and breeding Budgies and other types of cage birds. To find the address of a club or society near you, write *American Cage-Bird Magazine,* 3349 North Western Avenue, Chicago, Illinois 60618. The publication will tell you who to contact.

Membership in a bird club will enable you to meet people of like interest, gives you an opportunity to learn from experienced fanciers and will help you upgrade the quality level of your birds.

Although this portrait was painted before the turn of the century, Budgies similar to these, maintained by line breeding, can be seen today! *Greene*

Selective breeding from spontaneous mutations has resulted in a dazzling rainbow of Budgie colors. From the original green bird of the wild, breeders have developed Budgies in colors to suit every taste. *Australian Information Service*

Even if the club closest to you does not specialize in Budgies, join it anyway. There is much that can be learned and you might even broaden your horizons to embrace finches and canaries!

Even if the club's meeting place is a distant drive you should not reject the idea of joining since many people make the monthly meeting on outing and if you have the time to spare, it will benefit you to do the same.

Unless you intend to breed your Budgies, housing them is a rather simple matter as virtually all pet shops carry a wide variety of suitable cages. Although as a general rule "more is better" should guide you in your choice of cage, you must avoid providing one that is so large that the bird will be lost in it. Cages which are too large will sometimes cause a Parakeet to become insecure and instead of being playful and active, he will tend to sit quietly in a safe corner of his cage. Appropriate dimensions should be at least 15" by 15" by 15" but you can safely exceed these dimensions by at least another six inches.

Budgies. Lydekker

If you choose a cage which is too small, you will not only limit the bird's ability to exercise, but you will find that you have the additional problem of droppings falling onto perches as well as into water and food dishes. If you get into breeding pairs or groups of birds, cage size and requirements will increase dramatically.

Since Budgies love to chew, choose a cage made of metal. Stainless steel is expensive, but cleans beautifully. Chrome-plated cages are more common and cost less. Avoid cages which have been painted unless the painted area is not accessible to the bird or the paint has been bonded to the metal by baking.

It is always a good idea to wash down a new cage very thoroughly before putting it to use. This should be done with a detergent and a powerful spray of water to remove the detergent after washing. This will remove any bits of paint or metal which may have been left after the cage was constructed as well as any chemical residue that may have been left on the metal. I recently heard about a Budgie breeder who was losing birds that were housed in a new aviary. After much investigation, it was discovered that the new wire had been dipped in a rust inhibitor which was poisoning the birds as they clung to the wire with their claws and beaks. It is really a good idea to thoroughly wash any new object which you provide for your birds.

Three of four hardwood perches should be provided and positioned to allow the Parakeet to move from one to the other freely. They should, however, be far enough away from each other so the bird will not continually soil them. A swing may or may not be appreciated. If you do provide one, make sure that it is large enough so the bird does not have to stoop to avoid the top of the cage when he uses it.

An early rendering of a Budgie. *Animate Creations*

Most cages for Budgies are equipped with a hook or ring so that they can be hung from a stand or bracket. This is mainly to protect your pet if there is a cat in the house, if not, there is no reason why the cage cannot be kept on a suitable stand. A table or a small chest of drawers is excellent. Food, vitamins and all the other accessories that you will be buying for your new friend can be kept in a drawer, out of sight and dust-free.

In choosing a location for a cage, it is vital that it not be in an area where the bird could be subject to drafts. Although the Parakeet will appreciate plently of light, you should also make sure that the entire cage is not in strong, direct sunlight unless it is for a brief period of time. Thus, although it may be tempting to locate your Parakeet's cage on or near a window ledge, this is not an ideal location. This does not mean that during the late spring or summer that you cannot bring the cage out of doors. As a matter of fact, such a treat (which might also include a gentle shower) will be greatly appreciated. Just keep in mind, however, that the lenth of time you keep your pet in the sun should be brief.

If you have a single Budgie your best food bet is probably the quality seed mix available at supermarkets or pet shops. The basic Parakeet mix usually consists of canary seed, millet and oats, with the proportions generally being half canary and half millet with just a sprinkling of oats. If you have any doubts about the freshness of the seed, see if you can cause it to sprout. If most of your sample does not sprout, you ought to consider changing your brand as seed which does not sprout is probably old and less nutritious. Spray millet is also frequently given as a treat. If the large spray appears to intimidate your pet, you can simply break off small pieces for him.

Canary seed and millet are mainly sources of carbohydrates. The amount of fats and proteins they provide are limited. For good health and the opportunity to live a full lifetime, supplementary foods should be included to provide additional fats and proteins. Many successful breeders use protein rich foods such as milk, eggs, cheese and even small amounts of freshly chopped beef.

Your pet shop will also have gravel in small packages. Choose a brand which includes calcium and minerals and make sure you get the package marked especially for Parakeets as different species of birds require different sizes of gravel. The gravel (sometimes called grits) should be offered in a separate cup.

Small quantities of greens such as dandelion, carrot, and beet tops, will round out your Budgie's diet. Make sure they are fresh and clean and if you have any doubts, don't use them.

Water should be changed at least once a day and more often in warm weather. A good vitamin supplement may be added to your Parakeet's water. One or two drops a day is ample.

Your Budgie's nails and beak are very much like the antlers of a deer in that they grow continuously. Birds who have their freedom have plenty of opportunity to wear their beaks and nails down through contact with the hard bark of trees and other rough surfaces. You will have to make up for your pet's lost opportunities by providing him with a cuttlebone, a lava stone or both. The cuttlebone in addition to supplying calcium will aid in keeping the beak worn down. The lava stone which is really a man-made stone compounded of irregular particles, can help even more in keeping both beak and nails within reasonable limits. If you find that your bird's nails are not being worn down and are starting to curve into a "c" shape, you will have to clip his nails, or have them clipped. The proper technique is simple and painless. Hold your Budgie on his back in the palm of your left hand. Use a gentle but firm grip and with your index finger and thumb keep his head from moving. A fingernail clipper or a dog's nail clipper are ideal tools, but make sure that the clipper you use is sharp so that you actually cut rather than crush the nail.

Since the nail contains a blood vessel you must only remove a small part of it. It is possible to actually see the location of the blood vessel by holding the nail up to bright light. If in doubt cut only the pointed tip of the nail and if this is done frequently enough the blood vessel will recede. Eventually the chances of causing bleeding will be considerably reduced. If you should cut a bit too far don't panic as the bleeding can easily be stopped by using styptic or by dipping the entire claw into a capful of peroxide. Try to make the first nail trimming experience non-traumatic so that your pet does not learn to fear this important aspect of his grooming.

A normal Parakeet should not need his beak trimmed but if, for some reason, your bird is not wearing his beak down rapidly enough I would suggest that you have the beak trimmed by the vet the first time. Thereafter, you can judge for yourself if you are capable of managing this procedure.

Avoid the use of sandpaper perch covers in hopes of keeping the nails short. They are extremely hard on the feet (particularly in young birds) and can cause soreness and irritation.

Your Budgie can tolerate a fairly wide range of temperatures. The important thing is to avoid sudden changes in temperature. Parakeets, like many other birds, can become acclimated to fairly low temperatures if they are conditioned over a reasonable length of time.

259

Suddenly putting a bird who has lived most of his life at room temperature (65-72 degrees Fahrenheit) into an unheated basement or spare room is just asking for trouble. Going to the other extreme is not wise either. If the room in which your bird is kept is too warm (above 75 degrees Fahrenheit) you may find that he will start to molt out of season. A temperature of about 68 degrees is fine for the average pet. In the event of an emergency, such as a power failure, cover the cage with a blanket and bring it into the warmest room in the house. Since heat will be lost gradually there is no reason that your Budgie cannot be maintained in this manner until power is restored.

Mites and feather lice are threats to your Parakeet's health and care and also make him quite uncomfortable. Because of their size, mites are difficult to see but if your pet scratches continually (scratches, not preens) spraying him once and his cage several times with an anti-mite spray should help. Do not spray into food or water dishes and be sure to follow the directions on the can as these sprays are potent. If you suspect mites but are not sure, you can use the old trick of covering the cage with a piece of white cloth at night and then quickly checking it in the morning as soon as you have put the lights on. Tiny black or red specks would definitely be evidence of mites. A bird who had not had mites and who is in your home and not exposed to an infested bird will generally not suffer from these pests. They must be introduced into the cage before they can become a problem.

Young Budgies are easily tamed and even those older birds which are passed along to you by owners who no longer have the time to care for them have good potential. While it is true that Budgies are capable of giving a sharp pinch or nip, these birds cannot really hurt and this knowledge is a great advantage when beginning training.

A young Parakeet is defined as any bird which is less than four or five months old. If you can obtain a bird that is six to eight weeks of age it is a decided advantage in training but don't attempt to get one that is much younger than that as it may not yet be fully capable of eating seed and unless you have lots of spare time, hand-feeding such a bird can be quite a chore.

I have not found that either sex shows a greater degree of talent for learning but if you prefer a particular sex, the marking above the base of the beak (the cere) is an excellent way to distinguish between the sexes. In males the cere is bright blue while the female's is brown. All young Budgies have a light blue cere but after about six or eight weeks this becomes a darker blue in the male and turns to a light brown in the hen. The cere marking can also give you a general idea of age as a light tan cere indicates a young female with the color

The natural, basic color of the Cockatiel is gray with yellow and orange markings on the face and head and white markings across the wings.
Australian Information Service

As with Budgies, mutations have occured in Cockatiels which have been carefully cultivated by breeders. The specimen here is a pearly Cockatiel. *Kelley*

This aviary of healthy attractive Cockatiels offers some idea of the color mutations breeders have successfully developed with this species. *Kelley*

changing to light and then dark brown as the hen matures. The intensity of the blue marking would, of course, bear a relationship to age in males.

Cockatiels

For many people the Cockatiel is the first step upward from the Budgie into the world of larger parrots. This extremely popular bird is about 12 inches long and with its attractive little crest, bright markings and friendly personality, it tends to behave like a "mini" Cockatoo. As a matter of fact, the Cockatiel belongs to the same family as the Cockatoo but it is unique enough in its structure to have earned its own generic designation. Some of the many names used for this parrot include, the Quarrion, Cockatoo-Parrot, Weero, Crested-Ground Parakeet and even the Joey. It can, however, be readily identified anywhere in the world as *Nymphicus hollandicus* or the Cockatiel.

The basic color of these small natives of Australia is gray with a white marking across the wings. There are yellow and orange areas on the face which are quite dull in the female but which are really outstanding in males. Females also show yellowish lines on the under portions of their tails. This feather design is also found in the females of some species of the larger Cockatoos. Since the deep colors do not develop until at least six months of age, it is hard to determine sex accurately much before this.

In their native Australia Cockatiels are widely distributed throughout the entire continent. They are not found in Tasmania as their flying strength is apparently not sufficient to help them bridge the water barrier which separates the island of Tasmania from the main continent.

Cockatiels can learn to talk and whistle and they show a great deal of affection for their owners. Birds who are taken from the nest early and who are hand-fed by breeders become extremely tame and loving and make the best pets.

Cockatiels do quite well on a diet which includes canary seed, millet, hemp and oats. Sunflower seed as well as an occasional peanut will also be relished but should not be fed too freely, otherwise the bird would become overweight. Fruits and greens should be provided but only when they are in prime condition. Fresh water, every day, is a must for Cockatiels and a drop or two of liquid vitamins will keep feathers glossy and lengthen your bird's lifespan.

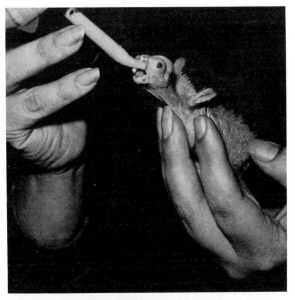

A baby albino Cockatiel at 12 days old, being hand-fed. *Mathews*

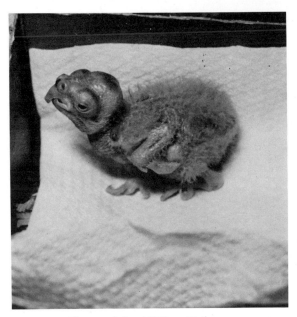

The same baby at 15 days. *Mathews*

At 20 days the baby Cockatiel has grown considerably.

At five weeks the young Cockatiel is almost fully feathered. It is interesting to note that even though this bird is albino, it does have color in its crest, cheek patches and under the tail. *Mathews*

If you are interested in breeding parrots, the Cockatiel is an excellent bird to begin with. Since the males and females show dimorphism (obvious external sexual differences) getting a true pair does not pose the difficult challenge that it does with many other parrot species. The Cockatiel is considered sexually mature at about two years of age although some individuals have succeeded in breeding them the first year.

A suitable nest box for a Cockatiel would be about ten inches by ten inches by fifteen inches with the largest dimension being the height. A concave depression in the bottom of the box will keep the eggs from rolling around. Of course, an entrance must be provided in the form of an opening to the box which should be about three inches across. A perch which extends through the box to the inside will make it easier for the parents to get in and out without climbing all over the babies.

A great deal of interest exists in color variations among the Cockatiels and many people breed to achieve these variations as well as to continue specific mutations. Colors and patterns which appear to have originated by mutation and which are quite popular today include cinnamon, albino, pearled and pied. A pied bird is one whose normal coloration is lacking in some areas of the body and thus gives the impression of being spotted. Popular colors have tended to change over the years much in the way that other fashions have fluctuated.

An unusual event in Cockatiel breeding occurred on St. Patrick's Day, March 17, 1978 when E. C. Dugan and his wife Roberta observed a pair of twin Cockatiels hatch from a single egg. The babies (appropriately named Pat and Mike) are both males. Pat is pied with a white upper chest, white pied spots on his back, and has dark gray wings. Mike is a white male with a yellow head and pink eyes. These birds have been exhibited at the Rochester and Greater Western New York Cage-Bird shows.

There is a good market for these little parrots and healthy birds can bring prices of between $50.00 and $75.00. Of course, this is not all profit as the money spent on equipment, supplies and advertising must all be deducted from the price paid for the babies. The breeder's time is also worth money but on the other hand the pleasure which results from keeping and breeding these parrots is a compensation in itself.

Keas. *Lydekker*

On several occasions the bird took sullen fits, during which it would eat nothing for two or three days at a time, screaming and defending itself with its beak when anyone attempted to touch it. It was at all times of an uncertain temper, sometimes biting severely when such a thing was least expected. It appeared to be always in the best of humor when first taken out of its box in the morning, hooking on eagerly with its upper mandible to the finger held down to lift it out. As soon as it was placed on the desk it would attack the first object which attracted its attention—sometimes the leg of my trousers, sometimes a slipper or a boot. Of the latter it was particularly fond; it would nestle down upon it, flapping its wings and showing every symptom of pleasure. It would then get up, rub against it with its sides, and roll upon its back, striking out with its feet whilst in this position.

Dr. Lyall writing on the New Zealand Kakapo in the
Proceedings of the Zoological Society of London, 1852

The Kea, famous or infamous? *New York Zoological*

A family of Keas. Their long, pointed beaks are useful for digging grubs. *New Zealand Consulate General.*

14

A Sampler of Other
Interesting Parrots and
the Mynah Birds

Most PEOPLE associate the term "parrot" with large-beaked, colorful birds who eat seeds and fruits and behave in a rather comical manner. Not every parrot fits this description and this chapter inclues birds who differ from the typical parrot in a number of ways.

Kea *(Nestor notabilis)*

The Kea has a long, thin upper beak. It is not a particularly striking bird as its olive green plumage lacks the interesting and colorful markings seen in Amazons and Macaws. It does have orange-red feathers under its wings but these would normally not be visible unless the bird were in flight.

This odd-looking parrot is a native of New Zealand. It favors the higher mountain regions and "Kea country" is generally considered to be the higher altitudes of southern New Zealand.

Like most parrots, they have a finely developed sense of curious-ity which almost borders on being aggressive as they have been known to boldly investigate ski lodges by entering through the chimney while apparently looking for food. Once inside, they behave like any other parrot and chew madly and destructively on whatever they can find.

This bird has long had the reputation of being a sheep killer and there has been much controversy as to whether or not this charge is credible. During the period 1943–1945, a bounty was paid for the Kea by the government of New Zealand and almost 7,000 birds were destroyed before the payment of bounties ceased.

The Kea's long upper beak is a useful tool for digging grubs out of rotted logs and is also helpful in cutting into the fruits and berries which it favors. In spite of this normal diet, the consistent reports by shepherds and others of sheep who have been killed or wounded by the Kea are continuous. Some of the reports indicate that the parrot has been seen flying from the bodies of dead sheep while others note wool and fat found in the crops of dead Keas. Very few eye-witness accounts of actual attacks on living sheep exist although there are a number of reports which indicate wounded sheep in areas where the Kea was known to feed.

Other circumstantial evidence includes reports that when Keas have been shot in a given vicinity, the killing of sheep in that area has ceased. In general, the current opinion seems to be that while the Kea may attack a sheep who is trapped, sick or injured, they are not important enemies and should not be penalized as such. If the Kea truly does attack sheep the habit is relatively recent as sheep were first introduced to New Zealand late in the 18th century.

Despite their poor reputations people who keep this parrot report that it does all the splendid and amusing things that other parrots do. They play with toys, swing from their owner's fingers and can learn to speak.

Sidney Porter kept Keas and they were among his favorite parrots. He felt that if they had been more widely available that they would have become quite popular as pets as they are intelligent and have pleasant personalities.

Porter's first Keas were acquired directly from New Zealand by a friend traveling in that country. The four birds (three males and a female) were transported in a huge crate made of thick lumber and lined with tin sheeting. A complicated double front was provided for this structure as Keas are notorious for their ability to open and get out of simple containers. On their native island they have the reputation of being able to gain access to houses and sheds by opening windows or even prying open doors.

Porter's Keas lived up to the reputation of their race by regularly escaping. They would open their inner door and then once in the smaller partition between the doors they would brace their bodies and use their feet to work open the outer door. It generally took the better part of the day to recapture them although it must be said in their favor that when they were caught they simply accepted the situation and permitted him to return them to their cage.

Mr. Porter brought a Kea to the meeting of a local society so that he could have the specimen show how clever it was. He provided a parrot cage which had its door ready to drop but which was held open with a bit of wire. The cage was baited with an apple placed in the middle of its tray so that the Kea would have to go inside to get it. The parrot approached the cage and after delibrating for a few minutes pulled the sand tray out to get the apple and thus avoided the trap.

The Keas did well on many varieties of fruits and vegetables which included artichokes, parsnips, carrots, beets and turnips. They also enjoyed apples, nuts and a mixture of kibble and corn. Porter reported that two of them had paired off and he had observed them copulating as well as feeding each other.

Lories and Lorikeets

The parrots classified as Lories and Lorikeets (you can keep track of who is who by remembering: short name, short tail; longer name, longer tail) are particularly pleasing in many ways. Their rich colors and glossiness of feather identify them almost immediately. They have a neat, compact and well proportioned parrot-shape. Healthy Lories show a curious nature. Since they are very active and agile birds they are able to satisfy their curiosity about new objects in or near their dwellings by getting into some very unusual positions and holding them for great lengths of time. Dr. Russ describes their movements quite accurately as "pert . . . odd, hasty and vio-lent. . ."

The *Loridae* are a very large family of parrots. This family feeds mainly on fruit, nectar and pollen. Their beaks and tongues have anatomical modifications which help them feed. The tongue, as pointed out by Dorst, retains some of the thickness of other parrots' tongues, but ends in a dense bundle of hair-like structures which form a little brush for licking nectar. It is possible that this structure is an adaptation to the shape of Australasian nectar-bearing flowers.

The Lories are examples of the general truth of the adage, "you are what you eat." Their soft, virtually liquid diet results in loose droppings which can quickly make a mess of their cage, their immediate area and their own feathers. Thus, they should be given as much space as possible and every opportunity for bathing.

271

Chattering Lory *(Lorius garrulus)*

This parrot tends to bear a closer resemblance to other members of the parrot race than most of the Lories because its beak is broader and less narrow at the tip and their tails are shorter and broader and more typically parrot-like.

The Chattering Lory is about 12 or 13 inches long which would make him the size of a small Amazon. His general plumage is flaming red with a yellow and green area on the back. The beak is orange and the eye yellow to orange. The feathers have (as with all Lories) an almost silky appearance. The texture and high gloss reminds one of the fur-like feathers of the Eclecti and perhaps there is a relationship between them. It is interesting to note that both birds can be found in the Moluccas and Indonesia and until relatively recently the Eclecti were classified as *Lorius* although current classification identifies them as *Eclectus*.

As you might have suspected this parrot's Latin name bears a relationship to the English word garrulous, a term often applied to someone who talks too much. Thus, its name is an allusion to its constant chattering.

Rutgers and Norris note that this Lory is also sometimes referred to as the Scarlet Lory. They pinpoint its area of origin as the Halmahera and Weda Islands of the Moluccas. Their description is similar to that of other authors when they indicate that this is a very active parrot who delights in tumbling head over heels among the branches of a tree (or his perches) while constantly chattering.

A.A. Prestwich lists many successful breedings for the Chattering Lory with the earliest being credited to Lord Poltimore who received a first breeding award for his success in 1913. Other early, successful attempts at breeding the Chattering Lory were made by Mrs. Bonestell of California in 1939, F.H. Rudkin in 1944 and Mr. Prestwich himself in 1945. A more recent breeding was reported by Phyllis Gale of South Africa who received her first pair of Chattering Lories in June, 1967. She was really not sure that they were a pair as the sexes show no differences. June is winter in South Africa so the birds were kept in the house until the weather began to warm up in September. They were then placed in an aviary with a large 25 inch by 15 inch nestbox. A number of holes were bored in the bottom of the nestbox so that the loose droppings typical of these birds would not accumulate. The hen appeared to be sitting on eggs by the end of October and about a month later a squeak was heard coming from the nestbox. After still another month a large baby could be seen but as big as he was he was only covered with white down. This big baby did

The Purple Capped Lory. *New York Zoological Society*

The White Capped Parrot, a member of the genus *Pionus*. *Marshall*

not leave the nest for almost three more months. By that time it looked much like its parents except that the beak was darker. The author reports a second breeding with two young being born in 1969.

Other well known members of this family include Swainson's Blue Mountain Lory, the Dusky Lory, the Black Capped Lory, the Purple Naped Lory and the extremely rare, beautiful and highly prized Tahitian Blue Lory.

The Pionus

The Pionus are a South American genus made up of eight species. They are easily recognized by their short, square tails and stocky build. They exhibit a close relationship to the Amazons in terms of appearance and behavior and to a casual observer the Spectacled Amazon or any other of the smaller Amazons could be mistaken for one of the Pionus. To avoid this error the observer should check the undertail coverts which are red in Pionus and green in Amazons. The length of birds in this group is between nine and 12 inches (most Amazons are at least several inches longer). There is' a distinct notch in the heavy upper beak as well as a prominent naked area above the beak.

Rosemary Low considers the Pionus to be almost ideal parrot pets. She feels this to be particularly true if there are children in the household. Ms. Low confirms the opinions of many other writers about their engaging personalities, steadiness and lack of propensity towards biting.

White Capped Parrot *(Pionus senilis)*

This parrot is also referred to as the White Crowned Parrot. This species of *Pionus* is nine or ten inches long. Its basic plumage is dark green with the under surface being a lighter, yellowish green. The forehead and the front of the crown are a milk white. The neck is also white. The wings are a mixture of dull, bluish green and a lighter green which gives a dappled effect. These pleasant little parrots originate in southern Mexico, Guatemala and western Panama where they are abundant.

The Duke of Bedford successfully bred this bird in 1934. It was the third effort for the parents and since they had failed to rear prior young this chick was taken from the nest and fed by hand.

Although early authors such as Dr. Russ classify these birds as Long Winged Parrots, using the Latin designation *Pioninae* for the genus, the description they give makes it evident that they are referring to the *Pionus* which were named by Johann Wagler early in the 19th century. Wagler's Latin choice is delightfully apt with *Pionus* translating, as being "plump or sleek" and *senilis* being a reference to old age because of the venerable white crown.

Other popular and frequently kept specimens of the *Pionus* includes the Red Vented Parrot, Maximillian's Parrot and the Bronze Winged Parrot.

The Caiques

These parrots are a group of small, brightly colored, solid looking birds with short square tails. They are only nine or ten inches long which makes them about as large as the smallest of the Amazons. Their area of distribution is the general region of northeastern South America. Their odd name rhymes with "dike" and may possibly bear a relationship to a sharply curved canoe used by certain South American Indian tribes; the inverted canoe resembling the sharply curved beak of the parrot.

Some writers see a relationship between this genus and some of the Conures based on the bone structure of their skulls. They are, however, dealt with as a separate genus by all modern authors.

White Bellied Caique *(Pionites leucogaster)*

The White Bellied Caique or as he is sometimes more politely referred to, the White Breasted Caique, has a largely orange colored head. The lores, throat and the sides of the head are yellow while the back and the wings are green. The lovely, ruffled, white breast and abdomen which gives the bird his name and the sudden way in which these feathers begin and end create the impression of a full-dress white shirt with a ruffled front if one choses to let their imagination follow its course. The beak is horn colored: the eye reddish-brown and the legs pink.

Edward J. Boosey speaks highly of the White Breasted Caique and describes one who loved to climb up the window cord as if he were a sailor climbing a rope. The same parrot would jump up the stairs and also push an imaginary wheelbarrow across the table. When his owner was ill this sweet little fellow would join him in bed with his tiny parrot head trustingly laid upon the pillow next to that of his master.

The Duke of Bedford who apparently was describing the same bird tells more about this unusual Caique. His name was Jot and in addition to the pleasant characteristics mentioned above he was also quite friendly with strangers and would test their patience and endurance with gentle pinches of their ears and fingers. If they showed distress he would laugh loudly.

Rutgers points out that it might be possible to sex these birds by noting that the cock has a slightly shorter and heavier beak.

There are several subspecies including *Pionites 1. xanthurus* and *Pionites 1. xanthomeria* (commonly referred to as the Yellow Tailed Caique and Yellow Thighed Caique, respectively). In addition to being slightly larger the colors mentioned in the common names describe the outstanding difference in the subspecies.

Rosemary Low considers them among the most intelligent, desirable and amusing of the parrots. Ms. Low goes so far as to say that they may be unique in their response to care and training. She recommends the Caiques as good subjects for behavioral studies for individuals who are interested in birds with strong personalities. Ms. Low further advises that the Caiques are highly social creatures and believes that it is positively cruel to keep any but the most tame Caique without a companion of its own kind.

What appears to be the first successful breeding of these parrots is credited by A.A. Prestwich to Gilbert Lee who had three young hatch out in April, 1932. Mr. Prestwich also credits the San Diego Zoo with a successful breeding in 1934. Ms. Low makes mention of later breedings at the Cincinnati Zoo in 1969 and in Tampa, Florida in the same year. A cross-breeding between a White Bellied Caique and a Black Headed Caique was achieved by Lady Poltimore in 1936.

Among the Caiques the Black Headed Caique is equal in popularity to the White Bellied Caique.

Hawk Headed Parrot *(Deroptyus accipitrinus)*

This unusual bird has a forehead and crown which are almost white. The lores are dark brown while the sides of the head are brown, streaked with white. The nape and the general region in the back of the neck are covered with dark red feathers which are edged in blue.

This parrot orginates in northern Brazil, Columbia and northeastern Peru. Although it is not commonly kept as a pet it is occasionally offered for sale and some are being bred in private aviaries.

Many writers classify the Hawk Headed parrot along with the Caiques *(Pionites)* while others prefer to place it in a group by itself as *Deroptyus*. Nevertheless, it is similar in many ways to the Caiques.

The Duke of Bedford considered them to be intelligent and playful. He also points out that they do not tend to lose their affection for their owners when kept with a member of their own species. This

A 10-week-old Maximilian's Parrot. *Ingels*　　　**A Black Headed Caique.** *Evans*

A Black Headed Caique and a White Breasted Caique preparing to box. *Photo by author*

277

The Hawk Headed parrot is an unusual, interesting bird. Its ability to form a complete ruff of its head feathers is unique among parrot species. *Photo by author*

is well worth noting as many a sweet parrot undergoes a drastic change in his relationship with humans when is is paired off with another bird.

The Hawk Headed Parrot raises the feathers on the back of his neck when he is excited. He will also raise them when he is angry or displays them for his owner or another bird. Most parrots can raise some of their feathers to a degree but the complete ruff produced by the Hawk Head is unique.

Doctor Russ tells of a Hawk Head belonging to a London gentlemen who could do many clever tricks. According to the owner, this bird would display his feathers on command.

Pesquet's Parrot *(Psittrichas fulgidus)*

The World of Birds Exhibit in the Bronx Zoo has several Pesquet's Parrots on display. These are rare birds which are native to the more mountainous regions of New Guinea. Although sightings are reported in its native land the chances of seeing the parrot in the United States may be rather limited as they are not commonly found in zoological collections. The Wassenaar Zoo at The Hague in Holland has a single Pesquet's and the San Diego Zoo also owns one. Rutgers and Norris indicate that the bird was first imported into England in 1919 with Lord Tavistock (later the Duke of Bedford) owning a hen. The Duke kept it for two years on a diet which was heavy in fruit and its next owner, Mrs. Dawson Burgess, continued the high fruit diet along with a sort of nectar of the type fed to Lories. The Duke reported that his bird was extremely sensitive to cold but thrived under warm conditions and became quite tame and friendly.

Pesquet's Parrot is the only member of its genus. Its elongated head, thin, hooked beak and almost complete lack of facial feathers provide the parrot's other name of Vulture Headed or Vulturine Parrot.

Pesquet's vary in size from about 17 to 20 inches and there may be a relationship between the altitude at which they live and their size. They are not particularly handsome birds, perhaps because of the odd shape of their head and beak. Their basic plumage is black with the feathers of the breast and abdomen being heavily tipped with gray to give a scalloped effect. Males have a red spot behind the eye which provides a fairly good indication of sex. The under-wing coverts and the lower underparts are a bright red. The beak is black and the eye is dark brown. It is possible that the lack of facial feathers is a survival characteristic as this feature would help the bird to avoid the problem of having its facial plumage matted by the sticky remains of the fruits and flowers which make up a large part of its diet in the wild.

Pesquet's parrot is a rare, striking species. The origin of their alternate name, Vulturine parrot, is obvious from their appearance. In this photograph, the male is in the foreground. *Kinnach*

Rutgers considers the Vulturine to be a relic of some ancient parrot form which is totally unrelated to any other group. There may also be a distant kinship to the *Eclecti* (whose own possible relationship to the *Loriidae* should also be noted).

Do not confuse these unusual birds with the small members of the South American genus *Gypopsitta* which have a bare region on their head and who are also called Vulturine Parrots. They have no real relationship to *Psittrichas.*

Eclectus Parrot *(Eclectus roratus)*

These vividly colored birds have also been referred to as the Red Sided Parrot, the Rocky River Parrot and the Sacred Temple Parrot. If they were actually worshipped at one time as sacred birds, it is probably due to their fantastic colors as they are among the most gaudily colored of all the parrots.

The multicolored Eclecti are found in Australia, New Guinea and various islands in the Pacific.

For many years the Eclecti (or Noble Parrots as they were called in Germany) were mistakenly thought to be two separate species. Even the famous ornithologist, Dr. Finsch (for whom Finsch's Amazon is named) was confused into thinking that the bright green male was one species while the red and blue female was another. Later, in the 19th century, Dr. A. B. Meyer, a director of the Natural History Museum in Dresden, was one of the first to realize that this was simply a case of sexual dimorphism with the male and female showing marked differences.

The rather obvious clue that gave Dr. Meyer the hint which led him to his correct conclusion was that whenever he collected a green specimen of Eclectus it was a male. The red specimens were always females. There was considerable discussion and dispute as well as expressions of disbelief when the claim that both birds were of the same species was first made. This is, of course, now an obvious and proven fact.

The male Eclectus is about 14 to 15 inches long. The feathers of a healthy specimen are so glossy that they actually look silky. The male is a brilliant green on his top surface while his wing coverts are yellowish-green with red patches on the breast as well as under the wing. The tail feathers are almost black with yellow tips. The upper beak is a waxy yellow color while the lower mandible is black. The iris varies from dark orange to brown.

The female of the species is a rich red color on her head and breast. The red feathers tend to become darker and fuller on her back and wings. Her belly is blue as is the nape of her neck. The female's

The brilliantly colored Eclectus parrot is an example of sexual dimorphism. The female (left) and the male show striking differences in color and markings. At one time it was thought that they were two entirely separate species. *Photo by author*

The Lesser Vasa parrot, a native of Malagasy, is now a protected species in its habitat.
New York Zoological Society

tail is tipped with orange. The bjll is black and the eye a yellowish color with an unusual blue circle around the eye. She is about the same size as the male.

Eclectus Parrots have been successfully bred and are regularly offered for sale. Some writers highly recommend the male over the female in terms of talking ability and tameness. The Duke of Bedford took the opposite point of view and preferred the female of the species. From my own observations I would tend to go along with the males as being more talented.

The basic variations between subspecies include size, head colors, brightness of plumage and location within the Pacific Islands.

The Eclecti which I have handled have been gentle and friendly. One is tempted to stroke the feathers of a clean and tame Eclectus as the texture is reminiscent of the mammalian fur of a cat or dog.

Vasa Parrot *(Coracopsis vasa)*

When we think of African parrots the birds which usually come to mind are the famous African Grey and the Lovebirds. There are, however, a substantial number of lesser-known genera distributed throughout the African continent as well as on a number of the offshore islands such as the Comoros, Reunion, the Seychelles and the large island nation of Madagascar.

The Vasa is particularly interesting as it appears that the original parrot population of Madagascar originated on the continent of Africa. It is possible that due to the isolation of the Vasa Parrot (since geologists believe no land connection with Africa existed for millions of years) that when we observe it, we are really studying an ancient specimen which has remained unchanged for many years. Incidentally, for those of you who no longer have children studying geography, I should point out the name of Madagascar was changed to Malagasy several years ago.

Most authors divide the members of the genus *Coracopsis* into the Greater Vasa Parrot and the Lesser Vasa Parrot which is an arrangement based mainly on size.

The bulk of the Lessers originate on the eastern end of Malagasy (as do the Greaters) although various subspecies are found in the western portion of the island as well as on the smaller islands to the north of and in the channel between Malagasy and the coast of Africa.

The Lesser Vasa Parrot is a fair-sized bird which reaches lengths of over 15 inches. Its feathers are dark brown and in some specimens almost black. The lower edges of the wings and flight feathers are tipped with silver. The eye is a deep brown and it is surrounded by a pink, naked ring. The beak varies with the time of the year and tends to be darker right after the molt. The feathers on the back of the head and neck are pointed (lanceolate) giving the bird a slightly ruffled look. The Greater Vasa is remarkably like the Lesser version except that the Greaters average about 20 inches in length. Although these parrots have been kept as pets and specimen birds for well over 100 years, they are seldom seen in private collections. This is not something that is likely to change for the better as all of the fauna of Malagasy are now protected and the only way that such a parrot could be exported would be through a special license.

Edward J. Boosey deals with the Greater and Lesser at the same time. He considers the Lesser to simply be a smaller edition of the Greater. He expresses surprise at the fact that two species who are so close could inhabit the same island and yet remain quite separate and distinct. Perhaps this is not the case. It is possible that subspecies are actually cases of interbreeding between these birds.

Boosey indicates that they are intelligent and make gifted mimics and talkers. He notes their affection and devotion to their owners but advises that they are delicate parrots in the sense that should they become ill, they are hard to cure. The Duke of Bedford notes this same lack of stamina.

Dr. Russ spells their name as the "Vaza Parrot." Russ also uses the term Black Parrot for both the Greater and the Lesser and differentiates between them by calling them the Large Black Parrot and the Small Black Parrot. He quotes a Mr. J. Audeberto, a long-time resident of Madagascar, who believed that there were few other parrots who could give as much pleasure to their owners. Mr. Audeberto reported that this was a quiet bird that did not chew or bite and which could speak and whistle quite well. In Mr. Audeberto's time the Vasa Parrot could be purchased in Madagascar for less than a dollar!

Dr. Greene describes the Vasa as looking like a rusty crow. Although he felt it was far from handsome, he did note its good qualities which included longevity, tameness, gentleness, and a musical whistle. He describes a specimen in the London Zoo which arrived in 1830 and died at the ripe old age of 52. An autopsy indicated that the parrot had been a female although she had not laid any eggs in all of her 52 years. Greene mentions that the bird was about the size of a Blue-Fronted Amazon which would indicate that it was the Lesser Vasa he was writing about.

Dr. Greene was aware of the larger species as he quotes a Mr. Janicke who owned a Greater Vasa and who reported that they were tame, good-natured and droll but had little talent for speaking. Dr.

Greene describes a popular misconception of his time which involved people believing that the Greater Vasa and the Lesser Vasa were actually the male and female of a single species.

Dr. Greene also tells how Mr. Groom (the manufacturer of the famous Groom's Indestructible Parrot Cage) exhibited a Vasa Parrot at the 24th Annual Exhibition of Canaries and Cage Birds in February, 1887. The show was held at the Crystal Palace and was well attended. Unfortunately, many of the visitors to the show attempted to get the parrot's attention by poking and prodding him with their walking sticks and umbrellas. The Vasa, who was tame (and not feeling too well) made no attempt to retaliate.

Dr. Greene indicates that the name of the Vasa Parrot was given to it by Linnaeus, the great Swedish naturalist, who wished to honor Gustave Vasa the founder of a Swedish dynasty of kings who ruled for almost 300 years. This poses an interesting conflict as A.A. Prestwich, advises that Vasa comes from the Malagasy word meaning "loud-voiced or clamorous."

Senegal Parrot *(Poicephalus senegalus)*

Another large group of African parrots belongs to the genus *Poicephalus* and the Senegal Parrot is typical of the genus. Although this species bears the name of the African country of Senegal it is also distributed throughout central-west Africa with the main species and several subspecies being found in Gambia, Guinea, the Ivory Coast and even as far inland as western Nigeria.

They are fairly small birds, only nine or ten inches long, but their temperament and colors are pleasing. The head is gray with the cheeks being a somewhat lighter gray in color. The ventral feathers blend from green to orange moving from the chest to the abdomen. Different degrees of yellow coloration are present in the abdomen of the subspecies. Thus, it is possible to have Senegals whose bellies are yellow, reddish or orange. The beak is gray and the legs are brown. The eyes are bright yellow and are set in dark, gray lores. The vivid contrast between the eyes and the lores (as well as the elongation of the region of the lores) gives the distinct impression that the Senegal is wearing a small mask making it quite easy to recognize this parrot.

The Senegal Parrot has been a popular pet for a very long time. Arthur Prestwich indicates that the Senegal was first identified by A. Goffin, the Dutch naturalist who had a Cockatoo named in his honor.

Greene believes that this parrot was one of the earlist members of its race to be mentioned in scientific writings and cites a source as early as 1445! That particular reference is somewhat obscure but a later one which he refers to, by the naturalist Brisson, in 1760, is without doubt a fine description of an adult male Senegal. Greene points out that an early nickname for the bird was the Blackheaded parrot. He tells of Senegals who could speak both German and French and describes Senegals he was acquainted with who ranged from wild to docile. Newly imported specimens could be purchased at the time of Greene's writing (1884) for less than two dollars each. Greene tells of many successful breedings of this bird and gives it further high recommendations as a pet.

Dr. Russ gives the 15th century date for the earliest description of the Senegal. I suspect, however, that Greene was quoting Dr. Russ when he used this date. Dr. Russ considered older specimens untamable but agrees with most authors that young Senegal Parrots are easily tamed and become very affectionate. He had one that was capable of opening virtually any cage and who loved to play and be petted.

Boosey describes how his Senegal Parrot would fly from room to room to follow him and he speculates that this constant opportunity for flight and exercise was helpful in extending the parrot's life-span. He considered it the most delightful of parrots and along with other authors mentions that this bird is hardy enough to be wintered in an outdoor aviary providing that it is introduced to the low temperatures in a gradual fashion. Mr. Boosey could do just about anything he wanted to with his Senegal and she trusted him to the point where if he opened his mouth she would put her head inside and emit clucking sounds which seemed to indicate that she was seeing an extraordinary sight!

Quaker Parakeet *(Myiopsitta monachus)*

This delightful but noisy parrot is a native of Argentina, Brazil, Uruguay and according to many reports on feral parrots is now making a valiant effort to establish itself as a native in parts of the United States and Puerto Rico. The Quaker is also referred to as the Green Parakeet, Gray Breasted Parakeet, Monk Parakeet and Montevideo Parakeet. It is the only member of its genus and has four recognized subspecies. The distinctions between them are made largely on size and variations in intensity of color.

Meyer de Schauensee describes these 11-inch-long parrots as having a gray forecrown and breast with the gray breast feathers having light edges. The lower breast is yellowish while the rest of the underparts are green. There are some blue outer wing feathers and a long pointed tail which is a mixture of yellow and bluish green. It is

The Senegal parrot has been familiar to naturalists and birc fanciers for centuries. Some authorities believe the Senegal was mentioned for the first time in scientific writings during the 15th century. *Photo by author*

The Quaker Parakeet is named for the gray bib pattern of facial feathers reminiscent of an old-fashioned Quaker costume. This hardy bird is attempting to establish itself in North America at the present time. *Evans*

287

the parrot's gray bib which provides the name Quaker as to the imaginative eye the bird's ventral gray coloration resembles the old fashioned Quaker costume.

A comparison of the parrot's appearance with the illustration on the Quaker Oats box easily illustrates the similarity. The Monk Parakeet designation is a direct translation of its species name, *monachus* and no doubt also is a reference to the gray breast. The light edges to the breast feathers provide a scalloped appearance quite similar to that of the African Grey except that in the Quaker these feathers end rather abruptly with the breast as the feathers of the abdomen are olive green.

Rutgers and Norris observe that this parrot is unique in that it is the only species which builds a community nest of twigs in the branches of trees. Inaccessible sites at the end of the branches and high above the ground are usually choosen. The nests of individual pairs are built together until the mass of material becomes quite large with the birds continuously repairing and adding to the community nest until it can weight as much as several hundred pounds. The parrots not only use the nest for breeding but will also roost in it throughout the year.

As noted by Rosemary Low, these are truly free-breeding birds which have been reared on many occasions during the past hundred years. Ms. Low describes a sophisticated pair of Quakers aboard a ship bound for Australia. They mated in their traveling box and then reared two chicks when the eggs hatched!

Dr. Greene comments that the Quaker may maintain his nest building habits in captivity. He describes a group which had numerous nest boxes at their disposal, but refused to have anything to do with them. Instead they covered up a seed box with twigs taken from a broom to make a nest more to their liking. The bits of broom were laced together over the seed box to produce a nest quite similar to those constructed by Quaker Parakeets living in the wild. Greene warns that this bird is also a master at shrieking. He tells of a splendid African Grey who was a highly accomplished talker and the delight of his owner. When the Grey was presented with a Quaker Parakeet as a neighbor he took up the hideous sounds produced by the Quaker and constantly repeated them at intervals thereafter even though the offending Quaker had been long since banished to another household.

Dr. Russ points out that the Quaker Parakeet was first described and named by Gmelin in 1783. Russ describes a Quaker living in the French city of Nice which made its reputation chiefly by trying furiously to bite all strangers. Because of its unfortunate personality it remained in the bird shop for an inordinate length of time and developed a number of vocal accomplishments. Russ relates that it could say, "To Arms!" in French and then imitate a drum roll. It could also say, "Rosetta, come here! Give me a kiss!" in Italian as well as coughing and laughing.

During the last five or six years there have been frequent reports in the press of parrots of various species flying freely in different parts of the United States. Descriptions and photographs seem to indicate the possibility that Blossom Headed Parakeets, Ringnecked Parakeets, Double Yellow Heads, Lovebirds, Canary Winged Parakeets, Nandays, Cockatiels and Budgies have fled their happy cage homes and are attempting to "make it" in the wild. There is some question as to how many of these parrots will be able to survive our North American winters but the Quaker Parakeet appears to be doing so and may actually be establishing its habitat in different parts of the country. Oddly enough, experiments with this parrot being kept as a free-flying pet were conducted as early as 1893 by von Prosch of Germany. According to Rutgers and Norris his free-fliers survived quite well and by 1898 had produced 23 young. A gentlemen named Pallisch set six pairs free in Vienna in 1925 and in spite of being shot at their numbers grew to about 60. Other experiments resulted in complaints by people whose crops were damaged and it is this problem of crop damage (rather than the charming concept of a species of parrot returning to North America to make up for the loss of the Carolina Conure) which is stressed in the various newspaper and magazine articles which have been appearing. John V. Dennis indicates that the easily recognized stick nests of the Quaker Parakeet were spotted in the Miami area in 1969 and as far north as New York by 1971. John Bull and Edward Riccituti report that the Quaker is a problem of such proportions to farmers in Argentina that authorities have responded with campaigns against the parrot which include bounties paid for indications of its death along with other gory activities.

They feed at bird feeders and have constructed their unusual nests between the rain gutters and leaders of buildings, on top of utility poles, in church bell towers and (without any respect for rank) under the eaves of both the enlisted men's quarters and the commanding officer's home at Fort Tilden (New York).

Ringneck Parrots

The large and highly popular genus *Psittacula* consists of parrots which are widely distributed throughout Asia and parts of Africa. One species, the Indian Ringneck, is the most freely scattered member of the entire race of parrots and is spread over Asia.

Ringnecks may be found in India, China, Ceylon, Africa, Tibet, Nepal and on many islands adjacent to these countries. (A parrot with Ringneck in its name which does not belong to this group is the Mallee Ringneck of Australia.)

Some of the members of this group are free breeders and thus they are frequently chosen by individuals who wish to make a start at breeding parrots. In general, they are gregarious birds which show affection for one another. I remember being greatly impressed during an early morning visit to an aviary with a large collection of Ringnecks and hearing them greet the arrival of dawn with weak, muttered squawks which finally exploded into discordant screams and busy conversation.

A number of Ringneck species are extremely common in India where they can be seen flying freely and visiting gardens. In the Hindi language the Indian Ringneck is called *Tota* while the Alexandrine is called *Hiraman Tota*. The Blossom Head is known as *Tiria Tota*.

Malcolm MacDonald who served as the British High Commissioner in India from 1955 to 1960 observed and photographed several of the Ringnecks in his Delhi garden much as you and I might take note of Bluejays and other attractive local birds. Delhi may well have been the city where Alexander The Great discovered the Indian Ringneck and collected specimens to bring home. MacDonald refers to the first Parakeets which he observed as Green Parakeets but from the photos it is obvious that he is talking about the Indian Ringneck. His apt description of "aristocratic-looking creatures with superlatively elegant figures" and his reference to their solemn but slightly supercilious manner is as good an account as anyone has given of this species. The pair in his garden showed a great deal of interest in a hole in a small Jacaranda tree which at that moment was serving as a nest for a family of Mynahs. The hen worked on the entrance when the Mynahs were not at home (a rather forward act and much like the owners of a new home moving in their cartons before the old occupants have left) and then quickly took possession when the Mynah Birds finally did leave. The Ringneck and her mate spent a lot of time in the nest with the hen occasionally peering out of the opening like a jack-in-the-box. This charming pair copulated successfully and thereafter drove away any trespassers who came too close to their nest. They even subjected the original Mynah owners of the nest to this same treatment. Eggs followed with the male showing a great sense of responsibility in that he fed the female who now refused to leave the area of the nest and continued this behavior until her young were well along in their growth. The chicks hatched out at the end of

March but it took until the first week in May for one of them to risk contact with the outside world.' This took the form of peering out of the nest opening very much the way in which a young child stares at a busy street from its window. By the end of May this single chick left the nest with its parents, flying happily away with them.

MacDonald noted that the Indian Ringneck is a fastidious eater. He observed one delicately stretched along the branch of a plum tree until it found a fruit whose appearance pleased it. It would then bend its head in a courteous manner (as if it were paying the fruit a compliment) and devour it in a series of nibbles and gulps.

Indian and African Ringnecks *(Psittacula krameri)*

Early authors (and a few current ones) use the name Rose Ringed Parakeet when referring to the African and Indian varieties. Although highly descriptive of these parrots' most outstanding markings, it is an older name which is less commonly used. The subspecies known as the African Ringneck *(P.k. krameri)* ranges from west Africa to the southern Sudan. Its general color is green with the ventral surface being lighter than the dorsal. A black ring runs through the region of the chin and then follows the cheeks to the nape where it blends into the pink collar which circles the nuchal area. The eyes are a yellowish pink and the beak a plum-red which becomes almost black at the tip. Immature birds and females lack the black band and rose collar. It is generally not possible to determine sex in a young Ringneck as it is at least two years before they mature and male markings appear.

Psittacula krameri manillensis is the subspecies referred to as the Indian Ringnecked Parakeet. Its name refers to Manila in the Philippines; but this is an error as this parrot originates in Ceylon. A.A. Prestwich infers that a complete translation of the name would be "smaller parrot named for Kramer." G.H. Kramer was an Austrian naturalist whose works were published early in the 18th century.

The Indian Ringneck has more prominent collar markings than the African. The beak is larger and the lower beak is practically black. All of the markings in the Indian variety seem to be brighter. The Indian Ringneck is also two or three inches longer than the African with the extra length in the tail. Dr. Russ calls the Ringnecks the *Noble Parakeets*. He indicates that they have earned this name because of the admiration and esteem that they have been held in from the most ancient times. He mentions that a further reason for this impressive group name lies in the superiority of their form, color, talent for

291

speech, intelligence, and the success with which they freely breed in the aviary. Somewhat high praise from Dr. Russ but certainly with an element of truth to all of it.

Dr. Greene refers to this bird as the Ring-Necked or Bengal Parakeet. He accurately notes that there are both Indian and African varieties and neatly sums up the major differences between the two as described herein. Greene, along with Dr. Russ, considered them highly desirable parrots but warned that if they were teased, they would learn the habit of screaming or shrieking with such loud voices that there would be no enduring them in the house.

The Duke of Bedford was well acquainted with these attractive parrots. A friend of his owned one which could thread beads on a bit of cotton; retrieve small objects; ring a miniature bell; and twirl a stick around his head like an acrobat. This bird was also able to choose a card mentioned by his owner from a group which was face down on the table. He would walk along the table lifting each card until he came to the one his master or visitor had named. The "trick" was that his owner would give his thumb a slight twitch when the bird lifted the right card. This is somehow all reminiscent of an old story about a talking dog in a bar, but the fact that the parrot could respond to a small thumb movement is nonetheless remarkable. The Duke successfully bred these birds and his description of the courtship dance is quite amusing. After hopping and bowing around the hen, the male rocks back and forth on the perch and at intervals provides a passionate kiss on the back of the hen's neck. He also will sing to the hen if it is their first meeting.

Many members of the Ringneck group are still readily available at realistic prices. Color mutations occur frequently and the cross breeding of these mutations to produce still other combinations is a challenge which fascinates many breeders. Friends who have recently returned from a visit to India advise me that the Indian Ringneck is as common as ever there and that a Sunday visit to the Phaki Hat bird market in Calcutta provides a fascinating view of native parrots as well as imports. One Ringneck that they almost purchased had been trained to shout, "Chor! Chor!" which means "Thief! Thief!" They did not say whether it actually frightened off potential robbers.

Other well known Asiatic Parakeets which are kept and bred include the Moustache Parakeet, the Plum Head, the Blossom Head, the Slaty Head, the Malabar and the Alexandrine. Experimenters have also been successful in breeding a color mutation of Indian Ringneck known as the Lutino variety.

A lutino mutation Indian Ringneck. *Buttstead*

The Indian Ringneck Parakeet is yet another old favorite among bird enthusiasts. The combination of beauty, trainability and ease of breeding is largely responsible for this species' durable popularity. *Vazquez*

The Alexandrine Ringneck, another well-known Asiatic Ringneck species. *Kelley*

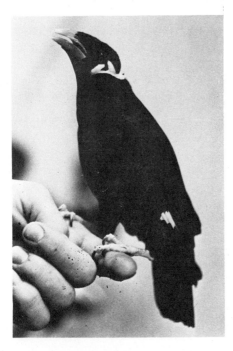

The Greater Hill Mynah is a gifted, if raucous, mimic. Unlike most parrots, the Mynah is not even slightly self-conscious about his ability and will talk for virtually anyone regardless of the surroundings or circumstances.

M. Morrone/S. Rosenblum

There is a number of other interesting Mynah species. Most, like this Bald Mynah, are more familiar to ornithologists and aviculturists than to pet owners.

New York Zoological Society

Mynah Birds

These shiny, metallic black, talking virtuosos are known throughout Asia although they are most commonly associated with India.

There are many types of Mynah birds but those which are kept as pets generally belong to the genus *Gracula* which should not link the bird (in your mind) with the common Grackle, a widely distributed creature better known for its vicious behavior towards dogs and cats (or even humans) who threaten its nest than its ability to mimic. The talking Mynah includes a large number of species but the two most popular and best known are the Greater Hill Mynah *(Gracula religiosa intermedia)* which is distributed throughout northern India and parts of China and the Lesser Hill Mynah *(Gracula religiosa indica)* found in India and Ceylon.

The Greater is about 11 inches (the size of a common pigeon) with the Lesser attaining only about $2/3$ of this size. The giant of the race, the Javan Hill Mynah *(Gracula religiosa religiosa)* found in Malaya, Java, and the Sunda Islands can reach almost 16 inches but this species is not commonly imported.

The Greater Hill Mynah is considered by many to be the finest talking Mynah and perhaps even the finest of all talking birds. The Lesser is not as talented but can be purchased for a lower price.

The Greater Hill Mynah has a yellowish beak with a light tip. The flight feathers, which are black, have a white marking which helps to relieve their somber appearance. The skin around the back of the eyes and the region of the ears is bare but colored a bright yellow and because of the looseness of its texture resembles the wrinkled wattles seen in poultry. The feet are also yellow. In young birds one can note that the yellowish colors and the wattles themselves are not fully developed.

Mynahs are among the most abundant of Indian birds. Although they spend most of their lifetimes in the trees they are found wherever man is present. They are often kept as pets in India and make themselves useful as they scream and react violently when snakes are present.

The spelling "Myna" is the Hindi version of the name with the English spelling differing only by the addition of a final "h" to make it Mynah.

In India the Common Mynah nests in February. Hollows in tree trunks are used for nesting with the birds bringing in large quantities of material with which to line the cavity. Malcolm MacDonald notes that Mynahs are fond of stuffing odd bits of material into their nests and will use brightly colored or shiny wrappings almost like decorations. The tree cavities are apparently highly desired by a number of species of birds and MacDonald describes lengthy battles between Mynah birds and the Indian Ringnecks over the occupancy of the more desirable residences.

The Mynahs are courageous birds and will protect their nests against larger and more powerful creatures than themselves. They are even willing to take on the Pariah Kite, an aggressive fighter from whom even parrots and other strongly beaked birds will flee.

MacDonald aptly describes the Common Mynah as being " . . . As typical an Indian figure as a fakir, maharajah or a babu." He notes how they strut around with great importance, talking ceaselessly and occasionally behaving in a vulgar manner. The Mynah bird has a trim figure and although his walk and manner is bold and commanding he generally spoils the effect by clownish or pompous behavior.

The Mynah's skill as a mimic is outstanding. Its normal voice is rather harsh and raucous but when imitating the song of other birds its voice can be quite beautiful. Mr. MacDonald notes having seen a Common Mynah physically imitating a woodpecker as it perched on a trunk of a tree and vainly hammered at a hole in the bark. He wondered whether it was actually trying to make a hole or simply attempting to reproduce the sound that a woodpecker makes as it hits a tree trunk with its beak.

Mynahs enunciate in a clear, distinct manner but have such loud voices that they sometimes change homes quite frequently as families become weary of having irrelevant remarks screamed out in a penetrating voice at strange or awkward moments.

MacDonald describes a meeting with a Mynah who was alone in a room in a friend's house. Apparently the bird felt it should act as host since it was the only one present. "How are you?" it inquired in English with a touch of Bengali accent. Mr. MacDonald answered "very well." At that the Mynah cocked his head curiously and replied with an unprintable remark. MacDonald notes that he felt truly welcome.

I had a similar meeting with a Mynah in the pet department of a large department store. As I walked among the cages I heard a voice exclaim, "Buy me!" the request was repeated a number of times and I was delighted when a little detective work showed that the voice came from the cage of a Greater Hill Mynah. Needless to say, I could not oblige him as the price asked for this talented bird exceeded my weekly salary at that time.

Another chance meeting with a clever Mynah occured in the Bird Market in Paris where my wife and I were fascinated by a French speaking Mynah Bird who greeted all comers with, *"Comment tu t'appelles?"* It is only fair that he would ask everyone their name as, after all this is how most people greeted him.

Charlie a Lesser Hill Mynah which I finally did get to own, could clearly scream the phrase, "Want an apple!" When I told my children about the parrot capable of saying, "Hail to the Emperor!" who fled captivity and taught all the local crows this greeting my offspring speculated that if Charlie were to escape he would probably greet the wild birds with his favorite phrase and then be pecked for his impudence.

General Care

Mynahs require a comfortable temperature and humidity. Their room should be kept at about 70 degrees and if necessary moisture should be added to the air. A Mynah should not be kept in direct sunlight for any length of time but there is no reason why your pet cannot enjoy having his cage brought out into a semi-shaded area while receiving a gentle spray of tepid water. Mynahs enjoy bathing and will do so on an almost daily basis if the opportunity is provided.

Feeding your Mynah

These soft-beaked birds are omnivorous but unlike the rest of the birds mentioned in this book they do not eat seeds. A Mynah can live on the prepared pellets sold for his species. These pellets are a ration prepared by grinding up appropriate ingredients, extruding them into long strands and then chopping them into pellets after drying. Although this is a convenience for you, it is best to vary this prepared diet with fruits, raw chopped meat, greens, orange juice, egg yolk (hard boiled), banana, hot peppers, grapes and raisins. Cut up the food you serve so that your Mynah does not attempt to swallow any object much larger than a pea as it is possible for a greedy Mynah to choke if he is careless about ingesting too large a piece of food.

In the wild, Mynah Birds extract grubs from decayed branches. They carry this appetite over into captivity and delight in taking meal worms from the fingers of their owners. A tame Mynah will eat these delicacies until you tire of supplying them but you should limit the amount to about two dozen a day so that there is an appetite for other foods. Meal worms can be maintained in a live and therefore fresh state for quite a while if they are stored in a container of oats or other dry cereal with air holes punched in the container. Water or milk should also be provided with a drop or two of a water soluble vitamin supplement added to the daily beverage.

Mynahs are clean birds and bathe frequently. In spite of this they have a reputation for sloppiness because they tend to shake their food vigorously in their beaks. This is probably a carry-over from life in the wild where a quick snap of the head will kill any live food which they have caught. The same action performed with a grape or cherry will, unfortunately, splatter part of the contents on the walls of the room in which the Mynah is kept.

With care and common sense these clever mimics can live as long as 20 to 30 years. They thrive on affection and as with most other things in life the pleasure they give will be a measure of the attention and care with which they are provided.

America's best-known Mynah, Raffles, was owned by Zetta and Carveth Wills.

Raffles was a Malay jungle orphan whose parents had been killed by a large snake. The Wells found him while he was still in his nest.

During the voyage back to United States Mrs. Wells was amazed to discover that without any great effort on her part Raffles had already learned to say such things as "Have a ball?" as well as calling her husband by name. When he began to whistle the National Anthem and to address his mistress as "darling" Mr. and Mrs. Wells knew that they had acquired an extremely talented bird.

The New York Customs Office originally refused to permit Raffles entry as "parrots" were not permitted into the United States in 1939. Somehow, Mrs. Wells convinced the customs officer that this black and yellow comedian was not a parrot and this along with Raffle's natural charm helped him to gain admission into the United States.

His career brought him into contact with most of the well-known radio and film personalities of the 1940s. He met and appeared with such celebrities as Fred Allen, Eddie Cantor, Bob Hope and Walt Disney.

Raffles also appeared in veterans' hospitals throughout the country and since most of the patients knew of him from listening to the radio they were thrilled to meet him in person.

Sources Cited and Suggested Reading

Alston, T. H. "Breeding of the Slaty-Headed Parrakeet" *Magazine of the Parrot Society*, 1 (November, 1967), 1–3.

———. "The Breeding of My Hahn's Macaws." *Magazine of the Parrot Society*, 3 (March, 1969), 80–83.

Ames, Felicia. *The Bird You Care For.* New York: Signet Books, 1970.

Armstrong, Edward A. *The Life & Lore of the Bird.* New York: Crown Publishers, 1975.

Arnall, L. and Keymer, I. F. *Bird Diseases.* Neptune, New Jersey: TFH Publications Inc., 1975.

Arthur, C. P. *Parrots For Pleasure and Profit.* London: F. Carl, c. 1900.

Aymer, Brandt. *The Personalities of Birds.* New York: Crown Publishers, 1965.

Barrett, Charles. *Parrots of Australasia.* Melbourne: N. H. Seward Pty. Ltd., 1949.

Benson, Wes. *Birds as Pets.* New Augusta, Indiana: Editors and Engineers, Ltd., 1965.

Berry, Robert J. "Precarious Perch for a Parrot." *Animal Kingdom,* 79 (October–November, 1976), 25–30.

Bertagnolio, Paolo. "Breeding of the Lesser Patagonian Conure." *Magazine of the Parrot Society,* Vol. 8 (September, 1974), 198–201.

Bloom, D. G. "Breeding of Black-Capped Lories." *Magazine of the Parrot Society,* 6 (November, 1972), 260–261.

Boosey, Edward J. *Parrots, Cockatoos and Macaws.* Silver Springs, Maryland: Denlingers, 1956.

Cayley, Neville W. *Australian Parrots.* Sydney: Angus and Robertson Ltd., 1938.

Chrystie, Frances N. *Pets.* Boston: Little, Brown and Company, 1974.

Day, R. K. "A Biography of A Goffin." *Magazine of the Parrot Society,* Vol. 11 (December, 1977), 269–73.

DeGrahl, W. *Farbiger Atlas Papageien.* Braunschweig: Horst Müller Verlag, 1972.

DeRochemont, R. *The Pet's Cookbook.* New York: Alfred A Knopf, 1964.

Derrett, David. "Breeding of the Golden-Crowned Conures." *Magazine of the Parrot Society,* 8 (October, 1973), 198–199.

Dolensek, Emil P. and Burn, Barbara. *A Practical Guide to Impractical Pets.* New York: The Viking Press, 1976.

Dorst, Jean. *The Life of Birds.* New York: Columbia University Press, 1974.

Eastman, William R., Jr. *The Parrots of Australia.* Narberth, Pennsylvania: Livingston Publishing Company, 1966.

Engholm, Eva. *Bird Infirmary.* New York: Taplinger Publishing Company, 1973.

Forshaw, Joseph M. *Australian Parrots.* Wynnewood, Pennsylvania: Livingston Publishing Company, 1969.

———. *Parrots of the World.* New York: Doubleday and Company, Inc., 1973.

Gale, Phyllis, S. "Chattering Lories." *Magazine of the Parrot Society,* 3 (April, 1969), 94–95.

———. "Roseate Cockatoos (Galahs)." *Magazine of the Parrot Society,* 6 (June, 1969), 141–142.

Graham, Anne D. *A Bird in My Bed.* New York: Taplinger Publishing Company, 1971.

Greene, W. T. *The Amateur's Aviary of Foreign Birds.* London: L. Upcott Gill, 1883.

———. *Birds I Have Kept in Years Gone.* London: George Bell & Sons, 1884.

———. *Parrots in Captivity.* London: George Bell & Sons, 1884.

———. *The Grey Parrot and How to Treat It.* London: Bazaar House c. 1895.

———. *Birds of the British Empire*. London: The Imperial Press, 1898.

Hargrove, Lyndon L. *Mexican Macaws: Comparative Osteology*. Tuscon: University Of Arizona Press, Anthropological Papers, No. 20, 1970.

Harper, Rex A. *Keeping A Parrot in the Family*. Cornwall, England: 1976.

Hausman, Leon A. *The Cage Bird Handbook*. New York: G. P. Putnam, 1954.

Hudson, W. H. *Birds and Man*. London: Duckworth & Co., 1915.

Laycock, George. "The Parrakeet Mystery." *South Carolina Wildlife*, 22 (May-June, 1975), 14–16, 38–40.

Lloyd-Jones, Buster. *The Animals Came One By One*. New York: The John Day Company, 1967.

Lorenz, Konrad Z. *King Solomon's Ring*. New York: Harper and Row Publishers, Inc., 1952.

Low, Rosemary. *The Parrots of South America*. London: John Gifford Ltd., 1972.

———. *Lories and Lorikeets*. London: Paul Ellek Ltd., 1977.

Lydekker, Richard. *The Royal Natural History*. London: Frederick Warne and Company, 1895.

MacDonald, Malcolm. *Birds in My Indian Garden*. New York: Alfred A. Knopf, 1961.

Marriner, George R. *The Kea, A New Zealand Problem*. Christchurch, New Zealand: 1908.

McPeek, R. "Finsch's Amazon." *Magazine of the Parrot Society*, 7 (November, 1973), 222–223.

Meyer de Schauensee, Rodolphe. *A Guide to the Birds of South America*. Wynnewood, Pennsylvania: Livingston Publishing Company, 1970.

Neal, Margaret W. "Feather Plucking in a Gang-Gang Cockatoo." *Magazine of the Parrot Society*, 5 (May, 1974), 95–97.

Noakes, Vivien. *Edward Lear*. Boston: Houghton Mifflin Company, 1969.

Norman, D. F. "Breeding of Scarlet Macaws." *Magazine of the Parrot Society*, 9 (March, 1975), 53–54.

Ogburn, Charlton. *The Adventure of Birds*. New York: William Morrow and Company, 1976.

Pasquier, Roger F. *Watching Birds, an Introduction to Ornithology.* Boston: Houghton Mifflin Co., 1977.

Plath, Karl. *Parrots Exclusively.* Fond du Lac, Wisconsin: All-Pets Books, Inc., 1957.

Pommery, Jean. *What to Do Till the Veterinarian Comes.* Radnor, Pennsylvania: Chilton Book Company, 1976.

Porter, S. "A West Indian Diary." *Avicultural Magazine,* (March, 1936), 66–82.

———. "The Kea." *Avicultural Magazine,* (July, 1936), 186–9.

Prestwich, Arthur A. *Records of Parrots Bred In Captivity.* London: 1954.

———. "I Name This Parrot . . ." Edenbridge: 1963.

———. *A Guide to the Names of the Parrots.* Edenbridge: 1969.

———. *English Names of the Parrots.* Edenbridge: 1970.

Ramen, N. "Breeding of Sun Conures." *Magazine of the Parrot Society,* (January, 1976), 2–3.

Reade, Brian. *Edward Lear's Parrots.* London: Gerald Duckworth, 1949.

Roberts, Sonia. *The Right Way to Keep Pet Birds.* New York: Gramercy Publishing Company, 1971.

———. *Bird-Keeping and Bird Cages—A History.* New York: Drake Publishers, Inc., 1973.

Robiller, Franz. *Cage and Aviary Birds.* London: Almark Publishing Co., 1974.

Rogers, Cyril H. *Encyclopedia of Cage and Aviary Birds.* New York: Macmillan Publishing Co., 1975.

Romero, Rolando. "Notes on the Red-Fronted Macaw." *Magazine of the Parrot Society,* Vol. 8 (July, 1974), 142–43.

Russ, Karl. *The Speaking Parrots.* London: L. Upcott Gill, 1884.

Rutgers, A. *The Handbook of Foreign Birds.* London: Blandford Press, 1965.

Rutgers, A. and Norris, K. A. *Encylopedia of Aviculture.* London: Blandford Press, 1972.

Sackett, Russell. "The Old Bird Won't Sell." LIFE, August 9, 1963.

Selby, P. J. *The Naturalist's Library.* London: Chatto and Windus, c. 1800.

Skutch, Alexander F. *A Bird Watcher's Adventures in Tropical America.* Austin: University of Texas Press, 1977.

Smith, George A. *Encyclopedia of Cockatiels*. Neptune, New Jersey: TFH Publications Inc., 1978.

Sparks, John. *Bird Behavior*. New York: Grosset & Dunlap, 1970.

Sutton, George M. *Portraits of Mexican Birds*. Norman, Oklahoma: University of Oklahoma Press, 1975.

Tavistock, Marquess of (Hastings William A. Russell.) *Parrots and Parrot-Like Birds in Aviculture*. London: F.V. White and Company, 1929.

Ter Horst, P. "Breeding the Great White-Crested Cockatoo." *Magazine of the Parrot Society,* 8 (March, 1974), 59.

Thomas, Arline. *Bird Ambulance*. New York: Charles Scribner's Sons, 1971.

Vane, E. N. T. "Breeding of the Moustache Parrakeet." *Avicultural Magazine,* 59 (September-October, 1953), 151–155.

Villiard, Paul. *Birds as Pets*. New York: Doubleday and Co., 1974.

Wells, Zetta, and Wells, Carveth. *Raffles, The Bird Who Thinks He is a Person*. New York: G. P. Putnam Sons, 1945.

Cockatoos. *Lydekker*